Wild Yosemite

Yosemite

Sound! Sound! Sound!
O colossal walls and crown'd
In one eternal thunder!
Sound! Sound! Sound!
O ye oceans overhead,
While we walk, subdued in wonder,
In the ferns and grasses, under
And beside the swift Merced!

Fret! Fret! Fret!
Streaming sounding banners, set
On the giant granite castles
In the clouds and in the snow!
But the foe he comes not yet,
We are loyal, valiant vassals,
And we touch the trailing tassles
Of the banners far below.

Surge! Surge! Surge!
From the white Sierra's verge
To the very valley blossom.
Surge! Surge! Surge!
Yet the song bird builds a home,
And the mossy branches cross them,
And the tasseled tree tops toss them
In the clouds of falling foam.

Sweep! Sweep! Sweep!
O ye heaven born and deep,
In one dread unbroken chorus!
We may wonder or we may weep,
We may wait on God before us;
We may shout or lift a hand,
We may bow down and deplore us,
But we may never understand.

Beat! Beat! Beat!
We advance, but would retreat
From this restless, broken breast
Of the earth in a convulsion.
We would rest, but dare not rest,
For the angel of expulsion
From this Paradise below
Waves us onward and . . . we go.

—Joaquin Miller

Wild Yosemite

25 Tales of Adventure, Nature, and Exploration

Edited by Susan M. Neider

Introduction by Bruce Hamilton

Skyhorse Publishing

Skyhorse Publishing books may be purchased in bulk at special discounts for sales promotion,
corporate gifts, fund-raising, or educational purposes. Special editions can also be created to
specifications. For details, contact the Special Sales Department, Skyhorse Publishing, 307
West 36th Street, 11th Floor, New York, NY 10018 or info@skyhorsepublishing.com.

Skyhorse® and Skyhorse Publishing® are registered trademarks of Skyhorse Publishing,
Inc.®, a Delaware corporation.

Visit our website at www.skyhorsepublishing.com.
10 9 8 7 6 5 4 3 2 1

Library of Congress Cataloging-in-Publication-Data

Wild Yosemite : personal accounts of adventure, discovery and nature /
Susan M. Neider, editor.
p. cm.
ISBN-13: 978-1-60239-056-0 (hardcover : alk. paper)
ISBN-10: 1-60239-056-8 (hardcover : alk. paper)
1. Yosemite National Park (Calif.)—Description and travel—Anecdotes. 2. Sierra Nevada
(Calif. and Nev.)—Description and travel—Anecdotes. 3. Yosemite National Park (Calif.)—
History—19th century—Anecdotes. 4. Yosemite National Park (Calif.)—Discovery and
exploration—Anecdotes. 5. Natural history—California—Yosemite National Park—Anecdotes. 6. Adventure and adventurers—California—Yosemite National Park—Biography—
Anecdotes. 7. Explorers—California—Yosemite National Park—Biography—Anecdotes.
8. Travelers—California—Yosemite National Park—Biography—Anecdotes. 9. Travelers'
writings.
I. Neider, Susan M.
F868.Y6W55 2007
979.4'47—dc22
2006039597

Cover design by Liz Driesbach

Front cover illustration: Albert Bierstadt "Domes of Yosemite," 1867/oil on canvas, 116 ×
180 inches, Collection of St. Johnsbury Athenaeum, St. Johnsbury, VT. Used by permission.

Back cover photo: Theodore Roosevelt and John Muir at Glacier Point, courtesy of Library
of Congress

All other illustrations © 2007 by Susan M. Neider

Print ISBN: 978-1-63220-311-3
Ebook ISBN: 978-1-63220-786-9

Printed in the United States of America

Other books by Susan M. Neider

Color Country: Touring the Colorado Plateau, Winner of five international awards including EVVY First Place in Coffee Table Books and IPPY Second Place in Travel Books

High Country: Touring the Colorado Rockies

Golden Country: Touring Scenic California

Some Like It Hot! Yellowstone's Favorite Geysers, Hot Springs, and Fumaroles

Classic Yellowstone: The Best of the World's First National Park

Table of Contents

Preface

The magnificent granite mountains of the Sierra Nevada impose a formidable presence of supreme elevation and length, extending for more than 400 miles along California's eastern flank. These are exuberant mountains full of wild energy, vigorous and youthful, probably less than ten million years old. The southern third of the range is the highest and most rugged, where eleven of the fifteen California peaks above 14,000 feet rise in a single dominant crest known as the High Sierra. The eastern edge of the range ends in a dramatic escarpment descending to the barren salt flats of Death Valley, 282 feet below sea level. The long and gradual western slopes are heavily forested, with occasional lava spews and rocky protrusions through the thin soil, a scene of gray-browns and greens.

Centuries ago, on these gentler slopes, man's gradual ascent to the High Sierra began. Trails and roads emerged, snaking and winding through hairpins and switchbacks, under sheer granite cliffs with peeling walls, light gray and stark. Loggers eyed the immense conifers, tall straight shooters with textured bark in a range of rich browns. Dappled light streamed through dense, mature forests and groves of giant sequoia. The air was dusty with glaciated granite, ground from massive domes into glacial flour, a reminder of the power of moving ice that a million years ago carved into this wild backcountry a charismatic central valley called Yosemite, beneath vast subalpine meadows in the heart of the High Sierra, under luminous skies and pitch nights.

With the California Gold Rush of 1849, word spread quickly of Yosemite's staggering beauty, attracting fortune hunters and travelers around the globe. Writers, artists, and photographers were awed by "the Incomparable Valley." Settlements, mining camps, hotels, and tourism exploded and the great trees were felled by the thousands. Finally on October 1, 1890, Congress created Yosemite National Park, answering the urgent cry of conservationist John Muir to protect this magnificent land from misuse, carelessness, and greed.

Yosemite National Park is an American wilderness treasure worthy of an anthology of historical writing. The focus of this collection is the spectacular natural features and their impact on those talented writers who were moved to describe them. The text is about two-thirds John Muir because he's so wonderful to read, but also includes the writings of President Teddy Roosevelt, philosopher Ralph Waldo Emerson, geologist Clarence King, editor and reformer Horace Greeley, landscape architect Frederick Olmsted, poet Joaquin Miller, and legendary humorist Mark Twain. Their sense of language is superb and timeless, so no heavy editing of structure and style was necessary—just cherry-picking what was already there in essays, journal entries, and speeches. I've modernized the punctuation for an easier read and put together a selection of the very best of these great writers—outstanding descriptive passages and paragraphs—blended and assembled in a sensible order so that the reader can learn about the natural features of Yosemite through their eyes and words. I've also included various accounts of early expeditions, adventures, and general exploration of the park. However, this is not a social or political history. Writings about life in the early settlements, territorial disputes, Native American life, and mining are purposefully left out in deference to the descriptions of natural features as these writers viewed them for the first time.

The earliest record of such first impressions is Lafayette Bunnell's *Entry of Yosemite Valley*, written on March 27, 1851 when he, as a private with the Mariposa Battalion, was part of the first known visit to Yosemite by non-Indian people.

In the *Discovery of the Yosemite*, published in 1881, he wrote:

We found the traveling much less laborious than before, and it seemed but a short time after we left the Indians before we suddenly came in full view of the valley in which was the village, or rather the encampments of the Yosemites. The immensity of rock I had seen, my vision on the Old Bear Valley trail from Ridley's Ferry, was here presented to my astonished gaze. The mystery of that scene was here disclosed. My awe was increased by this nearer view. The face of the immense cliff was shadowed by the declining sun; its outlines only had been seen at a distance. That stupendous cliff is now known as "El Capitan" (the Captain), and the plateau from which we had our first view of the valley, as Mount Beatitude.

It has been said that "it is not easy to describe in words the precise impressions which great objects make upon us." I cannot describe how completely I realized this truth. None but those who have visited this most wonderful valley can even imagine the feelings with which I looked upon the view that was there presented. The grandeur of the scene was but softened by the haze that hung over the valley, light as gossamer, and by the clouds, which partially dimmed the higher cliffs and mountains. This obscurity of vision but increased the awe with which I beheld it, and as I looked, a peculiar exalted sensation seemed to fill my whole being, and I found my eyes in tears with emotion.

During many subsequent visits to this locality, this sensation was never again so fully aroused. It is probable that the shadows fast clothing all before me, and the vapory clouds at the head of the valley, leaving the view beyond still undefined, gave a weirdness to the scene, that made it so impressive; and the conviction that it was utterly indescribable added strength to the emotion. It is not possible for the same intensity of feeling to be aroused more than once by the same object, although I never looked upon these scenes except with wonder and admiration.

Richardson, in his admirable, "Beyond the Mississippi," says: "See Yosemite and die! I shall not attempt to describe it; the subject is too large and my capacity too small. Painfully at first these stupendous walls confuse the mind. By degrees, day after day, the sight of them clears it, until at last one receives a just impression of their solemn immensity. Volumes ought to be and will be written about it."

Mr. Richardson has expressed in graphic language the impressions produced upon nearly all who for the first time behold this wonderful valley.

Bunnell added an additional thought many years later:

The public has now, to a certain degree, been prepared for these scenes. They are educated by the descriptions, sketches, photographs and masterly paintings of Hill and Bierstadt; whereas, on our first visit, our imagination had been misled by the descriptive misrepresentations of savages, whose prime object was to keep us from their safe retreat, until we had expected to see some terrible abyss. The reality so little resembled the picture of imagination, that my astonishment was the more overpowering.

Bunnell had it right; raw amazement—reaction without expectation—is a rare gift. Each of us has one chance at it. Others followed with their own powerful accounts, many included in this anthology, and by now, several hundred million visitors have traveled the same twisting roads into Yosemite to feel for themselves what Bunnell proclaimed: *I can depart in peace, for I have here seen the power and glory of a Supreme being; the majesty of His handywork is in that "Testimony of the Rocks."*

—Susan M. Neider

Introduction

Yosemite's history as a mecca for visitors began in the middle of the nineteenth century. State of California soldiers forcefully relocated the Native Americans from the central Sierra Nevada at the request of gold-seeking Forty-Niners and white settlers, and the troops came out of Yosemite Valley with tales of amazing cliffs and waterfalls and mountain marvels. Within a few short years the stories of Yosemite's splendor had spread from coast to coast. A fellow traveler en route to Yosemite with the painter Albert Bierstadt wrote, in 1863, "If report was true, we were going to the original site of the Garden of Eden." Inspired by the Yosemite landscape, Frederick Law Olmsted, the designer of Central Park in New York, convinced Congress and President Abraham Lincoln to create the "Yosemite Grant" in 1864 to preserve the Yosemite Valley and the Mariposa Grove of giant sequoias. This was eight years before the first national park, Yellowstone, was formally established.

John Muir made his way to the fabled Yosemite Valley as soon as he set foot in California in 1868. He was stunned by the beauty and wildness of the place: "Yosemite is the grandest, most divine of all earthly dwelling places, the Lord's mountain house."

Muir spent his first seven years in California mostly in and around Yosemite. He built a cabin at the foot of Yosemite Falls and took a job as a sheepherder in the high country, even though he detested the " hooved locusts" under his care. He also ran a small sawmill in the valley, cutting only trees that fell naturally. Most of his days were spent rambling, climbing mountains, sketching, writing in his journal, studying the rocks and remnant glaciers, and introducing others to the glory of the place.

"I drifted enchanted . . . gazing afar over domes and peaks, lakes and woods, and the billowy glaciated fields," he wrote. "In the midst of such beauty . . . one's body is all one tingling palate. Who wouldn't be a mountaineer!"

Muir realized that mountain temples like Yosemite would not be safe for long unless citizens organized to protect them. By 1892 he and some scientists, scholars, and other Yosemite enthusiasts had founded the Sierra Club, a conservation group that he hoped "would be able to do something for wildness and make the mountains glad." The club's initial purpose was: "To explore, enjoy, and render accessible the mountain regions of the Pacific Coast; to publish authentic information concerning them; to enlist the support and cooperation of the people and the government in preserving the forests and other features of the Sierra Nevada Mountains."

Introduction

Since Muir's time, millions of writers, painters, poets, politicians, photographers, backpackers, scientists, and plain ordinary people have flocked to Yosemite every year. They climb the mountains and "get their good tidings" as Muir would say, and emerge with a deeper love of the Earth and its wildness. For many, it's an annual family pilgrimage that has been going on for generations.

If you've never been to Yosemite, the writings of Muir, Emerson, Roosevelt and others who experienced Yosemite a hundred years ago will transport you and inspire you to plan a trip. If you've been there—once or a hundred times—they will build on your memories and beckon you back again.

You may be surprised to find how easily you can recognize the places these authors describe. There are some significant changes in the park, of course. Roads and tourist facilities have multiplied, fire suppression has led to an increase in dense forest cover in some areas, some lakes have silted in, rivers have flooded and changed course, and tragically Hetch Hetchy Valley was inundated. But, remarkably, much of Yosemite looks just as it did in John Muir's day. You can sit on the summit of the same peak and share the same view he wrote about with such spirit and eloquence.

But keeping Yosemite wild for future generations in all the grandeur that we have known will require our care and vigilance. John Muir fought dam builders, loggers, miners, and sheepherders who threatened and despoiled Yosemite in his day. We can carry on his work by reducing auto traffic and development, shielding stream banks from erosion, restoring the historic role of fires, and ultimately draining and restoring Hetch Hetchy Valley, to name just a few of the challenges we face today.

If Yosemite and these writings have given you a gift of inspiration, hopefully you will find a way in your lives to give something back to Yosemite, so that it will be there for your grandchildren. That would make the mountains glad indeed.

—Bruce Hamilton
Deputy Executive Director,
Sierra Club
San Francisco, California

"In Yosemite, grandeur of these mountains
perhaps unmatched in the globe;
for here they strip themselves like athletes
for exhibition and stand, perpendicular granite walls,
showing their entire height,
and wearing a liberty cap of snow on their head."

—*Ralph Waldo Emerson, journal entry, 1871*

Yosemite Valley

1

The Great Chasm of Yosemite

Frederick Law Olmsted

The main feature of Yosemite is best indicated in one word as a chasm. It is a chasm nearly a mile in average width, however, and more than ten miles in length. The central and broader part of this chasm is occupied at the bottom by a series of groves of magnificent trees, and meadows of the most varied luxuriant and exquisite herbage, through which meanders a broad stream of the clearest water, rippling over a pebbly bottom, and eddying among banks of ferns and rushes, sometimes narrowed into sparkling rapids and sometimes expanding into placid pools which reflect the wondrous heights on either side. The walls to the chasm are generally half a mile, sometimes nearly a mile in height above these meadows, and where most lofty are nearly perpendicular, sometimes overjutting. At frequent intervals, however, they are cleft, broken, terraced, and sloped, and in these places, as well as everywhere upon the summit, they are overgrown by thick clusters of trees.

There is nothing strange or exotic in the character of the vegetation. Most of the trees and plants, especially of the meadow and waterside, are closely allied to and are not readily distinguished from those most common in the landscapes of the Eastern States or the midland counties of England. Banks of heartsease and beds of cowslips and daisies are frequent, and thickets of alder, dogwood, and willow often fringe the shores.

At several points, streams of water flow into the chasm, descending at one leap from five hundred to fourteen hundred feet. One small stream falls, in three closely consecutive pitches, a distance of two thousand six hundred feet. In the spray of these falls superb rainbows are seen.

At certain points, the walls of rock are ploughed in polished horizontal furrows, at others, moraines of boulders and pebbles are found, both evincing the terrific force with which, in past ages of the earth's history, a glacier has moved down the chasm from among the adjoining peaks of the Sierras. Beyond the lofty walls still loftier mountains rise, some crowned by, others in simple rounded cones of, light gray granite.

The climate of the region is never dry like that of the lower parts of the state of California. Even for several months, not a drop of rain has fallen twenty miles to the westward, and the country there is parched, and all vegetation withered. Yosemite continues to receive frequent soft showers, and to be dressed throughout in living green. After midsummer, a light, transparent haze generally pervades the atmosphere, giving indescribable softness and exquisite dreamy charm to the scenery, like that produced by the Indian summer of the East. Clouds gathering at this season upon the snowy peaks, which rise within forty miles on each side of the chasm to a height of over twelve thousand feet, sometimes roll down over the cliffs in the afternoon, and under the influence of the rays of the setting sun, form the most gorgeous and magnificent thunderheads.

Flowering shrubs of sweet fragrance and balmy herbs abound in the meadows, and there is everywhere a delicate odor of the prevailing foliage in the pines and cedars. The water of the streams is soft and limpid, as clear as crystal, abounds with trout and, except near its sources, is, during the heat of summer, of an agreeable temperature for bathing. In the lower part of the valley, there are copious mineral springs, the water of one of which is regarded by the aboriginal inhabitants as having remarkable curative properties. A basin still exists to which weak and sickly persons were brought for bathing. The water has not been analyzed, but that it possesses highly tonic as well as other medical qualities can be readily seen. In the neighboring mountains there are also springs strongly charged with carbonic acid gas, and said to resemble in taste the Empire Springs of Saratoga.

The other district consists of four sections of land on which stand, in the midst of a forest composed of the usual trees and shrubs of the western slope of the Sierra Nevada, about six hundred mature trees of the Giant Sequoia. Among them is one known through numerous paintings and photographs as the Grizzly Giant, which probably is the noblest tree in the world. Besides this, there are hundreds of such beauty and stateliness that, to one who moves among them in the reverent mood to which they so strongly incite the mind, it will not seem strange that intelligent travelers have declared that they would rather have passed by Niagara itself than have missed visiting this grove.

In the region intermediate between the two districts, the scenery generally is of grand character, consisting of granite mountains and a forest composed mainly of coniferous trees of great size. It is not, however, in its grandeur or in its forest beauty that the attraction of this intermediate region consists, so much as in the more secluded charms of some of its glens formed by mountain torrents fed from the snow banks of the higher Sierras. These have worn deep and picturesque channels in the granite rocks, and in the moist shadows of their recesses grow tender plants of rare and peculiar loveliness. The broad parachute-like leaves of the peltate saxifrage, delicate ferns, soft mosses, and the most brilliant lichens abound. The difference in the elevation of different parts of the district amounts to considerably more than a mile. Owing to this difference, and the great variety of exposure and other circumstances, there is a larger number of species of plants within the district than probably found within a similar space anywhere else on the continent.

4

It is conceivable that any one or all of the cliffs of Yosemite might be changed in form and color, without lessening the enjoyment which is now obtained from the scenery. Nor is this enjoyment any more essentially derived from its meadows, its trees, streams, least of all can it he attributed to the cascades. These, indeed, are scarcely to be named among the elements of the scenery. They are mere incidents, of far less consequence any day of the summer than the imperceptible humidity of the atmosphere and the soil. The chasm remains when they are dry, and the scenery may be, and often is, more effective, by reason of some temporary condition of the air, of clouds, of moon-light, or of sunlight through mist or smoke, in the season when the cascades attract the least attention, than when their volume of water is largest and their roar like constant thunder.

There are falls of water elsewhere finer, there are more stu-pendous rocks, more beetling cliffs, there are deeper and more awful chasms, there may be as beautiful streams, as lovely meadows, there are larger trees. It is in no scene or scenes the charm consists, but in the miles of scenery where cliffs of awful height and rocks of vast magnitude and of varied and exquisite coloring are banked and fringed and draped and shadowed by the tender foliage of noble and lovely trees and bushes, reflected from the most placid pools, and associated with the most tranquil meadows, the most playful streams, and every variety of soft and peaceful pastoral beauty. This union of the deepest sublimity with the deepest beauty of nature, not in one feature or another, not in one part or one scene or another, not any landscape that can be framed by itself, but all around and wherever the visitor goes, constitutes the Yosemite, the greatest glory of nature.

Mount Whitney

2

The Sierra Nevada Range

Clarence King

T he western margin of this continent is built of a succession of mountain chains folded in broad corrugations, like waves of stone upon whose seaward base beat the mild, small breakers of the Pacific. By far, the grandest of all these ranges is the Sierra Nevada, a long and massive uplift lying between the arid deserts of the Great Basin and the Californian exuberance of grainfield and orchard; its eastern slope, a defiant wall of rock plunging abruptly down to the plain; the western, a long, grand sweep, well-watered and overgrown with cool, stately forests; its crest, a line of sharp, snowy peaks springing into the sky and catching the alpenglow long after the sun has set for all the rest of America.

The ancient history of the Sierras goes back to a period when the Atlantic and Pacific were one ocean, in whose depths great accumulations of sand and powdered stone were gathering and being spread out in level strata. It is not easy to assign the age in which these submarine strata were begun, nor exactly the boundaries of the embryo continents from whose shores the primeval breakers ground away sand and gravel enough to form such incredibly thick deposits. It appears most likely that the Sierra region was submerged from the earliest Paleozoic, or perhaps even the Azoic, age. Slowly the deep ocean valley filled up, until, in the late Triassic period, the uppermost tables were in water shallow enough to drift the sands and clays into wave and ripple ridges. Age succeeded age; form after form of animal and plant life perished in the unfolding of the great plan of development, while the suspended sands of that primeval sea sank slowly down and were stretched in level plains upon the floor of stone.

Early in the Jurassic period, an impressive and far-reaching movement of the earth's crust took place, during which the bed of the ocean rose in crumpled waves towering high in the air and forming the mountain framework of the western United States. This system of upheavals reached as far east as Middle Wyoming and stretched from Mexico probably into

Alaska. Its numerous ridges and chains, having a general northwest trend, were crowded together in one broad zone whose western and most lofty member is the Sierra Nevada. During all of the Cretaceous period, and a part of the Tertiary, the Pacific beat upon its seaward foothills, tearing to pieces the rocks, crumbling and grinding the shores, and, drifting the powdered stone and pebbles beneath its waves, scattered them again in layers. This submarine table-land fringed the whole base of the range and extended westward an unknown distance under the sea. To this perpetual sea-wearing of the Sierra Nevada base was added the detritus made by the cutting out of canyons, which in great volumes continually poured into the Pacific, and was arranged upon its bottom by currents.

In the late Tertiary period, a chapter of very remarkable events occurred. For a second time, the evenly-laid beds of the sea bottom were crumpled by the shrinking of the earth. The ocean flowed back into deeper and narrower limits, and fronting the Sierra Nevada appeared the present system of Coast Ranges. The intermediate depression, or sea trough as I like to call it, is the valley of California, and is therefore a more recent continental feature than the Sierra Nevada. At once then, from the folded rocks of the Coast Ranges, from the Sierra summits and the inland plateaus, and from numberless vents caused by the fierce dynamical action, there poured out a general deluge of melted rock. From the bottom of the sea sprang up those fountains of lava whose cooled material forms many of the islands of the Pacific, and all along the coast of America, like a system of answering beacons, blazed up volcanic chimneys. The rent mountains glowed with outpourings of molten stone. Sheets of lava poured down the slopes of the

Sierra, covering an immense proportion of its surface, only the high granite and metamorphic peaks reaching above the deluge. Rivers and lakes floated up in a cloud of steam and were gone forever. The misty sky of these volcanic days glowed with innumerable lurid reflections, and at intervals along the crest of the range, great cones arose, blackening the sky with their plumes of mineral smoke. At length, having exhausted themselves, the volcanoes burned lower and lower, and at last, the greater number went out altogether.

The vast amount of ocean water, which had been vaporized, floated over the land, condensed upon hilltops, chilled the lavas, and finally buried beneath an icy covering all the higher parts of the mountain system. According to well-known laws, the over-burdened summits unloaded themselves by a system of glaciers. The whole Sierra crest was one pile of snow, from whose base crawled out the ice-rivers, wearing their bodies into the rock, sculpturing as they went the forms of valleys and brightening the surface of their tracks by the friction of stones and sand, which were bedded, armor-like, in their nether surface. Having made their way down the slope of the Sierra, they met a lowland temperature of sufficient warmth to arrest and waste them. At last, they shrank slowly back into the higher summit fastnesses, and there gradually perished, leaving only a crest of snow. The ice melted, and upon the whole plateau, little by little, a thin layer of soil accumulated, and, replacing the snow, there sprang up a forest of pines whose shadows fall pleasantly today over rocks, which were once torrents of lava, and across the burnished pathways of ice. Rivers, pure and sparkling, thread the bottom of these gigantic glacier valleys. The volcanoes are extinct, and the whole theatre of this impressive geological drama is now the most glorious and beautiful region of America.

Five distinct periods divide the history of the range. First, the slow gathering of marine sediment within the early ocean, during which incalculable ages were consumed. Second, in the early Jurassic period, this level sea-floor came suddenly to be lifted into the air and crumpled in folds, through whose yawning fissures and ruptured axes outpoured wide zones of granite. Third, the volcanic age of fire and steam. Fourth, the glacial period, when the Sierras were one broad field of snow, with huge dragons of ice crawling down its slopes and wearing their armor into the rocks. Fifth, the present condition.

From latitude 35 degrees to latitude 39 degrees, 30 minutes north, the Sierra lifts a continuous chain, the profile culminating in several groups of peaks separated by deeply-depressed curves or sharp notches, the summits varying from eight to fifteen thousand feet, seven to twelve thousand being the common range of passes. Near its southern extremity, in San Bernardino County, the range is cleft to the base with magnificent gateways opening through into the desert. From Walkers Pass for two hundred miles northward, the skyline is more uniformly elevated, the passes averaging nine thousand feet high, the actual summit a chain of peaks from thirteen to fifteen thousand feet. This serrated snow and granite outline of the Sierra Nevada, projected against the cold, clear blue, is the blade of white teeth, which suggested its Spanish name.

Northward still, the range gradually sinks; high peaks covered with perpetual snow are rarer and rarer. Its summit rolls on in broken, forest-covered ridges, now and then overlooked by a solitary pile of metamorphic or irruptive rock. At length, in Northern California, where it breaks down in a compressed medley of ridges and open, level expanses of plain, the axis is maintained by a line of extinct volcanoes standing above the lowland in isolated positions. The most lofty of these, Mount Shasta, is a cone of lava fourteen thousand four hundred and forty feet high, its broad base girdled with noble forests, which give way at eight thousand feet to a cap of glaciers and snow. Beyond this to the northward, the extension of the range is quite difficult to definitely assign, for, geologically speaking, the Sierra Nevada system occupies a broad area in Oregon consisting of several prominent mountain groups, while in a physical sense the chain ceases with Shasta. It is not easy to point out the actual southern limit either, because where the mountain mass descends into the Colorado desert, it comes in contact with a number of lesser groups of hills, which ramify in many directions, all losing themselves beneath the tertiary and quaternary beds of the desert.

For four hundred miles, the Sierras are a definite ridge, broad and high, and having the form of a seawave. Buttresses of somber-hued rock, jutting at intervals from a steep wall, form the abrupt eastern slopes. Irregular forests, in scattered growth, huddle together near the snow. The lower declivities are barren spurs, sinking into the sterile flats of the Great Basin. Long ridges of comparatively gentle outline characterize the western side, but this sloping table is scored from summit to base by a system of parallel transverse canyons, distant from one another often by less than twenty-five miles. They are ordinarily two or three thousand feet deep, falling at times in sheer, smooth-fronted cliffs, again in sweeping curves like the hull of a ship, again in rugged V-shaped gorges, or with irregular, hilly flanks opening at last through gateways of low, rounded foothills out upon the horizontal plain of the San Joaquin and Sacramento.

Every canyon carries a river, derived from constant melting of the perpetual snow, which threads its way down the mountain—a feeble type of those vast ice-streams and torrents that formerly discharged the summit accumulation of ice and snow while carving the canyons out from solid rock. Nowhere on the continent of America is there more positive evidence of the cutting power of rapid streams than in these very canyons. Although much is due to this cause, the most impressive passages of the Sierra valleys are actual ruptures of the rock, either the engulfment of masses of great size or a splitting asunder in yawning cracks. From the summits down half the distance to the plains, the canyons are also carved out in broad, round curves by glacial action. The summit gorges themselves are altogether the result of frost and ice. Here, even yet, may be studied the mode of blocking out mountain peaks; the cracks riven by unequal contraction and expansion of the rock; the slow leverage of ice, the storm, the avalanche.

The western descent, facing a moisture-laden, aerial current from the Pacific, condenses on its higher portions a great amount of water, which has piled upon the summits in the form of snow, and is absorbed upon the upper plateau by an exuberant growth of forest. This prevalent wind, which during most undisturbed periods blows continuously from the ocean, strikes first upon the western slope of the Coast Range, and there discharges, both as fog and rain, a very great sum of moisture. But, being ever reinforced, it blows over their crest, and, hurrying eastward, strikes the Sierras at about four thousand feet above sea level. Below this line, the foothills are oppressed by an habitual dryness, which produces a rusty olive tone throughout nearly all the large conspicuous vegetation, scorches the red soil, and during the long summer, overlays the whole region with a cloud of dust. Dull and monotonous in color, there are, however, certain elements of picturesqueness in this lower zone. Its oak-clad hills wander out into the great, plain-like coast promontories, enclosing yellow or, in spring-time, green bays of prairie. The hill-forms are rounded, or stretch in long, longitudinal ridges, broken across by the river canyons. Above this zone of red earth, softly modeled undulations, and dull, grayish groves with a chain of mining towns, dotted ranches, and vineyards, rise the swelling middle heights of the Sierras, a broad, billowy plateau cut by sharp, sudden canyons, and sweeping upwards with its dark, superb growth of coniferous forest to the feet of the summit peaks.

For a breadth of forty miles, all along the chain, is spread this continuous belt of pines. From Walker's Pass to Sitka, one may ride through an unbroken forest and will find its character and aspect vary constantly in strict accordance with the laws of altitude and moisture, each of the several species of coniferous trees taking its position with an almost mathematical precision. Where low gaps in the Coast Range give free access to the western wind, there the forest sweeps downward and encamps upon the foothills, and, continuing northward, it advances toward the coast, securing for itself over this whole distance about the same physical conditions; so that a tree which finds itself at home on the shore of Puget's Sound, in the latitude of Middle California, has climbed the Sierras to a height of six thousand feet, finding there its normal requirements of damp, cool air. As if to economize the whole surface of the Sierra, the forest is mainly made up of twelve species of conifer, each having its own definitely circumscribed limits of temperature, and yet being able successively to occupy the whole middle Sierra up to the foot of the perpetual snow. The average range in altitude of each species is about twenty-five hundred feet, so that you pass imperceptibly from the zone of one species into that of the next. Frequently, three or four are commingled, their varied habit, characteristic foliage, and richly-colored trunks uniting to make the most stately of forests.

In the center of the coniferous belt is assembled the most remarkable family of trees. Those which approach the perpetual snow are imperfect, gnarled, storm-bent, full of character and suggestion, but lacking the symmetry, the rich, living green, and the great size of their lower neighbors. In the other extreme of the pine belt, growing side by side with foothill oaks, is an equally imperfect species, which, although attaining a very great size, still has the air of an abnormal tree. The conditions of drought on the one hand, and rigorous storms on the other, injure and blast alike, while the more verdant center, furnishing the finest conditions, produces a forest whose profusion and grandeur fill the traveler with the liveliest admiration.

Toward the south, the growth of the forest is more open and grove-like, the individual trees becoming proportionally larger and reaching their highest development. Northward, its density increases, to the injury of individual pines, until the branches finally interlock, and at last on the shores of British Columbia, the trunks are so densely assembled that a dead tree is held in its upright position by the arms of its fellows. At the one extremity are magnificent purple shafts ornamented with an exquisitely delicate drapery of pale golden and dark blue green; at the other, the slender spars stand crowded together like the fringe of masts girdling a prosperous port. The one is a great, continuous grove, on whose sunny openings are innumerable brilliant parterres; the other is a dismal thicket, a sort of gigantic canebrake, void of beauty, dark, impenetrable, save by the avenues of streams, where one may float for days between somber walls of forest. From one to the other of these extremes is an imperceptible transition. Only in the passage of hundreds of miles does the forest seem to thicken northward, or the majesty of the single trees appear to be impaired by their struggle for room.

Near the center is the perfection of forest. At the south are the finest specimen trees, at the north the densest accumulations of timber. In riding throughout this whole region and watching the same species—from the glorious ideal life of the south gradually dwarfed toward the north until it becomes a mere wand, or in climbing from the scattered, drought-scourged pines of the foothills up through the zone of finest vegetation to those summit crags, where, struggling against the power of tempest and frost, only a few of the bravest trees succeed in clinging to the rocks and to life—one sees with novel effect the inexorable sway which climatic conditions hold over the kingdom of trees.

Looking down from the summit, the forest is a closely-woven vesture, which has fallen over the body of the range, clinging closely to its form, sinking into the deep canyons, covering the hilltops with even, velvety folds, and only lost here and there where a bold mass of rock gives it no foothold, or where around the margin of the mountain lakes, bits of alpine

16

meadow lie open to the sun. Along its upper limit, the forest zone grows thin and irregular; black shafts of alpine pines and firs clustering on sheltered slopes, or climbing in disordered processions up broken and rocky faces. Higher, the last gnarled forms are passed, and beyond stretches the rank of silent, white peaks, a region of rock and ice lifted above the limit of life. In the north, domes and cones of volcanic formation are the summit, but for about three hundred miles in the south, it is a succession of sharp granite aiguilles and crags. Prevalent among the granitic forms are singularly perfect conoidal domes, whose symmetrical figures, were it not for their immense size, would impress one as having an artificial finish. The alpine gorges are usually wide and open, leading into amphitheaters whose walls are either rock or drifts of never-melting snow. The sculpture of the summit is very evidently glacial. Beside the ordinary phenomena of polished rocks and moraines, the larger general forms are clearly the work of frost and ice, and, although this ice-period is only feebly represented today, the frequent avalanches of winter and freshly-scored mountain flanks are constant suggestions of the past.

Strikingly contrasted are the two countries bordering the Sierra on either side. Along the western base is the plain of California, an elliptical basin four hundred and fifty miles long by sixty-five broad; level, fertile, well-watered, half tropically-warmed; checkered with farms of grain, ranches of cattle, orchard and vineyard, and homes of commonplace opulence, towns of bustling thrift. Rivers flow over it, bordered by lines of oaks, which seem characterless or gone to sleep when compared with the vitality, the spring, and attitude of the same species higher up on the foothills. It is a region of great industrial future within a narrow range, but quite without charms for the student of science. It has a certain impressive breadth when seen from some overlooking eminence, or when in early spring its brilliant carpet of flowers lies as a foreground over which the dark pineland and white crest of the Sierra loom indistinctly. From the Mexican frontier up into Oregon, a strip of actual desert lies under the east slope of the great chain and stretches eastward, sometimes as far as five hundred miles, varied by successions of bare, white ground, effervescing under the hot sun with alkaline salts, plains covered by the low, ashy-hued sage-plant, high, barren, rocky ranges, which are folds of metamorphic rocks, and piled-up lavas of bright red or yellow colors, all over-arched by a sky which is at one time of a hot, metallic brilliancy, and again the tenderest of evanescent purple or pearl.

Utterly opposed are the two aspects of the Sierras from these east and west approaches. I remember how stern and strong the chain looked to me when I first saw it from the Colorado desert.

It was in early May, 1866. My companion, Mr. James Terry Gardiner, and I got into the saddle on the bank of the Colorado River, and headed westward over the road from La Paz to San Bernardino. Far ahead of us, a white line traced across the barren plain marked our road. It seemed to lead to nowhere, except onward over more and more arid reaches of desert. Rolling hills of crude color and low, gloomy contour rose above the general level. Here and there the eye was arrested by a towering crag or an elevated, rocky mountain group, whose naked sides sank down into the desert, unrelieved by the shade of a solitary tree. The whole aspect of nature was dull in color, and gloomy with an all-pervading silence of death. Although the summer had not fairly opened, a torrid sun beat down with cruel severity, blinding the eye with its brilliance and inducing a painful slow fever. The very plants, scorched to a crisp, were ready, at the first blast of a sirocco, to be whirled away and ground to dust. Certain bare zones lay swept clean of the last dry stems across our path, marking the track of whirlwinds. Water was only found at intervals of sixty or seventy miles, and when reached, was more of an aggrava-tion than a pleasure—bitter, turbid, and scarce. We rode for it all day, and berated it all night, only to leave it at sunrise with a secret fear that we might fare worse next time.

About noon on the third day of our march, having reached the borders of the Chabazon Valley, we emerged from a rough, rocky gateway in the mountains, and I paused while my com-panion made up his quarter of a mile, that we might hold council and determine our course, for the water question was becoming serious. Springs which looked cool and seductive on our maps proving to be dried up and obsolete upon the ground.

Gardiner reached me in a few minutes, and we dismounted to rest the tired mules and to scan the landscape before us. We were on the margin of a great basin whose gently shelving rim sank from our feet to a perfectly level plain, which stretched southward as far as the eye could reach, bounded by a dim, level horizon, like the sea, but walled in to the west at a dis-tance of about forty miles by the high, frowning wall of the Sierras. This plain was a level floor, as white as marble, and into it the rocky spurs from our own mountain range descended like promontories into the sea. Wide, deeply-indented white bays wound in and out among the foothills, and, traced upon the barren slopes of this rocky coast was marked, at a considerable elevation above the plain, the shoreline of an ancient sea, white stain defining its former margin as clearly as if the water had but just receded. On the dim, distant base of the Sierras the same primeval beach could be seen. This watermark, the level, white valley, and the utter absence upon its surface of any vegetation, gave a strange and weird aspect to the country, as if a vast tide had but just ebbed, and the brilliant, scorching sun had hurriedly dried up its last traces of moisture.

In the indistinct glare of the southern horizon, it needed but slight aid from the imagination to see a lifting and tumbling of billows, as if the old tide were coming, but they were only shudderings of heat. As we sat there surveying this unusual scene, the white expanse became suddenly transformed into a placid blue sea along whose rippling shores were the white blocks of roofs, groups of spire-crowned villages, and cool stretches of green grove. A soft, vapory atmosphere hung over this sea. Shadows, purple and blue, floated slowly across it, producing the most enchanting effect of light and color. The dreamy richness of the tropics, the serene sapphire sky of the desert, and the cool, purple distance of mountains were grouped as by miracle. It was as if Nature were about to repay us a hundred-fold for the lie she had given the topographers and their maps.

In a moment the illusion vanished. It was gone, leaving the white desert unrelieved by a shadow; a blaze of white light falling full on the plain; the sun-struck air reeling in whirlwind columns, white with the dust of the desert, up, up, and vanishing into the sky. Waves of heat rolled like billows across the valley, the old shores became indistinct, the whole lowland unreal. Shades of misty blue crossed over it and disappeared. Lakes with ragged shores gleamed out, reflecting the sky, and in a moment disappeared. We eagerly scanned the distance, but were unable, among the phantom lakes and the ever-changing illusions of the desert, to fix upon any probable point. Indian trails led out in all directions, and our only clue to the right path was far in the northwest, where, looming against the sky, stood two conspicuous mountain piles lifted above the general wall of the Sierra, their bases rooted in the desert and their precipitous fronts rising boldly on each side of an open gateway. The two summits, high above the magical stratum of desert air, were sharply defined and singularly distinct in all the details of rockform and snowfield. From their position, we knew them to be walls of the San Gorgonio Pass, and through this gateway lay our road. Thus we rode down into the desert, and hour after hour traveled silently on, straining our eyes forward to a spot of green, which we hoped, might mark our oasis.

It was the oasis, and not the mirage.

Under the palms we hastily threw off our saddles and allowed the parched brutes to drink their fill. We lay down in the grass, drank, bathed our faces, and played in the water like children. By and by we plunged into the pool, which was perhaps thirty feet long and deep enough to give us a pleasant swim. The water being almost blood-warm, we absorbed it in every pore, dilated like sponges, and came out refreshed. With its isolation, its strange, warm fountain, its charming vegetation varied with grasses, trailing water-plants, bright parterres in which were minute flowers of turquoise blue, pale gold, mauve, and rose, and its two graceful palms, this oasis evoked a strange sentiment. I have never felt such a sense of absolute and remote seclusion. The hot, trackless plain and distant groups of mountain shut it away from all the world. Its humid and fragrant air hung over us in delicious contrast with the oven-breath through which we had ridden. Weary little birds alighted, panting, and drank and drank again, without showing the least fear of us. Wild doves fluttering down bathed in the pool and fed about among our mules.

After straining over one hundred and fifty miles of silent desert, hearing no sound but the shoes of our mules grating upon hot sand, after the white glare, and that fever-thirst which comes from drinking alkali water, it was a deep pleasure to lie under the palms and look up at their slow-moving green fans, and hear in those shaded recesses the mild, sweet twittering of our traveler-friends, the birds, who stayed, like ourselves, overcome with the languor of perfect repose.

Declining rapidly toward the west, the sun warned us to renew our journey. As I rode, I watched the western prospect. Completely bounding the basin in that direction rose the gigantic wall of the Sierra, its serrated line sharply profiled against the evening sky. This dark barrier became more and more shadowed, so that the old shore line and the lowland, where mountain and plain joined, were lost. The desert melted in the distance into the shadowed masses of the Sierra, which, looming higher and higher, seemed to rise as the sun went down. Scattered snowfields shone along its crest. Each peak and notch, every column of rock and detail of outline, were black and sharp. On either side of the San Gorgonio stood its two guardian peaks, San Bernardino and San Jacinto, capped with rosy snow, and the pass itself, warm with western light, opened hopefully before us. For a moment the sun rested upon the Sierra crest, and then, slowly sinking, suffered eclipse by its ragged, black profile. Through the slow hours of darkening twilight a strange, ashy gloom overspread the desert. The forms of the distant mountain chains behind us, and the old shore line upon the Sierra base, stared at us with a strange, weird distinctness. At last all was gray and vague, except the black silhouette of the Sierras cut upon a band of golden heaven.

Muir Woods

3

John Muir: An Appreciation

Theodore Roosevelt

Ordinarily, the man who loves the woods and mountains, the trees, the flowers, and the wild things, has in him some indefinable quality of charm, which appeals even to those sons of civilization who care for little outside of paved streets and brick walls. John Muir was a fine illustration of this rule. He was by birth a Scotchman—a tall and spare man, with the poise and ease natural to him who has lived much alone under conditions of labor and hazard. He was a dauntless soul, and also one brimming over with friendliness and kindliness.

He was emphatically a good citizen. Not only are his books delightful, not only is he the author to whom all men turn when they think of the Sierras and northern glaciers, and the giant trees of the California slope, but he was also—what few nature lovers are—a man able to influence contemporary thought and action on the subjects to which he had devoted his life. He was a great factor in influencing the thought of California and the thought of the entire country so as to secure the preservation of those great natural phenomena— wonderful canyons, giant trees, slopes of flower-spangled hill-sides—which make California a veritable Garden of the Lord.

It was my good fortune to know John Muir. He had written me, even before I met him personally, expressing his regret that when Emerson came to see the Yosemite, his (Emerson's) friends would not allow him to accept John Muir's invitation to spend two or three days camping with him, so as to see the giant grandeur of the place under surroundings more con-genial than those of a hotel piazza or a seat on a coach. I had answered him that if ever I got in his neighborhood I should claim from him the treatment that he had wished to accord Emerson. Later, when as President I visited the Yosemite, John Muir fulfilled the promise he had at that time made to me. He met me with a couple of pack mules, as well as with riding mules for himself and myself, and a first-class packer and cook, and I spent a delightful three days and two nights with him.

The first night we camped in a grove of giant sequoias. It was clear weather and we lay in the open, the enormous cinnamon-colored trunks rising about us like the columns of a vaster and more beautiful cathedral than was ever conceived by any human architect. One incident surprised me not a little. Some thrushes—I think they were western hermit thrushes—were singing beautifully in the solemn evening stillness. I asked some question concerning them of John Muir, and to my surprise found that he had not been listening to them and knew nothing about them. John Muir, I found, was not interested in the small things of nature unless they were unusually conspicuous. Mountains, cliffs, trees appealed to him tremendously, but birds did not unless they possessed some very peculiar and interesting as well as conspicuous traits, as in the case of the water ouzel. In the same way, he knew nothing of the wood mice; but the more conspicuous beasts, such as bear and deer, for example, he could tell much about.

All next day we traveled through the forest. Then a snowstorm came on, and at night we camped on the edge of the Yosemite, under the branches of a magnificent silver fir, and very warm and comfortable we were, and a very good dinner we had before we rolled up in our tarpaulins and blankets for the night. The following day we went down into the Yosemite and through the valley, camping in the bottom among the timber.

There was a delightful innocence and good will about the man, and an utter inability to imagine that anyone could either take or give offense. Of this I had an amusing illustration just before we parted. We were saying good-bye, when his expression suddenly changed, and he remarked that he had totally forgotten something. He was intending to go to the Old World with a great tree lover and tree expert from the Eastern States who possessed a somewhat crotchety temper. He informed me that his friend had written him, asking him to get from me personal letters to the Russian Czar and the Chinese

Emperor. And when I explained to him that I could not give personal letters to foreign potentates, he said, "Oh, well, read the letter yourself, and that will explain just what I want." Accordingly, he thrust the letter on me. It contained not only the request, which he had mentioned, but also a delicious preface, which, with the request, ran somewhat as follows:

"I hear Roosevelt is coming out to see you. He takes a sloppy, unintelligent interest in forests, although he is altogether too much under the influence of that creature Pinchot [Gifford Pinchot, first Chief of the U.S. Forest Service and a philosophical opponent of Muir, *ed.*] and you had better get from him letters to the Czar of Russia and the Emperor of China, so that we may have better opportunity to examine the forests and trees of the Old World."

Of course I laughed heartily as I read the letter, and said, "John, do you remember exactly the words in which this letter was couched?" Whereupon a look of startled surprise came over his face, and he said, "Good gracious! There was something unpleasant about you in it, wasn't there? I had forgotten. Give me the letter back."

So I gave him back the letter, telling him that I appreciated it far more than if it had not contained the phrases he had forgotten, and that while I could not give him and his companion letters to the two rulers in question, I would give him letters to our Ambassadors, which would bring about the same result.

John Muir talked even better than he wrote. His greatest influence was always upon those who were brought into personal contact with him. But he wrote well, and while his books have not the peculiar charm that a very, very few other writers on similar subjects have had, they will nevertheless last long. Our generation owes much to John Muir.

Glacier

4

Yosemite Glaciers

John Muir

Yosemite Valley
September 28, 1871

Two years ago, when picking flowers in the mountains back of Yosemite Valley, I found a book. It was blotted and storm-beaten; all of its outer pages were mealy and crumbly, and the paper seemed to dissolve like the snow beneath which it had been buried. But many of the inner pages were well preserved, and though all were more or less stained and torn, whole chapters were easily readable. In this condition is the great open book of Yosemite glaciers today; its granite pages have been torn and blurred by the same storms that wasted the castaway book. The grand central chapters of the Hoffman, and Tenaya, and Nevada glaciers are stained and corroded by the frosts and rains, yet, nevertheless, they contain scarcely one unreadable page. But the outer chapters of the Pohono, and the Illilouette, and the Yosemite Creek, and Ribbon, and Cascade glaciers, are all dimmed and eaten away on the bottom, though the tops of their pages have not been so long exposed, and still proclaim in splendid characters the glorious actions of their departed ice. The glacier which filled the basin of the Yosemite Creek was the fourth ice-stream that flowed to Yosemite Valley. It was about fifteen miles in length by five in breadth at the middle of the main stream, and in many places was not less than one thousand feet in depth. It united with the central glaciers in the valley by a mouth reaching from the east side of El Capitan to Yosemite Point, east of the falls. Its western rim was rayed with short tributaries, and on the north, its divide from the Tuolumne glacier was deeply grooved, but few if any of its ridges were here high enough to separate the descending ice into distinct tributaries. The main central trunk flowed nearly south and, at a distance of about ten miles, separated into three nearly equal branches, which were turned abruptly to the east. Those branch basins are laid among the highest spurs of the Hoffman range and abound in small, bright lakes, set in the solid granite without the usual terminal moraine dam. The structure of those dividing spurs is exactly similar, all three appearing as if ruins of one mountain, or rather as perfect units hewn from one mountain rock during long ages of glacial activity. As their north sides are precipitous, and as they extend east and west, they were enabled to shelter and keep alive their hiding glaciers long after the death of the main trunk. Their basins are still dazzling bright, and their lakes have as yet accumulated but narrow rings of border meadow, because their feeding streams have had but little time to carry the sand of which they are made. The east bank of the main stream, all the way from the three forks to the mouth, is a continuous, regular wall, which also forms the west bank of the Indian Canyon glacier-basin. The tributaries of the west side of the main basin touched the east tributaries of the cascade, and the great Tuolumne glacier from Mount Dana, the mightiest ice-river of this whole region, flowed past on the north. The declivity of the tributaries was great, especially those which flowed from the spurs of the Hoffman on the Tuolumne divide, but the main stream was rather level, and in approaching Yosemite was compelled to make a considerable ascent back of Eagle Cliff. To the concentrated currents of the central glaciers, and to the levelness and width of mouth of this one, we in a great measure owe the present height of the Yosemite Falls. Yosemite Creek lives the most tranquil life of all the large streams that leap into the valley. The others occupying the canyons of narrower and, consequently, of deeper glaciers, while yet far from the valley, abound in loud falls and snowy cascades, but Yosemite Creek flows straight on through smooth meadows and hollows, with only two or three gentle cascades, and now and then a row of soothing, rumbling rapids, biding its time and hoarding up the best music and poetry of its life for the one anthem at Yosemite, as planned by the ice.

When a bird's-eye view of Yosemite Basin is obtained from any of its upper domes, it is seen to possess a great number of dense patches of black forest, planted in abrupt contact with bare gray rocks. Those forest plots mark the number and the size of all the entire and fragmentary moraines of the basin, as the latter eroding agents have not yet had sufficient time to form a soil fit for the vigorous life of large trees. Wherever a deep-wombed tributary was laid against a narrow ridge, and was also shielded from the sun by compassing rock-shadows, there we invariably find more small terminal moraines, because when such tributaries were melted off from the trunk, they retired to those upper strongholds of shade, and lived and worked in full independence, and the moraines which they built are left entire because the water-collecting basins behind are too small to make streams large enough to wash them away. But in the basins of exposed tributaries there are no terminal moraines, because their glaciers died with the trunk. Medial and lateral moraines are common upon all the outside slopes, some of them nearly perfect in form, but down in the main basin there is not left one unaltered moraine of any kind, immense floods having washed down and leveled them into harder meadows for the present stream, and into sandy flower beds and fields for forests.

Such was Yosemite glacier, and such is its basin, the magnificent work of its hands. There is sublimity in the life of a glacier. Water rivers work openly, and so the rains and the gentle dews, and the great sea also grasping all the world. Even the universal ocean of breath, though invisible, yet speaks aloud in a thousand voices, and proclaims its modes of working and its power. But glaciers work apart from men, exerting their tremendous energies in silence and darkness, outspread, spirit-like, brooding above predestined rocks unknown to light, unborn, working on unwearied through unmeasured times, unhalting as the stars, until at length, their creations complete, their mountains brought forth, homes made for the meadows and the lakes, and fields for waiting forests, earnest, calm as when they came as crystals from the sky, they depart.

In the waning days of this mountain ice, when the main river began to shallow and break like a summer cloud, its crests and domes rising higher and higher, and island rocks coming to light far out in the main current, then many a tributary died, and this one, cut off from its trunk, moved slowly back amid the gurgling and gushing of its bleeding rills, until, crouching in the shadows of this half-mile hollow, it lived a feeble separate life. Here its days come and go, and the hiding glacier lives and works. It brings boulders and sand and fine dust polishings from its sheltering domes and canyons, building up a terminal moraine, which forms a dam for the waters which issue from it. Beneath, working in the dark, it scoops a shallow lake basin. Again the glacier retires, crouching under cooler shadows, and a cluster of steady years enables the dying glacier to make yet another moraine dam like the first. Where the granite begins to rise in curves to form the upper dam, it scoops another lake. Its last work is done, and it dies. The twin lakes are full of pure green water and floating masses of snow and broken ice. The domes, perfect in sculpture, gleam in newborn purity, lakes and domes reflecting each other bright as the ice which made them. God's seasons circle on, glad brooks born of the snow and the rain sing in the rocks and carry sand to the naked lakes, and, in the fullness of time, comes many a chosen plant; first a lowly carex with dark brown spikes, then taller sedges and rushes, fixing a shallow soil, and now come many grasses and daisies and blooming shrubs, until lake and meadow growing throughout the season like a flower in summer, develop to the perfect beauty of today.

Merced River

5

How The Valley Was Formed

John Muir

All California has been glaciated, the low plains and valleys as well as the mountains. Traces of an ice sheet, thousands of feet in thickness, beneath whose heavy folds the present landscapes have been molded, may be found everywhere, though glaciers now exist only among the peaks of the High

Sierra. No other mountain chain on this or any other of the continents that I have seen is so rich as the Sierra in bold, striking, well-preserved glacial monuments. Indeed, every feature is more or less tellingly glacial. Not a peak, ridge, dome, canyon, lake-basin, stream or forest will you see that does not in some way explain the past existence and modes of action of flowing, grinding, sculpturing, soil-making, scenery-making ice.

The landscapes of North Greenland, Antarctica, and some of those of our own Alaska, are still being fashioned beneath a slow-crawling mantle of ice, from a quarter of a mile to probably more than a mile in thickness, presenting noble illustrations of the ancient condition of California, when its sublime scenery lay hidden in process of formation. On the Himalaya, the mountains of Norway and Switzerland, the Caucasus, and on most of those of Alaska, their ice-mantle has been melted down into separate glaciers that flow river-like through the valleys, illustrating a similar past condition in the Sierra, when every canyon and valley was the channel of an ice-stream, all of which may be easily traced back to their fountains, where some sixty-five or seventy of their topmost residual branches still linger beneath protecting mountain shadows.

The change from one to another of those glacial conditions was slow as we count time. When the great cycle of snow years, called the Glacial Period, was nearly complete in California, the ice-mantle, wasting from season to season faster than it was renewed, began to withdraw from the lowlands and gradually became shallower everywhere. Then the highest of the Sierra domes and dividing ridges, containing distinct glaciers between them, began to appear above the icy sea. These first river-like glaciers remained united in one continuous sheet toward the summit of the range for many centuries. But as the snowfall diminished, and the climate became milder, this upper part of the ice-sheet was also in turn separated into smaller distinct glaciers, and these again into still smaller ones, while at the same time all were growing shorter and shallower, though fluctuations of the climate now and then occurred that brought their receding ends to a standstill, or even enabled them to advance for a few tens or hundreds of years.

Meanwhile, hardy, home-seeking plants and animals, after long waiting, flocked to their appointed places, pushing bravely on higher and higher, along every sun-warmed slope, closely following the retreating ice, which, like shreds of summer clouds, at length vanished from the newborn mountains, leaving them in all their main, telling features nearly as we find them now. Tracing the ways of glaciers, learning how Nature sculptures mountain-waves in making scenery-beauty that so mysteriously influences every human being, is glorious work.

The most striking and attractive of the glacial phenomena in the upper Yosemite region are the polished glacier pavements, because they are so beautiful, and their beauty is of so rare a kind, so unlike any portion of the loose, deeply weathered lowlands where people make homes and earn their bread. They are simply flat or gently undulating areas of hard, resisting granite, which present the unchanged surface upon which with enormous pressure the ancient glaciers flowed. They are found in most perfect condition in the subalpine region, at an elevation of from eight thousand to nine thousand feet. Some are miles in extent, only slightly interrupted by spots that have given way to the weather, while the best preserved portions reflect the sunbeams like calm water or glass, and shine as if polished afresh every day, notwithstanding they have been exposed to corroding rains, dew, frost, and snow for measureless thousands of years.

The attention of wandering hunters and prospectors, who see so many mountain wonders, is seldom commanded by other glacial phenomena, moraines however regular and artificial-looking, canyons however deep or strangely modeled, rocks however high. But when they come to these shining pavements, they stop and stare in wondering admiration, kneel again and again to examine the brightest spots, and try hard to account for their mysterious shining smoothness. They may have seen the winter avalanches of snow descending in awful majesty through the woods, scouring the rocks and sweeping away like weeds the trees that stood in their way, but conclude that this cannot be the work of avalanches because the scratches and fine polished strife show that the agent, whatever it was, moved along the sides of high rocks and ridges and up over the tops of them as well as down their slopes. Neither can they see how water may possibly have been the agent, for they find the same strange polish upon ridges and domes thousands of feet above the reach of any conceivable flood. Of all the agents of whose work they know anything, only the wind seems capable of moving across the face of the country in the directions indicated by the scratches and grooves. The Indian name of Lake Tenaya is "Pyweak"—the lake of shining rocks. One of the Yosemite tribe, Indian Tom, came to me and asked if I could tell him what had made the Tenaya rocks so smooth. Even dogs and horses, when first led up the mountains, study geology to this extent that they gaze wonderingly at the strange brightness of the ground and smell it, and place their feet cautiously upon it as if afraid of falling or sinking.

In the production of this admirable hard finish, the glaciers in many places flowed with a pressure of more than a thousand tons to the square yard, planing down granite, slate, and quartz alike, and bringing out the veins and crystals of the rocks with beautiful distinctness. Over large areas below the sources of the Tuolumne and Merced, the granite is porphyritic. Feldspar crystals an inch or two in length in many places form the greater part of the rock, and these, when planed off level with the general surface, give rise to a beautiful mosaic on which the happy sunbeams splash and glow in passionate enthusiasm. Here lie the brightest of all the Sierra landscapes.

One of the best general views of the brightest and best of the Yosemite Park landscapes that every Yosemite tourist should see is to be had from the top of Fairview Dome, a lofty conoidal rock near Cathedral Peak that long ago I named the Tuolumne Glacier Monument, one of the most striking and best preserved of the domes. Its burnished crown is about fifteen hundred feet above the Tuolumne Meadows and ten thousand above the sea. At first sight it seems inaccessible, though a good climber will find it may be scaled on the south side. About halfway up you will find it so steep that there is danger of slipping, but feldspar crystals, two or three inches long, of which the rock is full, having offered greater resistance to atmospheric erosion than the mass of the rock in which they are imbedded, have been brought into slight relief in some places, roughening the surface here and there, and affording helping footholds. The summit is burnished and scored like the sides and base, the scratches and strife indicating that the mighty Tuolumne Glacier swept over it as if it were only a mere boulder in the bottom of its channel. The pressure it withstood must have been enormous. Had it been less solidly built it would have been carried away, ground into moraine fragments, like the adjacent rock in which it lay imbedded. For, great as it is, it is only a hard residual knot like the Yosemite domes, brought into relief by the removal of less resisting rock about it, an illustration of the survival of the strongest and most favorably situated.

Hardly less wonderful is the resistance it has offered to the trying mountain weather since first its crown rose above the icy sea. The whole quantity of post-glacial wear and tear it has suffered has not degraded it a hundredth of an inch, as may readily be shown by the polished portions of the surface. A few erratic boulders, nicely poised on its crown, tell an interesting story. They came from the summit peaks twelve miles away, drifting like chips on the frozen sea, and were stranded here when the top of the monument emerged from the ice, while their companions, whose positions chanced to be above the slopes of the sides where they could not find rest, were carried farther on by falling back on the shallowing ice current.

The general view from the summit consists of a sublime assemblage of iceborn rocks and mountains, long wavering ridges, meadows, lakes, and forest-covered moraines, hundreds of square miles of them. The lofty summit peaks rise grandly along the sky to the east, the gray-pillared slopes of the Hoffman Range toward the west, and a billowy sea of shining rocks like the Monument, some of them almost as high and, which from their peculiar sculpture, seem to be rolling westward in the middle ground, something like breaking waves. Immediately beneath you are the Big Tuolumne Meadows, smooth lawns with large breadths of woods on either side, and watered by the young Tuolumne River, rushing cool and clear from its many snow- and ice-fountains. Nearly all the upper part of the basin of the Tuolumne Glacier is in sight, one of the greatest and most influential of all the Sierra ice-rivers. Lavishly flooded by many a noble affluent from the ice-laden flanks of Mounts Dana, Lyell, McClure, Gibbs, and Conness, it poured its majestic outflowing current full against the end of the Hoffman Range, which divided and deflected it to right and left, just as a river of water is divided against an island in the middle of its channel. Two distinct glaciers were thus formed, one of which flowed through the great Tuolumne Canyon and Hetch Hetchy Valley, while the other swept upward in a deep current two miles wide across the divide, five hundred feet high between the basins of the Tuolumne and Merced, into the Tenaya Basin, and thence down through the Tenaya Canyon and Yosemite.

The map-like distinctness and freshness of this glacial land-scape cannot fail to excite the attention of every beholder, no matter how little of its scientific significance may be recognized. These bald, westward-leaning rocks, with their rounded backs and shoulders toward the glacier fountains of the summit mountains, and their split, angular fronts looking in the opposite direction, explain the tremendous grinding force with which the ice-flood passed over them, and also the direction of its flow. And the mountain peaks around the sides of the upper general Tuolumne Basin, with their sharp unglaciated summits and polished rounded sides, indicate the height to which the glaciers rose, while the numerous moraines, curving and swaying in beautiful lines, mark the boundaries of the main trunk and its tributaries as they existed toward the close of the glacial winter. None of the commercial highways of the land or sea, marked with buoys and lamps, fences, and guideboards, is so unmistakably indicated as are these broad, shining trails of the vanished Tuolumne Glacier and its far-reaching tributaries.

I should like now to offer some nearer views of a few characteristic specimens of these wonderful old ice-streams, though it is not easy to make a selection from so vast a system intimately interblended. The main branches of the Merced Glacier are, perhaps, best suited to our purpose, because their basins, full of telling inscriptions, are the ones most attractive and accessible to the Yosemite visitors who like to look beyond the valley walls. They number five, and may well be called Yosemite glaciers, since they were the agents Nature used in developing and fashioning the grand valley. The names I have given them are, beginning with the northernmost, Yosemite Creek, Hoffman, Tenaya, South Lyell, and Illilouette Glaciers. These all converged in admirable poise around from northeast to southeast, welded themselves together into the main Yosemite Glacier, which, grinding gradually deeper, swept down through the valley, receiving small tributaries on its way from the Indian, Sentinel, and Pohono Canyons, and at length flowed out of the valley and on down the range in a general westerly direction. At the time that the tributaries mentioned above were well-defined as to their boundaries, the upper portion of the valley walls and the highest rocks about them, such as the Domes, the uppermost of the Three Brothers and the

Sentinel, rose above the surface of the ice. But during the valley's earlier history, all its rocks, however lofty, were buried beneath a continuous sheet, which swept on above and about them like the wind, the upper portion of the current flowing steadily, while the lower portion went mazing and swedging down in the crooked and dome-blocked canyons toward the head of the valley.

Every glacier of the Sierra fluctuated in width and depth and length, and consequently in degree of individuality, down to the latest glacial days. It must, therefore, be borne in mind that the following description of the Yosemite glaciers applies only to their separate condition, and to that phase of their separate condition that they presented toward the close of the glacial period after most of their work was finished, and all the more telling features of the valley and the adjacent region were brought into relief.

Yosemite Creek Glacier

The comparatively level, many-fountained Yosemite Creek Glacier was about fourteen miles in length by four or five in width, and from five hundred to a thousand feet deep. Its principal tributaries, drawing their sources from the northern spurs of the Hoffman Range, at first pursued a westerly course. Then, uniting with each other, and a series of short affluents from the western rim of the basin, the trunk thus formed swept around to the southward in a magnificent curve, and poured its ice over the north wall of Yosemite in cascades about two miles wide. This broad and comparatively shallow glacier formed a sort of crawling, wrinkled ice-cloud that gradually became more regular in shape and river-like as it grew older.

Encircling peaks began to overshadow its highest fountains, rock islets rose here and there amid its ebbing currents, and its picturesque banks, adorned with domes and round-backed ridges, extended in massive grandeur down to the brink of the Yosemite walls. In the meantime, the chief Hoffman tributaries, slowly receding to the shelter of the shadows covering their fountains, continued to live and work independently, spreading soil, deepening lake-basins, and giving finishing touches to the sculpture in general. At length these also vanished, and the whole basin is now full of light. Forests flourish luxuriantly upon its ample moraines, lakes and meadows shine and bloom amid its polished domes, and a thousand gardens adorn the banks of its streams.

It is to the great width and even slope of the Yosemite Creek Glacier that we owe the unrivaled height and sheerness of the Yosemite Falls. For had the positions of the ice-fountains and the structure of the rocks been such as to cause down-thrusting concentration of the Glacier as it approached the valley, then, instead of a high vertical fall we should have had a long slanting cascade, which after all would perhaps have been as beautiful and interesting, if we only had a mind to see it so.

Hoffman Glacier

The short, comparatively swift-flowing Hoffman Glacier, whose fountains extend along the south slopes of the Hoffman Range, offered a striking contrast to the one just described. The erosive energy of the latter was diffused over a wide field of sunken, boulder-like domes and ridges. The Hoffman Glacier, on the contrary, moved right ahead on a comparatively even surface, making descent of nearly five thousand feet in five miles, steadily contracting and deepening its current, and finally united with the Tenaya Glacier as one of its most influential tributaries in the development and sculpture of the great Half Dome, North Dome, and the rocks adjacent to them about the head of the valley.

The story of its death is not unlike that of its companion already described, though the declivity of its channel, and its uniform exposure to sun-heat prevented any considerable portion of its current from becoming torpid, lingering only well up on the mountain slopes to finish their sculpture and encircle them with a zone of moraine soil for forests and gardens. Nowhere in all this wonderful region will you find more beautiful trees and shrubs and flowers covering the traces of ice.

Tenaya Glacier

The rugged Tenaya Glacier, wildly crevassed here and there above the ridges it had to cross, instead of drawing its sources direct from the summit of the range, formed, as we have seen, one of the outlets of the great Tuolumne Glacier, issuing from this noble fountain like a river from a lake, two miles wide, about fourteen miles long, and from fifteen hundred to two thousand feet deep. In leaving the Tuolumne region, it crossed over the divide, as mentioned above, between the Tuolumne and Tenaya basins, making an ascent of five hundred feet. Hence, after contracting its wide current and receiving a strong affluent from the fountains about Cathedral Peak, it poured its massive flood over the northeastern rim of its basin in splendid cascades. Then, crushing heavily against the Clouds Rest Ridge, it bore down upon the Yosemite domes with concentrated energy.

Toward the end of the ice period, while its Hoffman companion continued to grind rock-meal for coming plants, the main trunk became torpid, and vanished, exposing wide areas of rolling rock-waves and glistening pavements, on whose channelless surface water ran wild and free. And because the trunk vanished almost simultaneously throughout its whole extent, no terminal moraines are found in its canyon channel; nor, since its walls are, in most places, too steeply inclined to admit of the deposition of moraine matter, do we find much of the two main laterals. The lowest of its residual glaciers lingered beneath the shadow of the Yosemite Half Dome, others along the base of Coliseum Peak above Lake Tenaya and along the precipitous wall extending from the lake to the Big Tuolumne Meadows. The latter, on account of the uniformity and continuity of their protecting shadows, formed moraines of considerable length and regularity that are liable to be mistaken for portions of the left lateral of the Tuolumne tributary glacier.

Spend all the time you can spare or steal on the tracks of this grand old glacier, charmed and enchanted by its magnificent canyon, lakes and cascades, and resplendent glacier pavements.

Nevada Glacier

The Nevada Glacier [probably referring to the South Lyell glacier, *ed.*] was longer and more symmetrical than the last, and the only one of the Merced system whose sources extended directly back to the main summits on the axis of the Sierra Range. Its numerous fountains were ranged side by side in three series, at an elevation of from ten thousand to twelve thousand feet above the sea. The first, on the right side of the basin, extended from the Matterhorn to Cathedral Peak; that on the left through the Merced group, and these two parallel series were united by a third that extended around the head of the basin at right angles to the others. The three ranges of high peaks and ridges that supplied the snow for these fountains, together with the Clouds Rest Ridge, nearly inclose a rectangular basin that was filled with a massive sea of ice, leaving an outlet toward the west through which flowed the main trunk glacier, three-fourths of a mile to a mile and a half wide, fifteen miles long, and from one thousand to fifteen hundred feet deep, and entered Yosemite between Half Dome and Mount Starr King.

Could we have visited Yosemite Valley at this period of its history, we should have found its ice cascades vastly more glorious than their tiny water representatives of the present day. One of the grandest of these was formed by that portion of the Nevada Glacier that poured over the shoulder of Half Dome. This glacier, as a whole, resembled an oak, with a gnarled swelling base and wide-spreading branches. Picturesque rocks of every conceivable form adorned its banks, among which glided the numerous tributaries, mottled with black and red and gray boulders from the fountain peaks, while ever and anon, as the deliberate centuries passed away, dome after dome raised its burnished crown above the ice-flood to enrich the slowly opening landscapes.

The principal moraines occur in short irregular sections along the sides of the canyons, their fragmentary condition due to interruptions caused by portions of the sides of the canyon walls being too steep for moraine matter to lie on, and to downsweeping torrents and avalanches. The left lateral of the trunk may be traced about five miles from the mouth of the first main tributary to the Illilouette Canyon. The corresponding section of the right lateral, extending from Cathedral tributary to Half Dome, is more complete because of the more favorable character of the north side of the canyon. A short side-glacier came in against it from the slopes of Clouds Rest; but being fully exposed to the sun, it was melted long before the main trunk, allowing the latter to deposit this portion of its moraine undisturbed. Some conception of the size and appearance of this fine moraine may be gained by following the Clouds Rest trail from Yosemite, which crosses it obliquely and conducts past several sections made by streams. Slate boulders may be seen that must have come from the Lyell group, twelve miles distant. But the bulk of the moraine is composed of porphyritic granite derived from Feldspar and Cathedral Valleys. On the sides of the moraines we find a series of terraces, indicating fluctuations in the level of the glacier, caused by variations of snowfall, temperature, etc., showing that the climate of the glacial period was diversified by cycles of milder or stormier seasons similar to those of postglacial time.

After the depth of the main trunk diminished to about five hundred feet, the greater portion became torpid, as is shown by the moraines, and lay dying in its crooked channel like a wounded snake, maintaining for a time a feeble squirming motion in places of exceptional depth, or where the bottom of the canyon was more steeply inclined. The numerous fountain-wombs, however, continued fruitful long after the trunk had vanished, giving rise to an imposing array of short residual glaciers, extending around the rim of the general basin a distance of nearly twenty-four miles. Most of these have but recently succumbed to the new climate, dying in turn as determined by elevation, size, and exposure, leaving only a few feeble survivors beneath the coolest shadows, which are now slowly completing the sculpture of one of the noblest of the Yosemite basins.

Illilouette Glacier

The comparatively shallow glacier that filled the Illilouette Basin more resembled a lake than a river of ice, being nearly half as wide as it was long. Its greatest length was about ten miles, and its depth perhaps nowhere much exceeded one thousand feet. Its chief fountains, ranged along the west side of the Merced group at an elevation of about ten thousand feet, gave birth to tributaries that flowed in a westerly direction, and united in the center of the basin. The broad trunk at first poured northwestward, then curved to the northward, deflected by the lofty wall forming its western bank, and finally united with the grand Yosemite trunk, opposite Glacier Point. All the phenomena relating to glacial action in this basin are remarkably simple and orderly, on account of the sheltered positions occupied by its ice-fountains, with reference to the disturbing effects of larger glaciers from the axis of the main range earlier in the period. From the eastern base of Starr King cone you may obtain a fine view of the principal moraines sweeping grandly out into the middle of the basin from the shoulders of the peaks, between which the ice-fountains lay. The right lateral of the tributary, which took its rise between Red and Merced Mountains, measures two hundred and fifty feet in height at its upper extremity, and displays three well-defined terraces, similar to those of the South Lyell [Nevada, *ed.*] Glacier. The comparative smoothness of the uppermost terrace shows that it is considerably more ancient than the others, many of the boulders of which it is composed having crumbled. A few miles to the westward, this moraine has an average slope of twenty-seven degrees, and an elevation above the bottom of the channel of six hundred and sixty feet. Near the middle of the main basin, just where the regularly formed medial and lateral moraines flatten out and disappear, there is a remarkably smooth field of gravel, planted with *Arctostaphylos* [manzanita, *ed.*] that looks at the distance of a mile like a delightful meadow. Stream sections show the gravel deposit to be composed of the same material as the moraines, but finer, and more waterworn from the action of converging torrents issuing from the tributary glaciers after the trunk was melted. The southern boundary of the basin is a strikingly perfect wall, gray on the top, and white down the sides and at the base with snow, in which many a crystal brook takes rise. The northern boundary is made up of smooth undulating masses of gray granite that lift here and there into beautiful domes, of which the Starr King cluster is the finest, while on the east tower the majestic fountain peaks, with wide canyons and névé amphitheaters between them, whose variegated rocks show out gloriously against the sky.

The iceplows of this charming basin, ranged side by side in orderly gangs, furrowed the rocks with admirable uniformity, producing irrigating channels for a brood of wild streams and abundance of rich soil adapted to every requirement of garden and grove. No other section of the Yosemite uplands is in so perfect a state of glacial cultivation, its domes and peaks and swelling rock-waves, however majestic in themselves, yet sub-missively subordinate to the garden center. The other basins we have been describing are combinations of sculptured rocks, embellished with gardens and groves, each of the five beautiful in its own way, and all as harmoniously related as are the five petals of a flower. After uniting in the Yosemite Valley, and expending the down-thrusting energy derived from their com-bined weight and the declivity of their channels, the grand trunk flowed on through and out of the valley. In effecting its exit, a considerable ascent was made, traces of which may still be seen on the abraded rocks at the lower end of the valley, while the direction pursued after leaving the valley is surely indicated by the immense lateral moraines extending from the ends of the walls at an elevation of from fifteen hundred to eighteen hundred feet. The right lateral moraine was dis-turbed by a large tributary glacier that occupied the basin of Cascade Creek, causing considerable complication in its struc-ture. The left is simple in form for several miles of its length, or to the point where a tributary came in from the southeast. But both are greatly obscured by the forests and underbrush growing upon them, and by the denuding action of rains and melting snows, etc. It is, therefore, the less to be wondered at that these moraines, made up of material derived from the dis-tant fountain-mountains, and from the valley itself, were not sooner recognized.

The action of flowing ice, whether in the form of river-like glaciers or broad mantles, especially the part it played in sculp-turing the earth, is as yet but little understood. Water rivers work openly where people dwell, and so does the rain, and the sea, thundering on all the shores of the world. The universal ocean of air, though invisible, speaks aloud in a thousand voices, and explains its modes of working and its power. But glaciers, back in their white solitudes, work apart from men, exerting their tremendous energies in silence and darkness. Outspread, spirit-like, they brood above the predestined landscapes, work on unwearied through immeasurable ages, until, in the fullness of time, the mountains and valleys are brought forth, channels furrowed for rivers, basins made for lakes and meadows, and arms of the sea, soils spread for forests and fields; then they shrink and vanish like summer clouds.

Tunnel View in August

6

The Incomparable Valley

John Muir

When I set out on the long excursion that finally led to California, I wandered afoot and alone, from Indiana to the Gulf of Mexico, with a plantpress on my back, holding a generally southward course, like the birds when they are going from summer to winter. From the west coast of Florida I crossed the gulf to Cuba, enjoyed the rich tropical flora there for a few months, intending to go thence to the north end of South America, make my way through the woods to the head-waters of the Amazon, and float down that grand river to the ocean. But I was unable to find a ship bound for South America—fortunately perhaps, for I had incredibly little money for so long a trip and had not yet fully recovered from a fever caught in the Florida swamps. Therefore, I decided to visit California for a year or two to see its wonderful flora and the famous Yosemite Valley. All the world was before me and every day was a holiday, so it did not seem important to which one of the world's wildernesses I first should wander.

Arriving by the Panama steamer, I stopped one day in San Francisco and then inquired for the nearest way out of town. "But where do you want to go?" asked the man to whom I had applied for this important information. "To any place that is wild," I said. This reply startled him. He seemed to fear I might be crazy and therefore the sooner I was out of town the better, so he directed me to the Oakland ferry.

So on the first of April, 1868, I set out afoot for Yosemite. It was the bloom-time of the year over the lowlands and Coast Ranges. The landscapes of the Santa Clara Valley were fairly drenched with sunshine, all the air was quivering with the songs of the meadowlarks, and the hills were so covered with flowers that they seemed to be painted. Slow indeed was my progress through these glorious gardens, the first of the California flora I had seen. Cattle and cultivation were making few scars as yet, and I wandered enchanted in long wavering curves, knowing by my pocket map that Yosemite Valley lay to the east and that I should surely find it.

The Sierra from the West

Looking eastward from the summit of the Pacheco Pass one shining morning, a landscape was displayed that after all my wanderings still appears as the most beautiful I have ever beheld. At my feet lay the Great Central Valley of California, level and flowery, like a lake of pure sunshine, forty or fifty miles wide, five hundred miles long, one rich furred garden of yellow *Compositae*. And from the eastern boundary of this vast golden flowerbed rose the mighty Sierra, miles in height, and so gloriously colored and so radiant, it seemed not clothed with light, but wholly composed of it, like the wall of some celestial city. Along the top, and extending a good way down, was a rich pearl-gray belt of snow; below it a belt of blue and lark purple, marking the extension of the forests; and stretching long the base of the range a broad belt of rose-purple; all these colors, from the blue sky to the yellow valley smoothly blending as they do in a rainbow, making a wall of light ineffably fine. Then it seemed to me that the Sierra should be called, not the Nevada or Snowy Range, but the Range of Light. And after ten years of wandering and wondering in the heart of it, rejoicing in its glorious floods of light, the white beams of the morning streaming through the passes, the noonday radiance on the crystal rocks, the flush of the alpenglow, and the irised spray of countless waterfalls, it still seems above all others the Range of Light.

The Sierra is about five hundred miles long, seventy miles wide, and from seven thousand to nearly fifteen thousand feet high. No mark of man is visible upon it, nor any thing to suggest the wonderful depth and grandeur of its sculpture. None of its magnificent forest-crowned ridges seems to rise much above the general level to publish its wealth. No great valley or river is seen, or group of well-marked features of any kind standing out as distinct pictures. Even the summit peaks, marshaled in glorious array so high in the sky, seem comparatively regular in form. Nevertheless, the whole range is furrowed with canyons two thousand to five thousand feet deep, in which once flowed majestic glaciers, and in which now flow and sing the bright rejoicing rivers.

Characteristics of the Canyons

Though of such stupendous depth, these canyons are not gloomy, jagged-walled gorges, savage and inaccessible. With rough passages here and there, they are flowery pathways conducting to the snowy, icy fountains, mountain streets full of life and light, graded and sculptured by the ancient glaciers and presenting throughout all their course a rich variety of novel and attractive scenery—the most attractive that has yet been discovered in the mountain ranges of the world. In many places, especially in the middle region of the western flank, the main canyons widen into spacious valleys or parks diversified like landscape gardens with meadows and groves and thickets of blooming bushes, while the lofty walls, infinitely varied in form, are fringed with ferns, flowering plants, shrubs of many species, and tall evergreens and oaks that find footholds on small benches and tables, all enlivened and made glorious with rejoicing streams that come chanting in chorus over the sunny brows of the cliffs and through side canyons in falls of every conceivable form, to join the rivers that flow in tranquil, shining beauty down the middle of each one of them.

The Incomparable Yosemite

The most famous and accessible of these canyon valleys, and also the one that presents their most striking and sublime features on the grandest scale, is the Yosemite, situated in the basin of the Merced River at an elevation of four thousand feet above the level of the sea. It is about seven miles long, half a mile to a mile wide, and nearly a mile deep in the solid granite flank of the range. The walls are made up of rocks, mountains in size, partly separated from each other by side canyons, and they are so sheer in front, and so compactly and harmoniously arranged on a level floor, that the valley, comprehensively seen, looks like an immense hall or temple lighted from above.

But no temple made with hands can compare with Yosemite. Every rock in its walls seems to glow with life. Some lean back in majestic repose; others, absolutely sheer or nearly so for thousands of feet, advance beyond their companions in thoughtful attitudes, giving welcome to storms and calms alike, seemingly aware, yet heedless, of everything going on about them. Awful in stern, immovable majesty, how softly these rocks are adorned, and how fine and reassuring the company they keep; their feet among beautiful groves and meadows, their brows in the sky, a thousand flowers leaning confidingly against their feet, bathed in floods of water, floods of light, while the snow and waterfalls, the winds and avalanches and clouds shine and sing and wreathe about them as the years go by, and myriads of small winged creatures—birds, bees, butterflies—give glad animation and help to make all the air into music. Down through the middle of the valley flows the crystal Merced, River of Mercy, peacefully quiet, reflecting lilies and trees and the onlooking rocks; things frail and fleeting and types of endurance meeting here and blending in countless forms, as if into this one mountain mansion Nature had gathered her choicest treasures, to draw her lovers into close and confiding communion with her.

The Approach to The Valley

Sauntering up the foothills to Yosemite by any of the old trails or roads in use before the railway was built from the town of Merced up the river to the boundary of Yosemite Park, richer and wilder become the forests and streams. At an elevation of six thousand feet above the level of the sea, the silver firs are two hundred feet high, with branches whorled around the colossal shafts in regular order, and every branch beautifully pinnate like a fern frond. The Douglas spruce [Douglas fir, *ed.*], the yellow and sugar pines and brown-barked *Libocedrus* [incense-cedar, *ed.*] here reach their finest developments of beauty and grandeur. The majestic sequoia is here too, the king of conifers, the noblest of all the noble race. All these colossal trees are as wonderful in fineness of beauty and proportion as in stature, growing together, an assemblage of conifers surpassing all that have ever yet been discovered in the forests of the world. Here indeed is the tree-lover's paradise; the woods, dry and wholesome, letting in the light in shimmering masses of half sunshine, half shade; the night air as well as the day air indescribably spicy and exhilarating; plushy fir-boughs for campers' beds and cascades to sing us to sleep as we gaze through the trees to the stars. On the highest ridges, over which these old Yosemite ways passed, the silver fir forms the bulk of the woods, pressing forward in glorious array to the very brink of the valley walls on both sides, and beyond the valley to a height of from eight thousand to nine thousand feet above the level of the sea. Thus it appears that Yosemite, presenting such stupendous faces of bare granite, is nevertheless imbedded in magnificent forests. All the main species of pine, fir, spruce, and *Libocedrus* are also found in the valley itself, but there are no "big trees" (*Sequoiadendron gigantea*) in the valley or about the rim of it. The nearest are about ten and twenty miles beyond the lower end of the valley on small tributaries of the Merced and Tuolumne Rivers.

The First View: The Bridal Veil

From the margin of these glorious forests, the first general view of the valley used to be gained—a revelation in landscape affairs that enriches one's life forever. Entering the valley, gazing overwhelmed with the multitude of grand objects about us, perhaps the first to fix our attention will be the Bridal Veil, a beautiful waterfall on our right. Its brow, where it first leaps free from the cliff, is about nine hundred feet above us, and as it sways and sings in the wind, clad in gauzy, sun-sifted spray, half falling, half floating, it seems infinitely gentle and fine. But the hymns it sings tell the solemn fateful power hidden beneath its soft clothing.

The Bridal Veil shoots free from the upper edge of the cliff by the velocity the stream has acquired in descending a long slope above the head of the fall. Looking from the top of the rock-avalanche talus on the west side, about one hundred feet above the foot of the fall, the under surface of the water arch is seen to be finely grooved and striated, and the sky is seen through the arch between rock and water, making a novel and beautiful effect.

Under ordinary weather conditions the fall strikes on flat-topped slabs, forming a kind of ledge about two-thirds of the way down from the top, and as the fall sways back and forth with great variety of motions among these flat-topped pillars, kissing and splashing notes as well as thunder-like detonations are produced, like those of Yosemite Fall, though on a smaller scale.

The rainbows of the Veil, or rather the spray- and foam-bows, are superb, because the waters are dashed among angular blocks of granite at the foot, producing abundance of spray of the best quality for iris effects, and also for a luxuriant growth of grass and maidenhair on the side of the talus, which lower down is planted with oak, laurel, and willows.

General Features Of The Valley

On the other side of the valley, almost immediately opposite Bridal Veil, there is another fine fall, considerably wider than the Veil when the snow is melting fast, and more than one thousand feet in height, measured from the brow of the cliff where it first springs out into the air to the head of the rocky talus on which it strikes and is broken up into ragged cascades. It is called Ribbon Fall or Virgins Tears. During the spring floods it is a magnificent object, but the suffocating blasts of spray that fill the recess in the wall which it occupies prevent a near approach. In autumn, however, when its feeble current falls in a shower, it may then pass for tears with the sentimental onlooker fresh from a visit to Bridal Veil.

Just beyond this glorious flood, El Capitan rock, regarded by many as the most sublime feature of the valley, is seen through the pine groves, standing forward beyond the general

60

line of the wall in most imposing grandeur, a type of permanence. It is thirty-three hundred feet high, a plain, severely simple, glacier-sculptured face of granite, the end of one of the most compact and enduring of the mountain ridges, unrivaled in height and breadth and flawless strength.

Across the valley from here, next to Bridal Veil, are the picturesque Cathedral Rocks, nearly twenty-seven hundred feet high, making a noble display of fine yet massive sculpture. They are closely related to El Capitan, having been hewn from the same mountain ridge by the great Yosemite Glacier when the valley was in process of formation.

Next to the Cathedral Rocks, on the south side, towers Sentinel Rock to a height of more than three thousand feet, a telling monument of the glacial period.

Almost immediately opposite the Sentinel are the Three Brothers, an immense mountain mass with three gables fronting the valley, one above another, the topmost gable nearly four thousand feet high. They were named for three brothers, sons of old Tenaya, the Yosemite chief, captured here during the Indian War, at the time of the discovery of the valley in 1852.

Sauntering up the valley through meadow and grove, in the company of these majestic rocks, which seem to follow us as we advance, gazing, admiring, looking for new wonders ahead where all about us is so wonderful, the thunder of Yosemite Fall is heard, and when we arrive in front of Sentinel Rock it is revealed in all its glory from base to summit, half a mile in height, and seeming to spring out into the valley sunshine direct from the sky. But even this fall, perhaps the most wonderful of its kind in the world, cannot at first hold our attention, for now the wide upper portion of the valley is displayed to view, with the finely modeled North Dome, the Royal Arches, and Washington Column on our left; Glacier Point, with its massive, magnificent sculpture on the right; and in the middle, directly in front, looms Tissiack or Half Dome, the most beautiful and most sublime of all the wonderful Yosemite rocks, rising in serene majesty from flowery groves and meadows to a height of four thousand seven hundred fifty feet.

Half Dome

7

Climbing Half Dome

John Muir

[South Dome is now called Half Dome, and is renamed as such in the text. *ed.*]

With the exception of a few spires and pinnacles, Half Dome is the only rock about the valley that is strictly inaccessible without artificial means, and its inaccessibility is expressed in severe terms. Nevertheless, many a mountaineer, gazing admiringly, tried hard to invent a way to the top of its noble crown—all in vain, until in the year 1875, George Anderson, an indomitable Scotchman, undertook the adventure. The side facing Tenaya Canyon is an absolutely vertical precipice from the summit to a depth of about sixteen hundred feet, and on the opposite side, it is nearly vertical for about as great a depth. The southwest side presents a very steep and finely-drawn curve from the top down a thousand feet or more, while on the northeast, where it is united with the Clouds Rest Ridge, one may easily reach a point called the Saddle, about seven hundred feet below the summit. From the Saddle, Half Dome rises in a graceful curve a few degrees too steep for unaided climbing.

A year or two before Anderson gained the summit, John Conway, the master trailbuilder of the valley, and his little sons, who climbed smooth rocks like lizards, made a bold effort to reach the top by climbing barefooted up the grand curve with a rope, which they fastened at irregular intervals by means of eye bolts driven into joints of the rock. But finding that the upper part would require laborious drilling, they abandoned the attempt, glad to escape from the dangerous position they had reached, some three hundred feet above the Saddle. Anderson began with Conway's old rope, which had been left in place, and resolutely drilled his way to the top, inserting eye bolts five to six feet apart, and making his rope fast to each in succession, resting his feet on the last bolt while he drilled a hole for the next above. Occasionally, some irregularity in the curve, or slight foothold, would enable him to climb a few feet without a rope, which he would pass and begin drilling again, and thus the whole work was accomplished in a few days. From this slender beginning he proposed to construct a substantial stairway which he hoped to complete in time for the next year's travel, but while busy getting out timber for his stairway and dreaming of the wealth he hoped to gain from tolls, he was taken sick and died all alone in his little cabin.

On the 10th of November, after returning from a visit to Mount Shasta, a month or two after Anderson had gained the summit, I made haste to the Dome, not only for the pleasure of climbing, but to see what I might learn. The first winter storm clouds had blossomed and the mountains and all the high points about the valley were mantled in fresh snow. I was, therefore, a little apprehensive of danger from the slipperiness of the rope and the rock. Anderson himself tried to prevent me from making the attempt, refusing to believe that any one could climb his rope in the now-muffled condition in which it then was. Moreover, the sky was overcast, and solemn snow-clouds began to curl around the summit, and my late experiences on icy Shasta came to mind. But reflecting that I had matches in my pocket, and that a little firewood might be found, I concluded that in case of a storm, the night could be spent on the Dome without suffering anything worth minding, no matter what the clouds might bring forth. I therefore pushed on and gained the top.

It was one of those brooding, changeful days that come between Indian summer and winter, when the leaf colors have grown dim and the clouds come and go among the cliffs like living creatures: now hovering aloft, now caressing rugged rock-brows with great gentleness, or, wandering afar over the tops of the forests, touching the spires of fir and pine with their soft silken fringes as if trying to tell the glad news of the coming of snow.

The first view was perfectly glorious. A massive cloud of pure pearl luster, apparently as fixed and calm as the meadows and groves in the shadow beneath it, was arched across the valley from wall to wall, one end resting on the grand abutment of El Capitan, the other on Cathedral Rock. A little later, as I stood on the tremendous verge overlooking Mirror Lake, a flock of smaller clouds, white as snow, came from the north, trailing their downy skirts over the dark forests, and entered the valley with solemn god-like gestures through Indian Canyon and over North Dome and Royal Arches. On they came with stately deliberation, nearer and nearer, gathering and massing beneath my feet and filling Tenaya Canyon. Then the sun shone free, lighting the pearly gray surface of the cloud-like sea and making it glow. Gazing, admiring, I was startled to see for the first time the rare optical phenomenon of the "Specter of the Brocken." My shadow, clearly outlined, about half a mile long, lay upon this glorious white surface with startling effect. I walked back and forth, waved my arms and struck all sorts of attitudes, to see every slightest movement enormously exaggerated. Considering that I have looked down so many times from mountain tops on seas of all sorts of clouds, it seems strange that I should have seen the "Brocken Specter" only this once. A grander surface and a grander standpoint, however, could hardly have been found in all the Sierra.

After this grand show, the cloud-sea rose higher, wreathing the Dome, and for a short time submerging it, making darkness like night, and I began to think of looking for a camp ground in a cluster of dwarf pines. But soon the sun shone free again, the clouds, sinking lower and lower, gradually vanished, leaving the Valley with its Indian summer colors apparently refreshed, while to the eastward the summit-peaks, clad in new snow, towered along the horizon in glorious array.

Though apparently it is perfectly bald, there are four clumps of pines growing on the summit, representing three species: *Pinus albicaulis, P. contorta* and *P. ponderosa*, var. Jeffreyi [whitebark pine, lodgepole pine, and Jeffrey pine, *ed.*]—all three, of course, repressed and storm-beaten. The alpine *Spiraea* grows here also and blossoms profusely with *Potentilla, Erigeron, Eriogonum, Pentstemon, Solidago* [cinquefoil, fleabane, buckwheat, beardtongue, goldenrod, *ed.*] and an interesting species of onion, and four or five species of grasses and sedges. None of these differs in any respect from those of other summits of the same height, excepting the curious little narrow-leaved, waxen-bulbed onion, which I had not seen elsewhere.

Notwithstanding the enthusiastic eagerness of tourists to reach the crown of Half Dome, the views of the valley from this lofty standpoint are less striking than from many other points comparatively low, chiefly on account of the foreshortening effect produced by looking down from so great a height. North Dome is dwarfed almost beyond recognition, the grand sculpture of the Royal Arches is scarcely noticeable, and the whole range of walls on both sides seem comparatively low and sunken, especially when the valley is flooded with noon sunshine. Half Dome itself, the most sublime feature of all the Yosemite views, is out of sight beneath one's feet. The view of Little Yosemite Valley is very fine, though inferior to one obtained from the base of the Starr King cone, but the summit landscapes towards Mounts Ritter, Lyell, Dana, Conness, and the Merced Group, are very effective and complete.

No one has attempted to carry out Anderson's plan of making the Dome accessible. For my part, I should prefer leaving it in pure wildness, though, after all, no great damage could be done by tramping over it. The surface would be strewn with tin cans and bottles, but the winter gales would blow the rubbish away. Avalanches might strip off any sort of stairway or ladder that might be built. Blue jays and Clark's crows [Clark's nutcracker, *ed.*] have trodden the Dome for many a day, and so have beetles and chipmunks, and Tissiack would hardly be more "conquered" or spoiled should man be added to her list of visitors. His louder scream and heavier scrambling would not stir a line of her countenance.

Yosemite Falls

8

In the Heart of the Sierras

James Mason Hutchings

But little seems to have been said, and that little very casually, about the marvelous grandeur of the Yosemite, at least but little found its way, impressibly, to the public through the press of that day. It was therefore only a historical verity to confess that, but for the contemplated publication of an illustrated California monthly—afterwards issued for a number of years in San Francisco—its merely fortuitous mention would probably have escaped the attention of the writer altogether as it seemed to have done that of the public. As the account given, however, mentioned the existence of "a waterfall nearly a thousand feet high," it was sufficient to suggest a series of ruminating queries. A waterfall a thousand feet in height, and that is in California? A thousand feet? Why, Niagara is only one hundred and sixty-four feet high! A thousand feet!! The scrap containing this valuable and startling statement, meager though it was, was carefully treasured.

The First Tourist Party

About the twentieth of June, 1855 [June 27, 1855, *ed.*]—some four years after Yosemite had been first seen by white men, and when entirely unaware of the sublime mountain scenery afterwards found there—the "waterfall a thousand feet high" induced the writer to form a party to visit it. That party consisted of the then well-known artist, Thomas Ayres (who had been specially engaged by the writer to portray the majesty and beauty of the lofty waterfall expected to be found there), Walter Millard, and J. M. Hutchings. Mr. Alexander Stair afterwards joined us at Mariposa.

Ho! For The Mountains

Believe me there is an indescribable charm steals over the heart when wandering among the untrodden fastnesses of the mountains for the first time, especially under circumstances similar to ours. We were entering a mysterious country, to us unknown. The journey before us was full of uncertain lights and shadows—so might its ending possibly be.

Successively and successfully, we passed through dark and apparently interminable forests, penetrated brushy thickets, ascended rocky ridges, and descended talus-covered slopes, until, on the afternoon of the third day of our deeply interesting expedition, we suddenly came in full view of the marvelous valley.

The inapprehensible, the uninterpretable profound, was at last opened up before us. That first vision into its wonderful depths was to me the birth of an indescribable "first love" for scenic grandeur that has continued, unchangeable, to this hour, and I gratefully treasure the priceless gift. I trust, moreover, to be forgiven for now expressing the hope that my long afterlife among the angel-winged shadows of her glorious cliffs, has given heart-felt proof of the abiding purity and strength of that "first love" for Yosemite.

This mere glimpse of the enchanting prospect seemed to fill our souls to overflowing with gratified delight that was only manifest in unbidden tears. Our lips were speechless from thanksgiving awe. Neither the language of tongue nor pen, nor the most perfect successes of art, can approximately present that picture. It was sublimity materialized in granite, and beauty crystallized into object forms, and both drawing us nearer to the Infinite One. It would be difficult to tell how long we looked lingeringly at this unexpected revelation; for, "With thee conversing, I forget all time."

A few advancing footsteps brought us to the foot of a fall, whose charming presence had long challenged our admiration; and, as we stood watching the changing drapery of its watery folds, the silence was eventually broken by my remark, "Is it not as graceful, and as beautiful, as the veil of a bride?" to which Mr. Ayres rejoined, "That is suggestive of a very pretty and most apposite name. I propose that we now baptize it, and call it, 'The Bridal Veil Fall,' as one that is both characteristic and euphonious." This was instantly concurred in by each of our party, and has since been so known, and called, by the general public. This, then, was the time, and these the circumstances, attending the origin of the name "Bridal Veil Fall."

Our progress upon the south side of the valley—the one on which we had entered it—was soon stopped by an immense deposit of rocky talus that compelled us to ford the Merced River. Advancing upward upon its northern bank, after threading our way among trees, or around huge blocks of granite that were indiscriminately scattered about, passing scene after scene of unutterable sublimity, and sketching those deemed most noteworthy, again crossing and recrossing the river, we found ourselves in immediate proximity to the "waterfall a thousand feet high," and which had been the magnetic incentive to our visit to Yosemite. This, from our measurements of prostrate pine trees, by which was estimated the height of those standing (as we had no instruments with us adapted to such purposes), we deduced its altitude to be from fifteen to eighteen hundred feet!

The oft-quoted phrase "A thing of beauty is a joy forever" was never more fully realized. The picture is photographed on the tablets of my memory in indelible colors, and is as fresh and bright today as was the first impression twenty-nine years ago. To the tourist who beholds it for the first time, the Nevada Fall, with its weird surroundings, is a view of rare and picturesque beauty and grandeur. The rugged cliffs, the summits fringed with stunted pine and juniper bounding the canyon on the southern side, the "Cap of Liberty" standing like a huge sentinel overlooking the scene at the north, the foaming caldron at the foot of the fall, the rapids below, the flume where the stream glides noiselessly but with lightning speed over its polished granite bed, making the preparatory run for its plunge over the Vernal Fall, form a combination of rare effects, leaving upon the mind an impression that years cannot efface. But the tourist is in a measure prepared. He has seen the engravings and photographic views, and read descriptions written by visitors who have preceded him. To us it was the opening of a sealed volume.

Tunnel View in December

9

In California—The Yosemite

Horace Greeley

Bear Valley, California
August 14, 1859

I left Sacramento on Monday morning last, traveling by stage to Stockton, forty-eight miles nearly due south, crossing the Mokelumne, and keeping first the Sacramento and then the San Joaquin a few miles on our right, and Mount Diablo conspicuous still further west. We traversed a level, fertile plain, sparsely wooded near the rivers—a plain which should be, but is not yet, densely peopled, and very productive. There are some fine orchard gardens near the cities, and might well be many; but a good part of the intermediate country is unin-closed, and the residue mainly devoted to large ranches, and in less degree, to the growing of small grain—wheat and barley. The stubble indicates good crops, but there is not a sufficient area devoted to them. Uncertainty of land titles—that para-mount curse of California—is assigned as the cause of this inadequacy of cultivation, which I trust is not to continue.

Stockton is situated on a bayou of the San Joaquin, at the head of regular steamboat navigation on that river, which makes it the third or fourth city of California, with fifteen thou-sand inhabitants, and an extensive carrying trade. The better dwellings are in good part surrounded by fine gardens, well filled with delicious fruit. In some of them, the primitive, wide-spreading oaks have been preserved, giving them an aspect of beauty and coolness most grateful to the traveler recently arrived from the plains. Stockton has the State Insane Asylum, and a very interesting commencement of a cabinet of natural history; better still, she has an Artesian well one thousand feet deep, bored at a cost of ten thousand dollars, and pouring forth a copious and unfailing stream, some feet above the sur-face of the earth. Deep as it is, it penetrates only successive strata of what appears to be alluvial deposit, never touching bedrock. Artesian wells are becoming common in California, and I trust are yet to play an important part in the develop-ment and extension not only of her agricultural but also of her mining industry, now crippled (especially in the south) by the general dearth of water. I have a suspicion that all the water hitherto obtained by canals or ditches, so expensively constructed, could have been procured far cheaper by digging Artesian wells, which, however multiplied, could hardly fail, at the foot of the Sierra Nevada, to strike copious fountains at no unreasonable depth.

I left Stockton next morning in a carriage with a friend who proposed to go through to Bear Valley (seventy-five miles) before sleeping—a feat which I doubted the ability of any span of livery horses to accomplish. My doubt was misplaced. Good horses, an early start, careful, considerate driving, frequent watering, and the dry, bracing air of California, carried us through by a little after 10 P.M., and our team would readily have gone ten miles further had we required it. I judge that sixty miles of just such roads would have been as hard a drive in any state east of the Rocky Mountains.

Our general course this day was east by south, passing mainly over moderately undulating prairie of very unequal but generally indifferent fertility, and crossing successively, at intervals of about twenty miles, the small rivers Stanislaus, Tuolumne, and Merced, all flowing from the mountains westward into the San Joaquin, and all rendered turbid by the mining operations in progress on their banks or in their beds. The Stanislaus runs through a belt of rather light and thin oak, some two or three miles wide; the others have a few scattering oaks and that is all. There is considerable husbandry—mainly of the ranching order, near Stockton and along the rivers aforesaid, but very little industry of any kind on the naked prairies between them, and not a drop of running water, except, perhaps, a spring or two under some of the low hills which have a tolerably steep side respectively. There are a very few deep holes in some of the winter watercourses at which cattle still find drink, though of a bad quality. One settler from Massachusetts, who lives mainly by cattle-growing, informed us that he came around Cape Horn eight or ten years since, has now about ninety head of cattle, which are fast increasing, and intends to erect a windmill this winter, by whose aid he will be able to have a good garden at once, and a fine fruit orchard within a few years. He has to go seven miles for his fuel, fencing stuff, etc., on the Stanislaus. His nearest neighbors, on the road we traveled, are some five to ten miles distant, but I believe he has nearer. He is doubtless richer here than in Massachusetts, but I cannot realize that his family are happier or more favorably situated for mental and moral improvement, there being no school within reach, and the children depending for instruction on their New England mother alone. But their children will not have New England mothers—and what then? I fear this cattle ranching, with long intervals between the ranches, is destined to half-barbarize many thousands of the next generation, whom schools can scarcely reach, and to whom "the sound of the church-going bell" will be a stranger. Most of the agriculturists of this region, however, came here from Missouri, Arkansas, or Texas—many of them from Missouri or Arkansas by way of Texas—and do not seem to regard common schools as essential to civilized life.

We crossed the Merced sixty miles from Stockton (all these rivers are crossed by toll bridges, or ferries—charges, one dollar each per wagon) just before sunset, and now our road became rugged and bad as we rose the first of the foothills of the Sierra. Thus far we had seen few traces of mining, save the muddy-colored waters of the rivers, but seven miles further brought us to Quartzburg, in the center of a nearly washed-out valley of gold-bearing gravel; and thence our way led seven miles further, over a far higher foothill, into Bear Valley, where we found friends and grateful rest. The next day I devoted to an examination of Colonel Fremont's mines and works, of which I may speak hereafter, but must now hurry on to Yosemite.

I left Bear Valley, two hours later than was fit, at 6 A.M., on Thursday, resolved to push through to my immediate destination that night. Every one assured us that to get through that day was impossible, yet I had no more time to give to the journey, and must try. My friend is a good rider, while I can barely ride at all, not having spent five hours on horseback, save in my visit to the Kansas gold mines, within the last thirty years. But the two gentlemen from Mariposa who accompanied and guided us knew all about the journey that we didn't— which is saying a great deal—so we pressed buoyantly, confidently on.

Hussey's steam sawmill, where we mounted, marks pretty fairly the division between the oaks of the lower and the firs of the higher elevations, though the two melt into each other. As we rose gradually but steadily, the white soon faded out, then the black, and last the live oak, though the genuineness of this last is disputed, while the yellow, pitch, and sugar pines, cedars, and balsam firs became more numerous and stately, till they at length had the ground almost wholly to themselves, save that the manzanita and other shrubs (mostly evergreens also) clustered on nearly every opening among the trees. There is little or no precipice or bare rock for miles, and we rose along the southern face of the ridge overlooking the Cholchilla Valley until we seemed to have half California spread out before us like a map. Our range of vision extended south to the Tulé Lake, or immense morass, in which the San Joaquin has its source, and west to the Coast Range, which alone barred the Pacific Ocean from our view. Still rising, we wound gradually around the peak of our first mountain through a slight depression or pass, and soon looked off upon the valley of the South Fork of the Merced, which opened for miles north and east of us. On this side, the descent is far steeper, and we traversed for miles a mere trace along the side of the mountain, where a misstep must have landed us at least a thousand feet below. In time, this too was left behind, and we descended fitfully and tortuously the east end of the mountain to the South Fork, whereon, sixteen miles from Hussey's and but five from the Big Trees of Mariposa, we halted for rest and food. Before 6 P.M., we were again in the saddle, crossing the fork and winding up over another mountain northward, with a precipitous descent of at least two thousand feet beside us for a mile or so. A steep ascent of half a mile carried us over the divide, whence we descended very rapidly to Alder Creek, at the northern base. Following up this creek over a succession of steep pitches, interleaved with more level patches, we bade adieu to daylight at Grizzly Flat, a spot noted for encounters with the monarch of our American forests, and thence crossed a ridge to Summit Meadows, a succession of mainly narrow grassy levels, which wind in and out among the promontories of more or less shattered granite which make down from the mountain peaks on either side, but pursue a generally eastward direction to pour their tiny tribute into the Great Chasm. Our route led us six or eight times across these meadows and, intermediately, across the generally wooded promontories, which deflected the probably continuous meadow into what seemed to us many, until we stood at length, about 10 P.M., on the brink of the awful abyss, and halted a moment to tighten girths and take breath for the descent.

And here let me renew my tribute to the marvelous bounty and beauty of the forests of this whole mountain region. The Sierra Nevadas lack the glorious glaciers, the frequent rains, the rich verdure, the abundant cataracts of the Alps; but they far surpass them—they surpass any other mountains I ever saw—in the wealth and grace of their trees. Look down from almost any of their peaks, and your range of vision is filled, bounded, satisfied, by what might be termed a tempest-tossed sea of evergreens, filling every upland valley, covering every hillside, crowning every peak but the highest, with their unfading luxuriance. That I saw during this day's travel many hundreds of pines eight feet in diameter, with cedars at least six feet, I am confident; and there were miles after miles of such and smaller trees of like genus standing as thick as they could grow. Steep mountainsides, allowing them to grow, rank above rank, without obstructing each other's sunshine, seem peculiarly favorable to the production of these serviceable giants. But the Summit Meadows are peculiar in their heavy fringe of balsam fir of all sizes, from those barely one foot high to those hardly less than two hundred, their branches surrounding them in collars, their extremities gracefully bent down by the weight of winter snows, making them here, I am confident, the most beautiful trees on earth. The dry promontories, which separate these meadows are also covered with a species of spruce, which is only less graceful than the fir aforesaid. I never before enjoyed such a tree feast as on this wearing, difficult ride.

Descent into Yosemite is only practicable at three points—one near the head of the valley, where a small stream makes in from the direction of the main ridge of the Sierra, down which there is a trail from the vicinity of Water River, Utah—a trail practicable, I believe, for men on foot only. The other two lead in near the outlet, from Mariposa and Coulterville respectively, on opposite banks of the Merced, and are practicable for sure-footed mules or horses. We, of course, made our descent by the Mariposa trail, on the south side of the little river, which here escapes from the famous valley by a canyon which water alone can safely, if at all, traverse, being shut in by lofty precipices, and broken by successive falls.

My friends insisted that I should look over the brink into the profound abyss before clambering down its side; but I, apprehending giddiness, and feeling the need of steady nerves, firmly declined. So we formed line again, and moved on.

The night was clear and bright, as all summer nights in this region are. The atmosphere cool, but not really cold. The moon had risen before 7 o'clock, and was shedding so much light as to bother us in our forest path, where the shadow of a standing pine looked exceedingly like the substance of a fallen one, and many semblances were unreal and misleading. It was often hard to realize that the dark, narrow current-like passage to the left was our trail, and not the winding, broader, moon-lighted opening on the right. The safest course was to give your horse a free rein, and trust to his sagacity or self-love for keeping the trail. As we descended by zigzags the north face of the all but perpendicular mountain, our moonlight soon left us, or was present only by reflection from the opposite cliff. Soon the trail became at once so steep, so rough, and so tortuous, that we all dismounted, but my attempt at walking proved a miserable failure. I had been riding with a bad Mexican stirrup, which barely admitted the toes of my left foot, and continual pressure on these had sprained and swelled them, so that walking was positive torture. I persevered in the attempt, till my companions insisted on my remounting, and thus floundering slowly to the bottom. By steady effort, we descended the three miles (four thousand feet perpendicular) in two hours, and stood at night by the rushing, roaring waters of the Merced.

That first full, deliberate gaze up the opposite height! Can I ever forget it? The valley is here scarcely half a mile wide, while its northern wall of mainly naked, perpendicular granite is at least four thousand feet high—probably more. But the modicum of moonlight that fell into this awful gorge gave to that precipice a vagueness of outline, an indefinite vastness, a ghostly and weird spirituality. Had the mountain spoken to me in audible voice, or began to lean over with the purpose of burying me beneath its crushing mass, I should hardly have been surprised. Its whiteness, thrown into bold relief by the patches of trees or shrubs which fringed or flecked it wherever a few handfuls of its moss, slowly decomposed to earth, could contrive to hold on, continually suggested the presence of snow, which suggestion, with difficulty refuted, was at once renewed. And, looking up the valley, we saw just such mountain precipices, barely separated by intervening watercourses of inconsiderable depth, and only receding sufficiently to make room for a very narrow meadow inclosing the river, to the furthest limit of vision.

We discussed the propriety of camping directly at the foot of the pass, but decided against it, because of the inadequacy of the grass at this point for our tired, hungry beasts, and resolved to push on to the nearest of the two houses in the valley, which was said to be four miles distant. To my dying day, I shall remember that weary, interminable ride up the valley. We had been on foot since daylight; it was now past midnight. All were nearly used up, and I in torture from over twelve hours' steady riding on the hardest trotting horse in America. Yet we pressed on, and on, through clumps of trees, and bits of forest, and patches of meadow, and over hillocks of mountain debris, mainly granite boulders of every size, often nearly as round as cannon balls, forming all but perpendicular banks to the capricious torrent that brought them hither—those stupendous precipices on either side glaring down upon us all the while. How many times our heavy eyes were lighted up by visions of that intensely desired cabin. Gladly could I have thrown myself recklessly from the saddle, and lain where I fell till morning, but this would never answer, and we kept steadily on.

"Time and the hour wear out the longest day."

I am told that none ever before traveled from Bear Valley to Yosemite in one day. The distance can hardly exceed thirty miles by an air line, but only a bird could traverse that line, while, by way of Mariposa and the South Fork, it must be fully sixty miles, with a rise and fall of not less than twenty thousand feet.

The fall of the Yosemite, so called, is a humbug. It is not the Merced River that makes this fall, but a mere tributary trout brook, which pitches in from the north by a barely once-broken descent of two thousand six hundred feet, while the

Merced enters the valley at its eastern extremity, over falls of six hundred and two hundred and fifty feet. But a river thrice as large as the Merced, at this season, would be utterly dwarfed by all the other accessories of this prodigious chasm. Only a Mississippi or a Niagara could be adequate to their exactions. I readily concede that a hundred times the present amount of water may roll down Yosemite Fall in the months of May and June, when the snows are melting from the central ranges of the Sierra Nevada, which bound this abyss on the east, but this would not add a fraction to the wonder of this vivid exemplification of the divine power and majesty. At present, the little stream that leaps down the Yosemite, and is all but shattered to mist by the amazing descent, looks like a tapeline let down from the cloud-capped height to measure the depth of the abyss. The Yosemite Valley is the most unique and majestic of Nature's marvels, but the Yosemite Fall is of little account. Were it absent, the valley would not be perceptibly less worthy of a fatiguing visit.

We traversed the valley from end to end the next day, but an accumulation of details on such a subject only serve to confuse and blunt the observer's powers of perception and appreciation. Perhaps the visitor who should be content with a long look into the abyss from the most convenient height, without braving the toil of a descent, would be wiser than all of us; and yet that first glance upward from the foot will long haunt me as more impressive than any look downward from the summit could be.

I shall not multiply details, nor waste paper in noting all the foolish names which foolish people have given to different peaks or turrets. Just think of two giant stone towers, or pillars, which rise a thousand feet above the towering cliff which form their base, being styled the "Two Sisters!" [Cathedral Spires, *ed.*] Could anything be more maladroit and lackadaisical? "The Dome" [Half Dome, *ed.*] is a high, round, naked peak, which rises between the Merced and its little tributary from the inmost recesses of the Sierra Nevada already instanced, and which towers to an altitude of over five thousand feet above the waters at its base. Picture to yourself a perpendicular wall of bare granite nearly or quite one mile high! Yet there are some dozen or score of peaks in all, ranging from three thousand to five thousand feet above the valley, and a biscuit tossed from any of them would strike very near its base, and its fragments go bounding and falling still further. I certainly miss here the glaciers of Chamonix, but I know no single wonder of nature on earth which can claim superiority over Yosemite. Just dream yourself for one hour in a chasm nearly ten miles long, with egress, save for birds and water, but at three points, up the face of precipices from three thousand to four thousand feet high, the chasm scarcely more than a mile wide at any point, and tapering to a mere gorge, or canyon, at either end, with walls of mainly naked and perpendicular white granite, from three thousand to five thousand feet high, so that looking up to the sky from it is like looking out of an unfathomable profound—and you will have some conception of Yosemite.

Lower Yosemite Fall

10

Waterfalls and Rainbows

John Muir

The Upper Canyons

Here the valley divides into three branches, the Tenaya, Nevada, and Illilouette Canyons, extending back into the fountains of the High Sierra, with scenery every way worthy the relation they bear to Yosemite.

In the south branch, a mile or two from the main valley, is the Illilouette Fall, six hundred feet high, one of the most beautiful of all the Yosemite choir, but to most people inaccessible as yet on account of its rough, steep, boulder-choked canyon. Its principal fountains of ice and snow lie in the beautiful and interesting mountains of the Merced group, while its broad open basin between its fountain mountains and canyon is noted for the beauty of its lakes and forests and magnificent moraines.

Returning to the valley, and going up the north branch of Tenaya Canyon, we pass between North Dome and Half Dome, and in less than an hour come to Mirror Lake, the Dome Cascades, and Tenaya Fall. Beyond the Fall, on the north side of the canyon, is the sublime El Capitan-like rock called Mount Watkins; on the south, the vast granite wave of Clouds Rest, a mile in height; and between them, the fine Tenaya Cascade with silvery plumes outspread on smooth glacier-polished folds of granite, making a vertical descent in all of about seven hundred feet.

Just beyond the Dome Cascades, on the shoulder of Mount Watkins, there is an old trail once used by Indians on their way across the range to Mono, but in the canyon above this point, there is no trail of any sort. Between Mount Watkins and Clouds Rest, the canyon is accessible only to mountaineers, and it is so dangerous that I hesitate to advise even good climbers, anxious to test their nerve and skill, to attempt to pass through it. Beyond the Cascades no great difficulty will be encountered. A succession of charming lily gardens and meadows occurs in filled-up lake basins among the rock-waves in the bottom of the canyon, and everywhere the surface of the granite has a smooth-wiped appearance, and in many places reflects the sunbeams like glass, a phenomenon due to glacial action, the canyon having been the channel of one of the main tributaries of the ancient Yosemite Glacier.

About ten miles above the valley, we come to the beautiful Tenaya Lake, and here the canyon terminates. A mile or two above the lake stands the grand Sierra Cathedral, a building of one stone, hewn from the living rock, with sides, roof, gable, spire and ornamental pinnacles, fashioned and finished symmetrically like a work of art, and set on a well-graded plateau about nine thousand feet high, as if Nature in making so fine a building had also been careful that it should be finely seen. From every direction its peculiar form and graceful, majestic beauty of expression never fail to charm. Its height from its base to the ridge of the roof is about twenty-five hundred feet, and among the pinnacles that adorn the front, grand views may be gained of the upper basins of the Merced and Tuolumne Rivers.

Passing the Cathedral we descend into the delightful, spacious Tuolumne Valley, from which excursions may be made to Mounts Dana, Lyell, Ritter, Conness, and Mono Lake, and to the many curious peaks that rise above the meadows on the south, and to the Big Tuolumne Canyon, with its glorious abundance of rock and falling, gliding, tossing water. For all these, the beautiful meadows near the Soda Springs form a delightful center.

Down the Yosemite Creek

In general views, the Yosemite Creek basin seems to be paved with domes and smooth, whaleback masses of granite in every stage of development—some showing only their crowns, others rising high and free above the girdling forests, singly or in groups. Others are developed only on one side, forming bold outstanding bosses usually well fringed with shrubs and trees, and presenting the polished surfaces given them by the glacier that brought them into relief. On the upper portion of the basin, broad moraine beds have been deposited and on these, fine, thrifty forests are growing. Lakes and meadows and small spongy bogs may be found hiding here and there in the woods or back in the fountain recesses of Mount Hoffman, while a thousand gardens are planted along the banks of the streams.

All the wide, fan-shaped upper portion of the basin is covered with a network of small rills that go cheerily on their way to their grand fall in the valley, now flowing on smooth pavements in sheets thin as glass, now diving under willows and laving their red roots, oozing through green, plushy bogs, splashing over small falls and dancing down slanting cascades, calming again, gliding through patches of smooth glacier meadows with sod of alpine *Agrostis* mixed with blue and white violets and daisies, breaking, tossing among rough boulders and fallen trees, resting in calm pools, flowing together until, all united, they go to their fate with stately, tranquil gestures like a full-grown river. At the crossing of the Mono Trail, about two miles above the head of Yosemite Fall, the stream is nearly forty feet wide, and when the snow is melting rapidly in the spring, it is about four feet deep, with a current of two and a half miles an hour. This is about the volume of water that forms the Fall in May and June when there had been much snow the preceding winter, but it varies greatly from month to month. The snow rapidly vanishes from the open portion of the basin, which faces southward, and only a few of the tributaries reach back to perennial snow and ice fountains in the shadowy amphitheaters on the precipitous northern slopes of Mount Hoffman. The total descent made by the stream from its highest sources to its confluence with the Merced in the valley is about six thousand feet, while the distance is only about ten miles, an average fall of six hundred feet per mile. The last mile of its course lies between the sides of sunken domes and swelling folds of the granite that are clustered and pressed together like a mass of bossy cumulus clouds. Through this shining way, Yosemite Creek goes to its fate, swaying and swirling with easy, graceful gestures and singing the last of its mountain songs before it reaches the dizzy edge of Yosemite to fall twenty-six hundred feet into another world, where climate, vegetation, inhabitants, all are different. Emerging from this last canyon, the stream glides in flat lace-like folds down a smooth incline into a small pool where it seems to rest and compose itself before taking the grand plunge. Then calmly, as if leaving a lake, it slips over the polished lip of the pool down another incline and out over the brow of the precipice in a magnificent curve thick-sown with rainbow spray.

The Yosemite Fall

Long ago before I had traced this fine stream to its head back of Mount Hoffman, I was eager to reach the extreme verge to see how it behaved in flying so far through the air, but after enjoying this view and getting safely away, I have never advised any one to follow my steps. The last incline down which the stream journeys so gracefully is so steep and smooth one must slip cautiously forward on hands and feet alongside the rushing water, which so near one's head is very exciting. But to gain a perfect view, one must go yet farther, over a curving brow to a slight shelf on the extreme brink. This shelf, formed by the flaking off of a fold of granite, is about three inches wide, just wide enough for a safe rest for one's heels. To me, it seemed nerve-trying to slip to this narrow foothold and poise on the edge of such precipice so close to the confusing whirl of the waters, and after casting longing glances over the shining brow of the fall and listening to its sublime psalm, I concluded not to attempt to go nearer, but, nevertheless, against reasonable judgment, I did. Noticing some tufts of *Artemisia* in a cleft of rock, I filled my mouth with the leaves, hoping their bitter taste might help to keep caution keen and prevent giddiness. In spite of myself, I reached the little ledge, got my heels well set, and worked sidewise twenty or thirty feet to a point close to the out-plunging current. Here the view is perfectly free down into the heart of the bright, irised throng of comet-like streamers into which the whole ponderous volume of the fall separates, two or three hundred feet below the brow. So glorious a display of pure wildness, acting at close range while cut off from all the world beside, is terribly impressive. A less nerve-trying view may be obtained from a fissured portion of the edge of the cliff about forty yards to the eastward of the fall. Seen from this point towards noon, in the spring, the rainbow on its brow seems to be broken up and mingled with the rushing comets until all the fall is stained with iris colors, leaving no white water visible. This is the best of the safe views from above, the huge steadfast rocks, the flying waters, and the rainbow light forming one of the most glorious pictures conceivable.

The Yosemite Fall is separated into an upper and a lower fall with a series of falls and cascades between them, but when viewed in front from the bottom of the Valley they all appear as one.

So grandly does this magnificent fall display itself from the floor of the valley, few visitors take the trouble to climb the walls to gain nearer views, unable to realize how vastly more impressive it is nearby than at a distance of one or two miles.

A Wonderful Ascent

The views developed in a walk up the zigzags of the trail leading to the foot of the Upper Fall are about as varied and impressive as those displayed along the favorite Glacier Point Trail. One rises as if on wings. The groves, meadows, fern-flats, and reaches of the river gain new interest, as if never seen before, and all become new over and over again as we go higher from point to point. The foreground also changes every few rods in the most surprising manner, although the earth-quake talus and the level bench on the face of the wall over which the trail passes seem monotonous and commonplace as seen from the bottom of the valley. Up we climb with glad exhilaration, through shaggy fringes of laurel, *Ceanothus*, glossy-leaved manzanita, and live oak, from shadow to shadow across bars and patches of sunshine, the leafy openings making charming frames for the valley pictures beheld through them, and for the glimpses of the high peaks that appear in the distance. The higher we go, the farther we seem to be from the summit of the vast granite wall. Here we pass a huge, projecting buttress whose grooved and rounded surface tells a plain story of the time when the valley, now filled with sunshine, was filled with ice, when the grand old Yosemite Glacier, flowing river-like from its distant fountains, swept through it with its crushing, grinding floods, wearing its way ever deeper, developing and fashioning these sublime rocks. Again we cross a white, battered gully, the pathway of rock avalanches or snow avalanches. Farther on we come to a gentle stream slipping down the face of the cliff in lace-like strips, and dropping from ledge to ledge—too small to be called a fall—trickling, dripping, oozing, a pathless wanderer from the upland meadows, seeking a way century after century to the depths of the valley without any appreciable channel. Every morning after a cool night, evaporation being checked, it gathers strength and sings like a bird, but as the day advances and the sun strikes its thin currents outspread on the heated precipices, most of its waters vanish ere the bottom of the valley is reached. Many a fine, hanging-garden aloft on breezy inaccessible heights owes to it its freshness and fullness of beauty; ferneries in shady nooks, filled with *Adiantum* [maidenhair fern, *ed.*], *Woodwardia* [chain fern, *ed.*], *Woodsia* [cliff fern, *ed.*], *Aspidium* [sword fern, *ed.*], *Pellaea* [cliffbrake, *ed.*], and *Cheilanthes* [lip fern, *ed.*], rosetted and tufted and ranged in lines, daintily overlapping, thatching the stupendous cliffs with softest beauty, some of the delicate fronds seeming to float on the warm moist air, without any connection with rock or stream. Nor is there any lack of colored plants wherever they can find a place to cling to; lilies and mints, the showy cardinal *Mimulus* [monkeyflower, *ed.*], and glowing cushions of the golden bahia, enlivened with butterflies and bees and all the other small, happy humming creatures that belong to them.

After the highest point on the lower division of the trail is gained, it leads up into the deep recess occupied by the great fall, the noblest display of falling water to be found in the valley, or perhaps in the world. When it first comes in sight it seems almost within reach of one's hand, so great in the spring is its volume and velocity, yet it is still nearly a third of a mile away and appears to recede as we advance. The sculpture of the walls about it is on a scale of grandeur, according nobly with the fall plain and massive, though elaborately finished, like all the other cliffs about the valley.

In the afternoon, an immense shadow is cast athwart the plateau in front of the fall, and far over the fields of chaparral that clothe the slopes and benches of the walls to the eastward, creeping upward until the fall is wholly overcast, the contrast between the shaded and illumined sections being very striking in these near views.

Under this shadow, during the cool centuries immediately following the breaking-up of the Glacial Period, dwelt a small residual glacier, one of the few that lingered on this sun-beaten side of the valley after the main trunk glacier had vanished. It sent down a long winding current through the narrow canyon on the west side of the fall, and must have formed a striking feature of the ancient scenery of the valley; the lofty fall of ice and fall of water side by side, yet separate and distinct.

The coolness of the afternoon shadow and the abundant dewy spray make a fine climate for the plateau ferns and grasses, and for the beautiful azalea bushes that grow here in profusion and bloom in September, long after the warmer thickets down on the floor of the valley have withered and gone to seed. Even close to the fall, and behind it at the base of the cliff, a few venturesome plants may be found undisturbed by the rock-shaking torrent.

The basin at the foot of the fall into which the current directly pours, when it is not swayed by the wind, is about ten feet deep and fifteen to twenty feet in diameter. That it is not much deeper is surprising, when the great height and force of the fall is considered. But the rock where the water strikes probably suffers less erosion than it would were the descent less than half as great, since the current is outspread, and much of its force is spent ere it reaches the bottom—being received on the air as upon an elastic cushion, and borne outward and dissipated over a surface more than fifty yards wide.

This surface, easily examined when the water is low, is intensely clean and fresh-looking. It is the raw, quick flesh of the mountain wholly untouched by the weather. In summer droughts when the snowfall of the preceding winter has been light, the fall is reduced to a mere shower of separate drops without any obscuring spray. Then we may safely go back of it and view the crystal shower from beneath, each drop wavering and pulsing as it makes its way through the air, and flashing off jets of colored light of ravishing beauty. But all this is invisible from the bottom of the valley, like a thousand other interesting things. One must labor for beauty as for bread, here as elsewhere.

The Grandeur of the Yosemite Fall

During the time of the spring floods, the best near view of the fall is obtained from Fern Ledge on the east side above the blinding spray at a height of about four hundred feet above the base of the fall. A climb of about fourteen hundred feet from the valley has to be made, and there is no trail, but to any one fond of climbing this will make the ascent all the more delightful. A narrow part of the ledge extends to the side of the fall and back of it, enabling us to approach it as closely as we wish. When the afternoon sunshine is streaming through the throng of comets, ever wasting, ever renewed, the marvelous firmness and variety of their forms are beautifully revealed. At the top of the fall they seem to burst forth in irregular spurts from some grand, throbbing mountain heart. Now and then, one mighty throb sends forth a mass of solid water into the free air far beyond the others, which rushes alone to the bottom of the fall with long streaming tail, like combed silk, while the others, descending in clusters, gradually mingle and lose their identity. But they all rush past us with amazing velocity and display of power, though apparently drowsy and deliberate in their movements when observed from a distance of a mile or two. The heads of these comet-like masses are composed of nearly solid water, and are dense white in color, like pressed snow, from the friction they suffer in rushing through the air, the portion worn off forming the tail between the white lustrous threads and films of which faint, grayish pencilings appear, while the outer, finer sprays of water-dust, whirling in sunny eddies, are pearly gray throughout.

At the bottom of the fall, there is but little distinction of form visible. It is mostly a hissing, clashing, seething, upwhirling mass of scud and spray, through which the light sifts in gray and purple tones, while at times, when the sun strikes at the required angle, the whole wild and apparently lawless, stormy, striving mass is changed to brilliant rainbow hues. The middle portion of the fall is the most openly beautiful; lower, the various forms into which the waters are wrought are more closely and voluminously veiled, while higher, towards the head, the current is more simple and undivided. But even at the bottom, in the boiling clouds of spray, there is no confusion, while the rainbow light makes all divine, adding glorious beauty and peace to glorious power. This noble fall has far the richest, as well as the most powerful, voice of all the falls of the valley, its tones varying from the sharp hiss and rustle of the wind in the glossy leaves of the live oak and the soft, sifting, hushing tones of the pines, to the loudest rush and roar of storm winds and thunder among the crags of the summit peaks. The low bass, booming, reverberating tones, heard under favorable circumstances five or six miles away, are formed by the dashing and exploding of heavy masses of water mixed with air upon two projecting ledges on the face of the cliff, the one on which we are standing and another about two hundred feet above it. The torrent of massive comets is continuous at time of high water, while the explosive, booming notes are wildly intermittent, because, unless influenced by the wind, most of the heavier masses shoot out from the face of the precipice, and pass the ledges upon which at other times they are wrecked. Occasionally the whole fall is swayed away from the front of the cliff, then suddenly dashed flat against it, or vibrated from side to side like a pendulum, giving rise to endless variety of forms and sounds.

Once during a violent windstorm, while I watched the fall from the shelter of a pine tree, the whole ponderous column was suddenly arrested in its descent at a point about midway between the base and top, and was neither blown upward or turned aside, but simply held stationary in midair as if gravitation below that point had ceased to act. Thus it remained for more than a minute, resting in the arms of the stormwind, the usual quantity of water meanwhile coming over the brow of the cliff and accumulating in the air as if falling upon an invisible floor, swedging and widening. Then, as if commanded to go on, scores of arrowy water-comets shot forth from the base of the suspended fountain, and the grand anthem of the fall once more began to sound.

The Nevada Fall

The Nevada Fall is six hundred feet high and is usually ranked next to the Yosemite in general interest among the five main falls of the valley. Coming through the Little Yosemite in tranquil reaches, the river is first broken into rapids on a moraine boulder-bar that crosses the lower end of the valley. Thence it pursues its way to the head of the fall in a very rough channel, cut in the solid granite, dashing on side angles, heaving in heavy surging masses against elbow knobs, and swirling and swashing in potholes without a moment's rest. Thus, already chafed and dashed to foam, overfolded and twisted, it plunges over the brink of the precipice as if glad to escape into the open air. But before it reaches the bottom, it is pulverized yet finer by impinging upon a sloping portion of the cliff about halfway down, thus making it the whitest of all the falls of the valley, and altogether one of the most wonderful in the world.

On the north side, close to its head, a slab of granite projects over the brink, forming a fine point for a view over its throng of streamers and wild plunging thunderbolts; through the broad drifts of spray, to the river far below, gathering its spent waters and rushing on again down the canyon in glad exultation into Emerald Pool, where at length it grows calm and gets rest for what still lies before it. All the features of the view correspond with the waters in grandeur and wildness. The glacier-sculptured walls of the canyon on either hand, with the sublime mass of the Glacier Point Ridge in front, form a huge triangular pit-like basin, which, filled with the roaring of the falling river seems as if it might be the hopper of one of the mills of the gods in which the mountains were being ground to dust.

The Vernal Fall

The Vernal, famous for its rainbows, is four hundred feet high, a staid, orderly, graceful, easy-going fall, proper and exact in every movement and gesture, with scarce a hint of the passionate enthusiasm of Yosemite or of the impetuous Nevada, whose chafed and twisted waters hurrying over the cliff seem glad to escape into the open air, while its deep, booming, thundertones reverberate over the listening landscape. Nevertheless, it is a favorite with most visitors, doubtless because it is more accessible than any other, more closely approached, and better seen and heard. A good stairway ascends the cliff beside it and the level plateau at the head enables one to saunter safely along the edge of the river as it comes from Emerald Pool and to watch its waters, calmly bending over the brow of the precipice, in a sheet eighty feet wide, changing in color from green to purplish gray and white until broken into spray at the bottom. Thence issuing from beneath its fine broad spray-clouds we see the adventurous river, still unspent, beating its way down the wildest and deepest of all its canyons in gray roaring rapids, dear to the ouzel, and below the confluence of the Illilouette, sweeping around the shoulder of

Half Dome on its approach to the head of the tranquil levels of the valley.

The Illilouette Fall

The Illilouette, in general appearance, most resembles the Nevada. The volume of water is less than half as great, but it is about the same height (six hundred feet) and its waters receive the same kind of preliminary tossing in a rocky, irregular channel. Therefore it is a very white and fine-grained fall. When it is in full springtime bloom, it is partly divided by rocks that roughen the lip of the precipice, but this division amounts only to a kind of fluting and grooving of the column, which has a beautiful effect. It is not nearly so grand a fall as the Upper Yosemite, or so symmetrical as the Vernal, or so airily graceful and simple as the Bridal Veil, nor does it ever display so tremendous an outgush of snowy magnificence as the Nevada. But in the exquisite fineness and richness of texture of its flowing folds it surpasses them all.

One of the finest effects of sunlight on falling water I ever saw in Yosemite or elsewhere I found on the brow of this beautiful fall. It was in Indian summer, when the leaf colors were ripe and the great cliffs and domes were transfigured in the hazy golden air. I had scrambled up its rugged talus-dammed canyon of the Illilouette, oftentimes stopping to take breath and look back to admire the wonderful views to be had there of the great Half Dome, and to enjoy the extreme purity of the water, which in the motionless pools on this stream is almost perfectly invisible; the colored foliage of the maples, dogwoods, *Rubus* tangles, etc., and the late goldenrods and asters. The voice of the fall was now low, and the grand spring and summer floods had waned to sifting, drifting gauze and thin-broidered folds of linked and arrowy lacework. When I reached the foot of the fall, slant sunbeams were glinting across its head, leaving all the rest of it in shadow. On its illumined brow a group of yellow spangles of singular form and beauty were playing, flashing up and dancing in large flame-shaped masses, wavering at times, then steadying, rising and falling in accord with the shifting forms of the water. But the color of the dancing spangles changed not at all. Nothing in clouds or flowers, on bird-wings or the lips of shells, could rival it in fineness. It was the most divinely beautiful mass of rejoicing yellow light I ever beheld—one of Nature's precious sights that come to us but once in a lifetime.

The Beauty Of The Rainbows

The Bridal Veil and Vernal Falls are famous for their rainbows, and special visits to them are often made when the sun shines into the spray at the most favorable angle. But amid the spray and foam and fine-ground mist ever rising from the various falls and cataracts, there is an affluence and variety of iris bows scarcely known to visitors who stay only a day or two. Both day and night, winter and summer, this divine light may be seen wherever water is falling, dancing, singing, telling the heart-peace of Nature amid the wildest displays of her power. In the bright spring mornings, the black-walled recess at the foot of Lower Yosemite Fall is lavishly fine with irised spray; and not simply does this span the dashing foam, but the foam itself, the whole mass of it, beheld at a certain distance, seems to be col-ored, and drips and wavers from color to color, mingling with the foliage of the adjacent trees, without suggesting any relationship to the ordinary rainbow. This is perhaps the largest and most reservoir-like fountain of iris colors to be found in the valley.

Lunar rainbows or spraybows also abound in the glorious affluence of dashing, rejoicing, hurrahing, enthusiastic spring floods, their colors as distinct as those of the sun and regularly and obviously banded, though less vivid. Fine specimens may be found any night at the foot of Upper Yosemite Fall, glowing gloriously amid the gloomy shadows and thundering waters of the canyon, whenever there is plenty of moonlight and spray. Even the secondary bow is at times distinctly visible.

The best point from which to observe them is on Fern Ledge. For some time after moonrise, at time of high water, the arc has a span of about five hundred feet, and is set upright, one end planted in the boiling spray at the bottom, the other in the edge of the fall, creeping lower, of course, and becoming less upright as the moon rises higher. This grand arc of color, glowing in mild, shapely beauty in so weird and huge a chamber of night shadows, and amid the rush and roar and tumultuous dashing of this thunder-voiced fall, is one of the most impressive and most cheering of all sights offered in all this wonder-filled valley.

Smaller bows may be seen in the gorge on the plateau between the Upper and Lower Falls. Once toward midnight, after spending a few hours with the wild beauty of the Upper Fall, I sauntered along the edge of the gorge, looking in here and there, wherever the footing felt safe, to see what I could learn of the night aspects of the smaller falls that dwell there. And down in an exceedingly black, pit-like por-

tion of the gorge, at the foot of the highest of the intermediate falls, while the moonbeams were pouring into it
through a narrow opening, I saw a well-defined spray-bow,
beautifully distinct in colors, spanning the pit from side to
side, while pure white foam-waves beneath the beautiful bow
were constantly springing up out of the dark into the moonlight like dancing ghosts.

An Unexpected Adventure

A wild scene, but not a safe one, is made by the moon as it
appears through the edge of Yosemite Fall when one is
behind it. Once, after enjoying the nightsong of the waters
and watching the formation of the colored bow as the moon
came round the domes and sent her beams into the wild
uproar, I ventured out on the narrow bench that extends
back of the fall from Fern Ledge and began to admire the
dim-veiled grandeur of the view. I could see the fine gauzy
threads of the fall's filmy border by having the light in front.
Wishing to look at the moon through the meshes of some of
the denser portions of the fall, I ventured to creep farther
behind it while it was gently wind-swayed, without taking sufficient thought about the consequences of its swaying back
to its natural position after the wind-pressure should be
removed. The effect was enchanting: fine, savage music
sounding above, beneath, around me, while the moon,
apparently in the very midst of the rushing waters, seemed to
be struggling to keep her place, on account of the ever-
varying form and density of the water masses through which
she was seen, now darkly veiled or eclipsed by a rush of thick-
headed comets, now flashing out through openings between

their tails. I was in fairyland between the dark wall and the wild throng of illumined waters, but suffered sudden disenchantment; for, like the witch-scene in Alloway Kirk, "in an instant all was dark." Down came a dash of spent comets, thin and harmless-looking in the distance, but they felt desperately solid and stony when they struck my shoulders, like a mixture of choking spray and gravel. Instinctively dropping on my knees, I gripped an angle of the rock, curled up with my face pressed against my breast, and in this attitude submitted as best I could to my thundering bath. The heavier masses seemed to strike like cobblestones, and there was a confused noise of many waters about my ears—hissing, gurgling, clashing sounds that were not heard as music. The situation was quickly realized. How fast one's thoughts burn in such times of stress! I was weighing chances of escape. Would the column be swayed a few inches away from the wall, or would it come yet closer? The fall was in flood and not so lightly would its ponderous mass be swayed. My fate seemed to depend on a breath of the "idle wind." It was moved gently forward, the pounding ceased, and I was once more visited by glimpses of the moon. But fearing I might be caught at a disadvantage in making too hasty a retreat, I moved only a few feet along the bench to where a block of ice lay. I wedged myself between the ice and the wall and lay face downwards, until the steadiness of the light gave encouragement to rise and get away. Somewhat nerve-shaken, drenched, and benumbed, I made out to build a fire, warmed myself, ran home, reached my cabin before daylight, got an hour or two of sleep, and awoke sound and comfortable, better, not worse for my hard midnight bath.

Climate And Weather

Owing to the westerly trend of the valley and its vast depth, there is a great difference between the climates of the north and south sides—greater than between many countries far apart—for the south wall is in shadow during the winter months, while the north is bathed in sunshine every clear day. Thus there is mild spring weather on one side of the valley while winter rules the other. Far up the northside cliffs, many a nook may be found closely embraced by sun-beaten rock-bosses in which flowers bloom every month of the year. Even butterflies may be seen in these high winter gardens except when snowstorms are falling and a few days after they have ceased. In January, near the head of Lower Yosemite Fall, I found the ant lions lying in wait in their warm sand-cups, rock ferns being unrolled, club mosses covered with fresh-growing plants, the flowers of the laurel nearly open, and the honeysuckle rosetted with bright young leaves. Every plant seemed to be thinking about summer. Even on the shadowside of the valley, the frost is never very sharp. The lowest temperature I ever observed during four winters was 7° Fahrenheit. The first twenty-four days of January had an average temperature at 9 A.M. of 32 degrees, minimum 22 degrees; at 3 P.M. the average was 40 degrees, the minimum 32 degrees. Along the top of the walls, seven thousand and eight thousand feet high, the temperature was, of course, much lower. But the difference in temperature between the north and south sides is due not so much to the winter sunshine as to the heat of the preceding summer, stored up in the rocks, which rapidly melts the snow in contact with them. For though summer sun-heat is stored in the rocks of the south side also, the amount is much less because the rays

106

fall obliquely on the south wall even in summer and almost vertically on the north.

The great annual spring thaw usually begins in May in the
forest region, and in June and July on the High Sierra, varying
somewhat both in time and fullness with the weather and the
depth of the snow. Toward the end of summer, the streams are
at their lowest ebb, few even of the strongest singing much
above a whisper they slip and ripple through gravel and
boulder-beds from pool to pool in the hollows of their channels, and drop in pattering showers like rain, and slip down
precipices and fall in sheets of embroidery, fold over fold. But,
however low their singing, it is always ineffably fine in tone, in
harmony with the restful time of the year.

The first snow of the season that comes to the help of
the streams usually falls in September or October, sometimes even in the latter part of August, in the midst of yellow
Indian summer when the goldenrods and gentians of the
glacier meadows are in their prime. This Indian summer
snow, however, soon melts, the chilled flowers spread their
petals to the sun, and the gardens as well as the streams are
refreshed as if only a warm shower had fallen. The snowstorms that load the mountains to form the main fountain
supply for the year seldom set in before the middle or end
of November.

Winter Beauty Of The Valley

When the first heavy storms stopped work on the high mountains, I made haste down to my Yosemite den, not to "hole up"
and sleep the white months away. I was out every day, and often
all night, sleeping but little, studying the so-called wonders and

common things ever on show, wading, climbing, sauntering among the blessed storms and calms, rejoicing in almost everything alike that I could see or hear: the glorious brightness of frosty mornings; the sunbeams pouring over the white domes and crags into the groves and waterfalls, kindling marvelous iris fires in the hoarfrost and spray; the great forests and mountains in their deep noon sleep; the good-night alpenglow; the stars; the solemn gazing moon, drawing the huge domes and headlands one by one glowing white out of the shadows hushed and breathless like an audience in awful enthusiasm, while the meadows at their feet sparkle with frost-stars like the sky; the sublime darkness of storm-nights, when all the lights are out; the clouds in whose depths the frail snowflowers grow; the behavior and many voices of the different kinds of storms, trees, birds, waterfalls, and snow avalanches in the ever-changing weather.

In winter, the thin outer folds and whirling spray of Upper Yosemite Fall are frozen while falling, and are deposited around the base of the fall in the form of a hollow truncated cone, which sometimes reaches a height of five hundred feet or more, into the heart of which the whole volume of the fall descends with a tremendous roar as if pouring down the throat of a crater. In the building of this ice cone, part of the frozen spray falls directly to its place in the form of minute particles like the dust of wind-beaten snow, but a considerable portion is first frozen upon the face of the cliff on both sides of the fall. Every clear frosty morning, loud sounds are heard booming and reverberating from side to side of the valley at intervals of a few minutes, beginning soon after sunrise and continuing an hour or two, like a thunderstorm. In my first winter in the valley, I could not make out the source of this noise. I thought of falling boulders, rock blasting, etc. Not till I saw what looked like hoarfrost dropping from the side of the Fall was the problem explained. The strange thunder is made by the fall of sections of ice formed of spray that is frozen on the face of the cliff along the sides of Upper Yosemite Fan—a sort of crystal plaster, a foot or two thick, racked off by the sunbeams, awakening all the valley like cock-crowing, announcing the finest weather, shouting aloud Nature's infinite industry and love of hard work in creating beauty.

Exploring An Ice Cone

This frozen spray gives rise to one of the most interesting winter features of the valley—a cone of ice at the foot of the fall, four or five hundred feet high. From the Fern Ledge standpoint its crater-like throat is seen, down which the fall plunges with deep, gasping explosions of compressed air, and, after being engulfed and churned in the stormy interior, the water bursts forth through arched openings at its base, apparently scourged and weary and glad to escape, while belching spray, spouted up out of the throat past the descending current, is wafted away in irised drifts to the adjacent rocks and groves. It is built during the night and early hours of the morning; only in spells of exceptionally cold and cloudy weather is the work continued through the day. The greater part of the spray material falls in crystalline showers direct to its place, something like a small local snowstorm, but a considerable portion is first frozen on the face of the cliff along the sides of the fall and stays there until expanded and cracked off in irregular masses, some of them tons in weight. In windy, frosty weather, when the fall is swayed from side to side, the cone is well drenched and the loose ice masses and spray-dust are all firmly welded and frozen together. Thus the finest of the downy wafts and curls of spray-dust, which in mild nights fall about as silently as dew, are held back until sunrise to make a store of heavy ice to reinforce the waterfall's thundertones.

While the cone is in process of formation, growing higher and wider in the frosty weather, the surface is smooth and pure white, the outlines finely drawn, the whole presenting the appearance of a beautiful crystal hill wreathed with folds of irised spray. But when it is wasting and breaking up in the spring, its surface is strewn with leaves, pine branches, stones, sand, etc., that have been brought over the fall, making it look like a heap of avalanche detritus.

Anxious to learn what I could about the structure of this curious ice-hill, I often approached it in calm weather and tried to climb it, carrying an ax to cut steps. Once I nearly succeeded in gaining the summit. At the base I was met by a current of spray and wind that made seeing and breathing difficult. I pushed on backward however, and soon gained the slope of the hill, where by creeping close to the surface, most of the choking blast passed over me and I managed to crawl up with but little difficulty. Thus I made my way nearly to the summit, halting at times to peer up through the wild whirls of spray at the veiled grandeur of the fall, or to listen to the thunder beneath me. The whole hill was sounding as if it were a huge, bellowing drum. I hoped that by waiting until the fall was blown aslant I should be able to climb to the lip of the crater and get a view of the interior, but a suffocating blast, half air, half water, followed by the fall of an enormous mass of frozen spray from a spot high up on the wall, quickly discouraged me. The whole cone was jarred by the blow and some fragments of the mass sped past me dangerously near, so I beat a hasty retreat, chilled and drenched, and lay down on a sunny rock to dry.

El Capitan

11

Around Yosemite Walls

Clarence King

Late in the afternoon of October 5, 1864, a party of us reached the edge of Yosemite, and, looking down into the valley, saw that the summer haze had been banished from the region by autumnal frosts and wind. We looked in the gulf through air as clear as a vacuum, discerning small objects upon valley floor and cliff-front. That splendid afternoon shadow, which divides the face of El Capitan, was projected far up and across the valley, cutting it in halves—one a mosaic of russets and yellows with dark pine and glimpse of white river; the other a cobalt blue zone, in which the familiar groves and meadows were suffused with shadow-tones.

It is hard to conceive a more pointed contrast than this same view in October and June. Then, through a slumberous yet transparent atmosphere, you look down upon emerald freshness of green, upon arrowy rush of swollen river, and here and there, along pearly cliffs, as from the clouds, tumbles white, silver dust of cataracts. The voice of full, soft winds swells up over rustling leaves, and, pulsating, throbs like the beating of far-off surf. All stern sublimity, all geological terribleness, are veiled away behind magic curtains of cloud-shadow and broken light. Misty brightness, glow of cliff and sparkle of foam, wealth of beautiful details, the charm of pearl and emerald, cool gulfs of violet shade stretching back in deep recesses of the walls—these are the features which lie under the June sky.

Now all that has gone. The shattered fronts of walls stand out sharp and terrible, sweeping down in broken crag and cliff to a valley whereon the shadow of autumnal death has left its solemnity. There is no longer an air of beauty. In this cold, naked strength, one has crowded on him the geological record of mountain work, of granite plateau suddenly rent asunder, of the slow, imperfect manner in which Nature has vainly striven to smooth her rough work and bury the ruins with thousands of years' accumulation of soil and debris.

The rock fell under us in one sheer sweep of thirty-two hundred feet. Upon its face we could trace the lines of fracture and all prominent lithological changes. Directly beneath, outspread like a delicately tinted chart, lay the lovely park of Yosemite, winding in and out about the solid white feet of precipices which sank into it on either side; its sunlit surface invaded by the shadow of the south wall; its spires of pine, open expanses of buff and drab meadow, and families of umber oaks rising as background for the vivid green river-margin and flaming orange masses of frosted cottonwood foliage. Deep in front, the Bridal Veil brook made its way through the bottom of an open gorge, and plunged off the edge of a thousand-foot cliff, falling in white waterdust and drifting in pale, translucent clouds out over the treetops of the valley. Directly opposite us, and forming the other gatepost of the valley's entrance, rose the great mass of Cathedral Rocks.

But our grandest view was eastward, above the deep, sheltered valley and over the tops of those terrible granite walls, out upon rolling ridges of stone and wonderful granite domes. Nothing in the whole list of irruptive products, except volcanoes themselves, is so wonderful as these domed mountains. They are of every variety of conoidal form, having horizontal sections accurately elliptical, ovoid, or circular, and profiles varying from such semicircles as the cap behind the Sentinel to the graceful, infinite curves of North Dome. Above and beyond these stretch back long, bare ridges connecting with sunny summit peaks. The whole region is one solid granite mass, with here and there shallow soil layers, and a thin, variable forest which grows in picturesque mode, defining the leading lines of erosion as an artist deepens here and there a line to hint at some structural peculiarity.

A complete physical exposure of the range, from summit to base, lay before us. At one extreme stand sharpened peaks, white in fretwork of glistening icebank, or black where tower straight bolts of snowless rock; at the other stretch away plains smiling with a broad, honest brown under autumn sunlight. They are not quite lovable, even in distant tranquility of hue, and just escape being interesting, in spite of their familiar rivers and associated belts of oaks. Nothing can ever render them quite charming, for in the startling splendor of flower-clad April you are surfeited with an embarrassment of beauty; at all other times stunned by their poverty. Not so the summits. Forever new, full of individuality, rich in detail, and coloring themselves anew under every cloud change or hue of heaven, they lay you under their spell. From them, the eye comes back over granite waves and domes to the sharp precipice-edges overhanging Yosemite. We look down those vast, hard, granite fronts, cracked and splintered, scarred and stained, down over gorges crammed with debris, or dark with files of climbing pines. Lower, the precipice feet are wrapped in meadow and grove, and beyond, level and sunlit, lies the floor—that smooth, river-cut park, with exquisite perfection of finish. The dome-like cap of El Capitan is formed of concentric layers like the peels of an onion, each one about two or three feet thick. Upon the precipice itself, either from our station on an over-hanging crevice, or from any point of opposite cliff or valley bottom, this structure is seen to be superficial, never descending more than a hundred feet.

An excursion which Cotter and I made to the top of the Three Brothers proved of interest. A half-hour's walk from camp, over rolling granite country, brought us to a ridge which jutted boldly out from the plateau to the edge of the Yosemite wall. Upon the southern side of this eminence heads a broad, debris-filled ravine, which descends to the valley bottom. Upon the other side, the ridge sends down its waters along a steep declivity into a lovely mountain basin, where, surrounded by forest, spreads out a level expanse of emerald meadow, with a bit of blue lakelet in the midst. The outlet of this little valley is through a narrow rift in the rocks leading down into Yosemite Fall.

Along the crest of our jutting ridge we found smooth pathway, and soon reached the summit. Here again we were upon the verge of a precipice, this time forty-two hundred feet high. Beneath us the whole upper half of the valley was as clearly seen as the southern half had been from El Capitan. The sinuosities of the Merced, those narrow, silvery gleams which indicated the channel of Yosemite Creek, the broad expanse of meadow, and debris trains, which had bounded down the Sentinel slope, were all laid out under us, though diminished by immense depth. The loftiest and most magnificent parts of the walls crowded in a semicircle in front of us. Above them, the domes, lifted even higher than ourselves, swept down to the precipice-edges. Directly to our left we overlooked the goblet-like recess into which the Yosemite tumbles, and could see the white torrent leap through its granite lip, disappearing a thousand feet below, hidden from our view by projecting crags, its roar floating up to us, now resounding loudly, and again dying off in faint reverberations like the sounding of the sea.

Looking up upon the falls from the valley below, one utterly fails to realize the great depth of the semicircular alcove into which they descend.

Looking back at El Capitan, its sharp, vertical front was projected against far blue foothills, the creamy whiteness of sunlit granite cut upon aerial distance, clouds, and cold blue sky shutting down over white crest and jetty pine-plumes, which gather helmet-like upon its upper dome. Perspective effects are marvelously brought out by the stern, powerful reality of such rock bodies as El Capitan. Across their terrible, blade-like precipice-edges you look on and down over vistas of canyon and green hillswells, the dark color of pine and fir broken by bare spots of harmonious red or brown, and changing with distance into purple, then blue, which reaches on farther into the brown monotonous plains. Beyond, where the earth's curve defines its horizon, dim serrations of Coast Range loom indistinctly on the hazy air. From here those remarkable fracture results, the Royal Arches, a series of recesses carved into the granite front, beneath North Dome, are seen in their true proportions. The concentric structure, which covers the dome with a series of plates, penetrates to a greater depth than usual. The Arches themselves are only fractured edges of these plates, resulting from the intersection of a cliff-plane with the conoidal shells.

We had seen the Merced group of snowpeaks heretofore from the west, but now gained a more oblique view, which began to bring out the thin obelisk-form of Mount Clark, a shape of great interest from its marvelous thinness. Mount Starr King, too, swelled up to its commanding height, the most elevated of the domes.

Looking in the direction of Half Dome, I was constantly impressed with the inclination of the walls, with the fact that they are never vertical for any great depth. This is observed, too, remarkably in the case of El Capitan, whose apparently vertical profile is very slant, the actual base standing twelve hundred feet in advance of the brow.

An excursion to the summit of North Dome was exceedingly interesting. From the rear of our camp we entered immediately a dense forest of conifers, which stretched southward along the summit of the ridge until solid granite, arresting erosion, afforded but little foothold. As usual, among the cracks, and clinging around the bases of boulders, a few hardy pines manage to live, almost to thrive, but as we walked, groups became scarcer, trees less healthy, all at last giving way to bare, solid stone. North Dome itself, which is easily reached, affords an impressive view up the Illilouette and across upon the fissured front of Half Dome. It is also one of the most interesting specimens of conoidal structure, since not only is its mass divided by large, spherical shells, but each of these is subdivided by a number of lesser, divisional planes. No lithological change is, however, noticeable between the different shells. The granite is composed chiefly of orthoclase, transparent vitreous quartz, and about an equal proportion of black mica and hornblende. Here and there adularia occurs, and, very sparingly, albite.

With no difficulty, but some actual danger, I climbed down a smooth granite roof-slope to where the precipice of Royal Arches makes off, and where, lying upon a sharp, neatly fractured edge, I was able to look down and study those purple markings which are vertically striped upon so many of these granite cliffs. I found them to be bands of lichen growth, which follow the curves of occasional waterflow. During any great rainstorm, and when snow upon the uplands is suddenly melted, innumerable streams, many of them of considerable volume, find their way to the precipice-edge, and pour down its front. Wherever this is the case, a deep purple lichen spreads itself upon the granite, and forms those dark cloudings which add so greatly to the variety and interest of the cliffs.

I found it extremest pleasure to lie there alone on the dizzy brink, studying the fine sculpture of cliff and crag, overlooking the arrangement of debris piles, and watching that slow, grand growth of afternoon shadows. Sunset found me there, still disinclined to stir, and repaid my laziness by a glorious spectacle of color. At this hour, there is no more splendid contrast of light and shade than one sees upon the western gateway itself—dark-shadowed El Capitan upon one side profiled against the sunset sky, and the yellow mass of Cathedral Rocks rising opposite in full light, while the valley is divided equally between sunshine and shade. Pine groves and oaks, almost black in the shadow, are brightened up to clear red-browns where they pass out upon the lighted plain. The Merced, upon its mirror-like expanses, here reflects deep blue from El Capitan, and there the warm Cathedral gold. The last sunlight reflected from some curious, smooth surfaces upon rocks east of the Sentinel, and about a thousand feet above the valley. I at once suspected them to be glacier marks, and booked them for further observation.

My next excursion was up to Mount Hoffmann, among a group of snowfields, whose drainage gathers at last through lakes and brooklets to a single brook, the Yosemite, and flows twelve miles in a broad arc to its plunge over into the valley. From the summit, which is of a remarkably bedded, conoidal mass of granite, sharply cut down in precipices fronting the north, is obtained a broad, commanding view of the Sierras from afar, by the heads of several San Joaquin branches, up to the ragged volcanic piles about Silver Mountain. From the top I climbed along slopes, and down by a wide detour among frozen snowbanks and many little basins of transparent blue water, amid black shapes of stunted fir, and over the confused wreck of rock and treetrunk thrown rudely in piles by avalanches whose tracks were fresh enough to be of interest. Upon reaching the bottom of a broad, open glacier-valley, through whose middle flows the Yosemite Creek and its branches, I was surprised to find the streams nearly all dry. The snow itself, under influence of cold, was a solid ice mass, and Yosemite Creek, even after I had followed it down for miles, had entirely ceased to flow. At intervals, the course of the stream was carried over slopes of glacier-worn granite, ending almost uniformly in shallow rock basins, where were considerable ponds of water, in one or two instances expanding to the dignity of lakelets.

The valley describes an arc whose convexity is, in the main, turned to the west, the stream running nearly due west for about four miles, turning gradually to the southward, and, having crossed the Mono trail, bending again to the southeast, after which it discharges over the verge of the cliff. An average breadth of this valley is about half a mile, its form a shallow, elliptical trough, rendered unusually smooth by the erosive action of old glaciers. Roches moutonnées break its surface here and there, but in general, the granite has been planed down into remarkable smoothness. All along its course, a varying rubbish of angular boulders has been left by the retiring ice whose material, like that of the whole country, is of granite, but I recognized prominently black sienitic granite from the summit of Mount Hoffmann, which, from superior hardness, has withstood disintegration, and is perhaps the most frequent material of glacier-blocks. The surface modeling is often of the most finished type. Especially is this the case wherever the granite is highly silicious, its polish becoming then as brilliant as a marble mantel. In very feldspathic portions, and particularly where orthoclase predominates, the polished surface becomes a crust, usually about three-quarters of an inch thick, in which the ordinary appearance of the minerals has been somewhat changed, the rock surface, by long pressure, rendered extremely dense, and in a measure separated from the underlying material. This smooth crust is constantly breaking off in broad flakes. The polishing extended up the valley sides to a height of about seven hundred feet.

The average section of the old glacier was perhaps six hundred feet thick by half a mile in width. I followed its course from Mount Hoffmann down as far as I could ride, and then, tying my horse only a little way from the brink of the cliff, I continued downward on foot, walking upon the dry streambed. I found here and there a deep pit-hole, sometimes twenty feet deep, carved in midchannel, and often full of water. Just before reaching the cliff verge, the stream enters a narrow, sharp cut about one hundred and twenty feet in depth, and probably not over thirty feet wide. The bottom and sides of this granite lip, here and there, are evidently glacier-polished, but the greater part of the scorings have been worn away by the attrition of sands. A peculiar, brilliant polish, which may be seen there today, is wholly the result of recent sand friction.

It was noon when I reached the actual lip, and crept with extreme caution down over smooth, rounded granite, between towering walls, to where the Yosemite Fall makes its wonderful leap. Polished rock curved over too dangerously for me to lean out and look down over the cliff-front itself. A stone gate dazzlingly gilded with sunlight formed the frame through which I looked down upon that lovely valley.

Contrast with the strength of yellow rock and severe adamantine sculpture threw over the landscape beyond a strange unreality, a soft, aerial depth of purple tone quite as new to me as it was beautiful beyond description. There, twenty-six hundred feet below, lay meadow and river, oak and pine, and a broad shadow-zone cast by the opposite wall. Over it all, even through the dark sky overhead, there seemed to be poured some absolute color, some purple air, hiding details, and veiling with its soft, amethystine obscurity all that hard, broken roughness of the Sentinel cliffs. In this strange, vacant, stone corridor, this pathway for the great Yosemite torrent, this sounding-gallery of thunderous tumult, it was a strange sensation to stand, looking in vain for a drop of water, listening vainly, too, for the faintest whisper of sound, and I found myself constantly expecting some sign of the returning flood.

From the lip I climbed a high point just to the east, getting a grand view down the cliff, where a broad, purple band defined the Yosemite spray line. There, too, I found unmistakable ice-striae, showing that the glacier of Mount Hoffmann had actually poured over the brink. At the moments of such discovery, one cannot help restoring in imagination pictures of the past. When we stand by riverbank or meadow of that fair valley, looking up at the torrent falling bright under fullness of light, and lovely in its graceful, wind-swayed airiness, we are apt to feel its enchantment; but how immeasurably grander must it have been when the great, living, moving glacier, with slow, invisible motion, crowded its huge body over the brink, and launched blue ice-blocks down through the foam of the cataract into that gulf of wild rocks and eddying mist!

I had always felt a desire to examine Bridal Veil canyon and the southwest Cathedral slope. Accordingly, one fine morning I set out alone, and descended through chaparral and over rough debris slopes to the stream, which at this time, unlike the other upland brooks, flowed freely, though with far less volume than in summer. At this altitude, only such streams as derive their volume wholly from melting snow dry up in the cold autumnal and winter months. Spring-fed brooks hold their own, and rather increase as cold weather advances.

It was a wild gorge down which I tramped, following the streambed, often jumping from block to block, or letting myself down by the chaparral boughs that overhung my way. Splendid walls on either side rose steep and high, for the most part bare, but here and there on shelf or crevice bearing clusters of fine conifers, their lower slopes one vast wreck of boulders and thicket of chaparral plants. Not without some difficulty, I at length got to the brink, and sat down to rest, looking over at the valley, whose meadows were only a thousand feet below. A cool, stirring breeze blew up the Merced Canyon, swinging the lace-like scarf of foam which fell from my feet, and, floating now against the purple cliff, again blew out gracefully to the right or left. While I looked, a gust came roaming round the Cathedral Rocks, impinging against our cliff near the fall, and apparently got in between it and the cliff, carrying the whole column of falling water straight out in a streamer through the air.

I went back to camp by way of the Cathedral Rocks, finding much of interest in the conoidal structure, which is yet perfectly apparent, and unobscured by erosion or the terrible splitting asunder they have suffered. Upon a ridge connecting these rocks with the plateaus just south, there were many instructive and delightful points of view, especially the crag just above the Cathedral Spires, from which I overlooked a large part of valley and cliff, with the two sharp, slender minarets of granite close beneath me. That great block forming the plateau between the Yosemite and Illilouette canyons afforded a fine field for studying granite, pine, and many remarkably characteristic views of the gorge below and peaks beyond. From our camp, I explored every ravine and climbed each eminence, reaching at last, one fine afternoon, the top of that singular, hemispherical mass, the Sentinel Dome. From this point, one sweeps the horizon in all directions. You stand upon the crest of half a globe, whose smooth, white sides, bearing here and there stunted pines, slope away regularly in all directions from your feet. Below, granite masses, blackened here and there with densely clustered forest, stretch through varied undulations toward you. At a little distance from the foot of Half Dome, trees hold upon sharp brinks, and precipices plunge off into Yosemite upon one side, and the dark, rocky canyon of Illilouette upon the other. Eastward, soaring into clouds, stands the thin, vertical mass of Half Dome.

From this view, the snowy peak of the Obelisk, flattened into broad, dome-like outline, rises, shutting out the more distant Sierra summits. This peak, from its peculiar position and thin, tower-like form, offers one of the most tempting summits of the region. From that slender top one might look into the Yosemite, and into that basin of ice and granite between the Merced and Mount Lyell groups. I had longed for it through the last month's campaign, and now made up my mind, with this inspiring view, to attempt it at all hazards.

A little way to the east, and about a thousand feet below the brink of Glacier Point, the crags appeared to me particularly tempting, so in the late afternoon I descended, walking over a rough, gritty surface of granite, which gave me secure foothold. Upon the very edge, the immense, splintered rocks lay piled one upon another; here a mass jutting out and over-hanging upon the edge, and here a huge slab pointed out like a barbette gun. I crawled out upon one of these projecting blocks and rested myself while studying the view.

From here, the one very remarkable object is Half Dome. You see it now edgewise and in sharp profile, the upper half of the conoid fronting the north with a sharp, sheer, frac-ture-face of about two thousand feet vertical. From the top of this a most graceful helmet curve sweeps over to the south, and descends almost perpendicularly into the valley of the Little Yosemite, and here, from the foot, springs up the block of Mount Broderick—a single, rough-hewn pyramid, three thousand feet from summit to base, trimmed upon its crest with a few pines, and spreading out its southern base into a precipice, over which plunges the white Nevada torrent. Observation had taught me that a glacier flowed over the Yosemite brink. As I looked over now, I could see its shallow valley and the ever-rounded rocks over which it crowded itself and tumbled into the icy valley below. Up the Yosemite gorge, which opened straight before me, I knew that another great glacier had flowed, and also that the valley of the Illilouette and the Little Yosemite had been the beds of rivers of ice.

It was impossible for me, as I sat perched upon this jutting rock mass, in full view of all the canyons which had led into this wonderful converging system of ice-rivers, not to imagine a picture of the glacier period. Bare or snow-laden cliffs over-hung the gulf. Streams of ice, here smooth and compacted into a white plain, there riven into innumerable crevasses, or tossed into forms like the waves of a tempest-lashed sea, crawled through all the gorges. Torrents of water and ava-lanches of rock and snow spouted at intervals all along the cliff walls. Not a tree nor a vestige of life was in sight, except far away upon ridges below, or out upon the dimly expanding plain. Granite and ice and snow, silence broken only by the howling tempest and the crash of falling ice or splintered rock, and a sky deep freighted with cloud and storm—these were the elements of a period which lasted immeasurably long, and only in comparatively the most recent geological times have given way to the present marvelously changed con-dition. Nature in her present aspects, as well as in the records of her past, here constantly offers the most vivid and terrible contrasts. Can anything be more wonderfully opposite than that period of leaden sky, gray granite, and desolate stretches of white, and the present, when of the old order we have only left the solid framework of granite, and the indelible inscrip-tions of glacier work? Today their burnished pathways are leg-ibly traced with the history of the past. Every ice-stream is represented by a feeble river, every great glacier cascade by a torrent of white foam dashing itself down rugged walls, or spouting from the brinks of upright cliffs. The very avalanche tracks are darkened by clustered woods, and over the level pathway of the great Yosemite glacier itself is spread a park of green, a mosaic of forest, a thread of river.

Bierstadt's Domes of Yosemite

12

The Domes of The Yosemite

Mark Twain

New York
June 2nd, 1867

"The Domes Of The Yosemite"

That is the name of Bierstadt's last picture. The art critics here
abused it without stint when its exhibition began, a month ago.
They ridiculed it so mercilessly that I thought it surely could
not be worth going to see, and so I stayed away.

I went to-day, however, and I think it is very well worth going to see. It is very beautiful—considerably more beautiful than the original.

You stand twelve hundred feet above the valley, and look up it toward the east, with the North Dome on the left and the South Dome [Half Dome, *ed.*] on the right. The rugged mountain range beyond the latter sweeps round to the right and shuts up the Valley, and, springing up among the clouds in the distance, you see one or two great peaks clad in robes of snow.

Well, the bird's-eye view of the level valley, with its clusters of diminished trees and its little winding river, is very natural, and familiar, and pleasant to look upon.

The pine trees growing out of clefts in a bold rock wall, in the right foreground, are very proper trees, and the grove of large ones, in the left foreground, and close at hand, are a true copy of Nature, and so are the various granite boulders in the vicinity.

Now, to sum up the picture's merits, those snow-peaks are correct—they look natural; the valley is correct and natural; the pine trees clinging to the bluff on the right, and the grove on the left, and the boulders, are all like nature; we will assume that the domes and things are drawn accurately.

One sees these things in all sorts of places throughout California, and under all sorts of circumstances, and gets so familiar with them that he knows them in a moment when he sees them in a picture. I knew them in Bierstadt's picture, and checked them off one by one, and said "These things are correct—they all look just as they ought to look, and they all belong to California."

But when I got around to the atmosphere, I was obliged to say "This man has imported this atmosphere; this man has surely imported this atmosphere from some foreign country, because nothing like it was ever seen in California."

I may be mistaken, for all men are liable to err, but I honestly think I am right. The atmospheric effects in that picture are startling, are full of variety, and are charming. It is more the atmosphere of Kingdom-Come than of California.

The time is early morning; the eastern heavens are filled with shredded clouds, and these afford the excuse for the dreamy lights and shadows that play about the leftward precipices and the great dome—a rich blending of softest purple, and gray, and blue, and brown and white, instead of the bald, glaring expanse of rocks and earth splotched with cloud-shadows like unpoetical ink-blots which one ought to see in a Californian mountain picture when correctly painted.

Some of Mr. Bierstadt's mountains swim in a lustrous, pearly mist, which is so enchantingly beautiful that I am sorry the Creator hadn't made it instead of him, so that it would always remain there.

In the morning, the outlines of mountains in California, even though they be leagues away, are painfully bold and sharp, because the atmosphere is so pure and clear—but the outlines of Mr. Bierstadt's mountains are soft and rounded and velvety, which is a great improvement on nature.

As a picture, this work must please, but as a portrait I do not think it will answer. Portraits should be accurate. We do not want feeling and intelligence smuggled into the pictured face of an idiot, and we do not want this glorified atmosphere smuggled into a portrait of the Yosemite, where it surely does not belong.

I may be wrong, but still I believe that this atmosphere of Mr. Bierstadt's is altogether too gorgeous.

Sequoias in winter

13

The Trees of The Valley

John Muir

For the use of the ever-increasing number of Yosemite visitors who make extensive excursions into the mountains beyond the valley, a sketch of the forest trees in general will probably be found useful. The different species are arranged in zones and sections, which brings the forest as a whole

133

within the comprehension of every observer. These species are always found as controlled by the climates of different elevations, by soil, and by the comparative strength of each species in taking and holding possession of the ground. So appreciable are these relations the traveler need never be at a loss in determining within a few hundred feet his elevation above sea level by the trees alone. Some of the species range upward for several thousand feet, yet even those species possessing the greatest vertical range are available in measuring the elevation, as they take on new forms corresponding with variations in altitude. Entering the lower fringe of the forest composed of Douglas oaks (*sic*) and Sabine pines [gray pine, *ed.*], the trees grow so far apart that not one-twentieth of the surface of the ground is in shade at noon. After advancing fifteen or twenty miles towards Yosemite and making an ascent of from two to three thousand feet, you reach the lower margin of the main pine belt, composed of great sugar pine, yellow pine, incense-cedar, and sequoia. Next you come to the magnificent silver-fir belt and lastly to the upper pine belt, which sweep up to the feet of the summit peaks in a dwarfed fringe, to a height of from ten to twelve thousand feet. That this general order of distribution depends on climate as affected by height above the sea, is seen at once, but there are other harmonies that become manifest only after observation and study. One of the most interesting of these is the arrangement of the forest in long curving bands, braided together into lace-like patterns in some places and outspread in charming variety. The key to these striking arrangements is the system of ancient glaciers; where they flowed, the trees followed, tracing their courses along the sides of canyons, over ridges, and high plateaus. All the forests of the Sierra are growing upon moraines, but moraines vanish like the glaciers that make them. Every storm that falls upon them wastes them, carrying away their decaying, disintegrating material into new formations, until they are no longer recognizable without tracing their transitional forms down the range. It appears, therefore, that the Sierra forests indicate the extent and positions of ancient moraines as well as they do belts of climate.

The Sugar Pine, King of Pine Trees

Of all the world's eighty or ninety species of pine trees, the sugar pine (*Pinus lambertiana*) is king, surpassing all others, not merely in size but in lordly beauty and majesty. In the Yosemite region it grows at an elevation of from three thousand to seven thousand feet above the sea and attains most perfect development at a height of about five thousand feet. The largest specimens are commonly about two hundred and twenty feet high and from six to eight feet in diameter four feet from the ground, though some grand old patriarch may be met here and there that has enjoyed six or eight centuries of storms and attained a thickness of ten or even twelve feet, still sweet and fresh in every fiber. The trunk is a remarkably smooth, round, delicately-tapered shaft, straight and regular as if turned in a lathe, mostly without limbs, purplish brown in color and usually enlivened with tufts of a yellow lichen. Toward the head of this magnificent column, long branches sweep gracefully outward and downward, sometimes forming a palm-like crown, but far more impressive than any palm crown I ever beheld. The needles are about three inches long in fascicles of five, and arranged in rather close tassels at the ends of slender branchlets that clothe the long outsweeping limbs. How well they sing in the wind, and how strikingly harmonious an effect is made by the long cylindrical cones, depending loosely from the ends of the long branches! The cones are about fifteen to eighteen inches long, and three in diameter, green, shaded with dark purple on their sunward sides. They are ripe in September and October of the second year from the flower. Then the flat, thin scales open and the seeds take wing, but the empty cones become still more beautiful and effective as decorations, for their diameter is nearly doubled by the spreading of the scales, and their color changes to yellowish brown while they remain, swinging on the tree all the following winter and summer, and continue effectively beautiful even on the ground many years after they fall. The wood is deliciously fragrant, fine in grain and texture and creamy yellow, as if formed of condensed sunbeams. The sugar from which the common name is derived is, I think, the best of sweets. It exudes from the heartwood where wounds have been made by forest fires or the ax, and forms irregular, crisp, candy-like kernels of considerable size, something like clusters of resin beads. When fresh it is white, but because most of the wounds on which it is found have been made by fire, the sap is stained and the hardened sugar becomes brown. Indians are fond of it, but on account of its laxative properties only small quantities may be eaten. No tree lover will ever forget his first meeting with the sugar pine. In most pine trees there is the sameness of expression, which to most people is apt to become monotonous, for the typical spiral form of conifers, however beautiful, affords little scope for appreciable individual character. The sugar pine is as free from conventionalities as the most picturesque oaks. No two are alike, and though they toss out their immense arms in what might seem extravagant gestures they never lose their expression of serene majesty. They are the priests of pines and seem ever to be addressing the surrounding forest. The yellow pine is found growing with them on warm hillsides, and the silver fir on cool northern slopes but, noble as these are, the sugar pine is easily king, and spreads his arms above them in blessing while they rock and wave in sign of recognition. The main branches are sometimes forty feet long, yet persistently simple, seldom dividing at all, excepting near the end; but anything like a bare cable appearance is prevented by the small, tasseled branchlets that extend all around them; and when these superb limbs sweep out symmetrically on all sides, a crown sixty or seventy feet wide is formed, which, gracefully poised on the summit of the noble shaft, is a glorious object. Commonly, however, there is a preponderance of limbs toward the east, away from the direction of the prevailing winds.

Although so unconventional when full-grown, the sugar pine is a remarkably proper tree in youth—a strict follower of coniferous fashions—slim, erect, with leafy branches kept exactly in place, each tapering in outline and terminating in a spiry point. The successive forms between the cautious neatness of youth and the bold freedom of maturity offer a delightful study. At the age of fifty or sixty years, the shy, fashionable form begins to be broken up. Specialized branches push out and bend with the great cones, giving individual character, that becomes more marked from year to year. Its most constant companion is the yellow pine. The Douglas spruce [Douglas fir, *ed.*], *Libocedrus* [incense-cedar, *ed.*], sequoia, and the silver fir are also more or less associated with it, but on many deep-soiled mountainsides, at an elevation of about five thousand feet above the sea, it forms the bulk of the forest, filling every swell and hollow and down-plunging ravine. The majestic crowns, approaching each other in bold curves, make a glorious canopy through which the tempered sunbeams pour, silvering the needles, and gilding the massive boles and the flowery, park-like ground into a scene of enchantment. On the most sunny slopes the white-flowered, fragrant *Chamaebatia* [bearclover, *ed.*] is spread like a carpet, brightened during early summer with the crimson *Sarcodes* [snowplant, *ed.*], the wild rose, and innumerable violets and gilias. Not even in the shadiest nooks will you find any rank, untidy weeds or unwholesome darkness. In the north sides of ridges the boles are more slender, and the ground is mostly occupied by an underbrush of hazel, *Ceanothus*, and flowering dogwood, but not so densely as to prevent the traveler from sauntering where he will, while the crowning branches are never impenetrable to the rays of the sun, and never so interblended as to lose their individuality.

The Yellow or Silver Pine

The silver pine or yellow pine [ponderosa pine, *ed.*], as it is commonly called, ranks second among the pines of the Sierra as a lumber tree, and almost rivals the sugar pine in stature and nobleness of port. Because of its superior powers of enduring variations of climate and soil, it has a more extensive range than any other conifer growing on the Sierra. On the western slope it is first met at an elevation of about two thousand feet, and extends nearly to the upper limit of timberline. Thence, crossing the range by the lowest passes, it descends to the eastern base, and pushes out for a considerable distance into the hot, volcanic plains, growing bravely upon well-watered, coarsely-stratified moraines between the talus slopes and meadows, upon gravelly lake basins, climbing old volcanoes, and dropping ripe cones among ashes and cinders.

The average size of full-grown trees on the western slope, where it is associated with the sugar pine, is a little less than two hundred feet in height and from five to six feet in diameter, though specimens considerably larger may easily be found. Where there is plenty of free sunshine and other conditions are favorable, it presents a striking contrast in form to the sugar pine, being a symmetrical spire, formed of a straight round trunk, clad with innumerable branches that are divided over and over again. Unlike the Yosemite form, about one-half of the trunk is commonly branchless, but where it grows at all close, three-fourths or more is naked, presenting then a more slender and elegant shaft than any other tree in the woods. The bark is mostly arranged in massive plates, some of them measuring four or five feet in length by eighteen inches in width, with a thickness of three or four inches, forming a quite marked and distinguishing feature. The needles are of a fine, warm, yellow-green color, six to eight inches long, firm and elastic, and crowded in handsome, radiant tassels on the upturning ends of the branches. The cones are about three or four inches long, and two and a half wide, growing in close, sessile clusters among the leaves.

The species attains its noblest form in filled-up lake basins, and as we have seen, so prominent a part does it form of their groves that it may well be called the Yosemite Pine. The largest that I have measured is standing alone almost opposite Sentinel Rock, or a little to the westward of it. It is a little over eight feet in diameter and about two hundred twenty feet high. Climbing these grand trees, especially when they are waving and singing in worship in wind-storms, is a glorious experience. Ascending from the lowest branch to the topmost is like stepping up stairs through a blaze of white light, every needle thrilling and shining as if with religious ecstasy.

The Jeffrey variety attains its finest development in the northern portion of the range, in the wide basins of the McCloud and Pitt Rivers, where it forms magnificent forests scarcely invaded by any other tree. It differs from the ordinary form in size, being only about half as tall, in its redder and more closely-furrowed bark, grayish-green foliage, less divided branches, and much larger cones. But intermediate forms come in which make a clear separation impossible, although some botanists regard it as a distinct species. It is this variety of ponderosa that climbs storm-swept ridges alone, and wanders out among the volcanoes of the Great Basin. Whether exposed to extremes of heat or cold, it is dwarfed like many other trees, and becomes all knots and angles, wholly unlike the majestic forms we have been sketching. Old specimens, bearing cones about as big as pineapples, may sometimes be found clinging to rifted rocks at an elevation of seven thousand or eight thousand feet, whose highest branches scarce reach above one's shoulders.

I have often feasted on the beauty of these noble trees when they were towering in all their winter grandeur, laden with snow—one mass of bloom; in summer, too, when the brown, staminate clusters hang thick among the shimmering needles, and the big purple burrs are ripening in the mellow light. But it is during cloudless wind-storms that these colossal pines are most impressively beautiful. Then they bow like willows, their leaves streaming forward all in one direction, and, when the sun shines upon them at the required angle, entire groves glow as if every leaf were burnished silver. The fall of tropic light on the crown of a palm is a truly glorious spectacle, the fervid sun-flood breaking upon the glossy leaves in long lance-rays, like mountain water among boulders at the foot of an enthusiastic cataract. But to me, there is something more impressive in the fall of light upon these noble, silver pine pillars: it is beaten to the finest dust and shed off in myriads of minute sparkles that seem to radiate from the very heart of the tree as if like rain, falling upon fertile soil, it had been absorbed to reappear in flowers of light. This species also gives forth the finest wind music. After listening to it in all kinds of winds, night and day, season after season, I think I could approximate to my position on the mountain by this pine music alone. If you would catch the tone of separate needles, climb a tree in breezy weather. Every needle is carefully tempered and gives forth no uncertain sound, each standing out with no interference excepting during head gales. Then you may detect the click of one needle upon another, readily distinguishable from the free wind-like hum.

When a sugar pine and one of this species equal in size are observed together, the latter is seen to be more simple in manners, more lively and graceful, and its beauty is of a kind more easily appreciated; on the other hand, it is less dignified and original in demeanor. The yellow pine seems ever eager to shoot aloft, higher and higher. Even while it is drowsing in autumn sun-gold, you may still detect a skyward aspiration, but the sugar pine seems too unconsciously noble and too complete in every way to leave room for even a heavenward care.

The Douglas Spruce

The Douglas spruce (*Pseudotsuga Douglasii*) [Douglas fir, *Pseudotsuga menziesii, ed.*] is one of the largest and longest-lived of the giants that flourish throughout the main pine belt, often attaining a height of nearly two hundred feet, and a diameter of six or seven feet. Where the growth is not too close, the stout, spreading branches, covering more than half of the trunk, are hung with innumerable slender, drooping sprays, handsomely feathered with the short leaves which radiate at right angles all around them. This vigorous tree is ever beautiful, welcoming the mountain winds and the snow as well as the mellow summer light, and it maintains its youthful freshness undiminished from century to century through a thousand storms. It makes its finest appearance during the months of June and July, when the brown buds at the ends of the sprays swell and open, revealing the young leaves, which at first are bright yellow, making the tree appear as if covered with gay blossoms. The pendulous bracted cones, three or four inches long, with their shell-like scales, are a constant adornment.

The young trees usually are assembled in family groups, each sapling exquisitely symmetrical. The primary branches are whorled regularly around the axis, generally in fives, while each is draped with long, feathery sprays that descend in lines as free and as finely drawn as those of falling water.

In Oregon and Washington it forms immense forests, growing tall and mast-like to a height of three hundred feet, and is greatly prized as a lumber tree. Here it is scattered among other trees, or forms small groves, seldom ascending higher than fifty-five hundred feet, and never making what would be called a forest. It is not particular in its choice of soil: wet or dry, smooth or rocky, it makes out to live well on them all. Two of the largest specimens, as we have seen, are in Yosemite. One of these, more than eight feet in diameter, is growing on the terminal moraine of the small residual glacier that lingered in the shady Illilouette Canyon. The other is growing at the foot of Liberty Cap near Nevada Fall. No other tree in the Sierra seems so much at home on earthquake taluses, and many of these huge boulder-slopes are almost exclusively occupied by it.

The Incense-Cedar

The incense-cedar (*Libocedrus decurrens*), with cinnamon-colored bark and yellow-green foliage, is one of the most interesting of the Yosemite trees. Some of them are one hundred and fifty feet high, from six to ten feet in diameter, and they are never out of sight as you saunter among the yellow pines. Their bright brown shafts and towers of flat, frondlike branches make a striking feature of the landscapes throughout all the seasons. In midwinter, when most of the other trees are asleep, this cedar puts forth its flowers in millions—the pistillate pale green and inconspicuous, but the staminate bright yellow, tingeing all the branches and making the trees as they stand in the snow look like gigantic goldenrods.

Incense-cedar is quite generally distributed throughout the pine belt without exclusively occupying any considerable area, or even making extensive groves. On the warmer mountain slopes, it ascends to about five thousand feet, and reaches the climate most congenial to it at a height of about four thousand feet, growing vigorously at this elevation in all kinds of soil. In particular, it is capable of enduring more moisture about its roots than any of its companions excepting only the sequoia.

Casting your eye over the general forest from some ridgetop, you can identify it by the color alone of its spiry summits, a warm yellow-green. In its youth up to the age of seventy or eighty years, none of its companions forms so strictly tapered a cone from top to bottom. The branches, outspread in flat plumes and, beautifully fronded, sweep gracefully downward and outward, except those near the top, which aspire; the lowest, especially in youth and middle age, droop to the ground, overlapping one another, shedding off rain and snow like shingles, and making fine tents for birds and campers. As it becomes older, it oftentimes grows strikingly irregular and picturesque. Large branches push out at right angles to the trunk, forming stubborn elbows and shoot up parallel with the axis. This tree frequently lives more than a thousand years; very old trees are usually dead at the top. The flat fragrant plumes are exceedingly beautiful: no waving fern-frond is finer in form and texture. In its prime the whole tree is thatched with them, but if you would see the *Libocedrus* in all its glory, you must go to the woods in midwinter when it is laden with myriads of yellow flowers about the size of wheat grains, forming a noble illustration of Nature's immortal virility and vigor. The mature cones, about three-fourths of an inch long, born on the ends of the plumy branchlets, serve to enrich still more the surpassing beauty of this winter-blooming tree-goldenrod.

The Silver Firs

We come now to the most regularly planted and most clearly defined of the main forest belts, composed almost exclusively of two silver firs—*Abies concolor* and *Abies magnifica* [white fir and red fir, *ed.*]—extending with but little interruption four hundred and fifty miles at an elevation of from five thousand to nine thousand feet above the sea. In its youth, *A. concolor* is a charmingly symmetrical tree with its flat, plumy branches arranged in regular whorls around the whitish-gray axis, which terminates in a stout, hopeful shoot, pointing straight to the zenith like an admonishing finger. The leaves are arranged in two horizontal rows along branchlets that commonly are less than eight years old, forming handsome plumes, pinnated like the fronds of ferns. The cones are grayish-green when ripe, cylindrical, from three to four inches long, and one and a half to two inches wide, and stand upright on the upper horizontal branches. Full-grown trees in favorable situations are usually about two hundred feet high and five or six feet in diameter. As old age creeps on, the rough bark becomes rougher and grayer, the branches lose their exact regularity of form, many that are snow-bent are broken off and the axis often becomes double or otherwise irregular from accidents to the terminal bud or shoot. Nevertheless, throughout all the vicissitudes of its three or four centuries of life, come what may, the noble grandeur of this species, however obscured, is never lost.

The magnificent silver fir, or California red fir (*Abies magnifica*) is the most symmetrical of all the Sierra giants, far surpassing its companion species in this respect and easily distinguished from it by the purplish-red bark, which is also more closely furrowed than that of the white, and by its larger cones, its more regularly whorled and fronded branches, and its shorter leaves, which grow all around the branches and point upward instead of being arranged in two horizontal rows. The branches are mostly whorled in fives, and stand out from the straight, red-purple bole in level, or in old trees in drooping collars, every branch regularly pinnated like fernfronds, making broad plumes, singularly rich and sumptuous-looking. The flowers are in their prime about the middle of June; the male red, growing on the underside of the branches in crowded profusion, giving a very rich color to all the trees; the female greenish-yellow, tinged with pink, standing erect on the upper side of the topmost branches, while the tufts of young leaves, about as brightly colored as those of the Douglas spruce [Douglas fir, *ed.*], make another grand show. The cones mature in a single season from the flowers. When mature they are about six to eight inches long, three or four in diameter, covered with a fine gray down and streaked and beaded with transparent balsam, very rich and precious-looking, and stand erect like casks on the topmost branches. The inside of the cone is, if possible, still more beautiful. The scales and bracts are tinged with red and the seed-wings are

146

purple with bright iridescence. Both of the silver firs live between two and three centuries when the conditions about them are at all favorable. Some venerable patriarch may be seen heavily storm-marked, towering in severe majesty above the rising generation, with a protecting grove of hopeful saplings pressing close around his feet, each dressed with such loving care that not a leaf seems wanting. Other groups are made up of trees near the prime of life, nicely arranged as if Nature had culled them with discrimination from all the rest of the woods. It is from this tree, called Red Fir by the lumbermen, that mountaineers cut boughs to sleep on when they are so fortunate as to be within its limit. Two or three rows of the sumptuous plushy-fronded branches, overlapping along the middle, and a crescent of smaller plumes mixed to one's taste with ferns and flowers for a pillow, form the very best bed imaginable. The essence of the pressed leaves seems to fill every pore of one's body. Falling water makes a soothing hush, while the spaces between the grand spires afford noble openings through which to gaze dreamily into the starry sky. The fir woods are fine sauntering-grounds at almost any time of the year, but finest in autumn when the noble trees are hushed in the hazy light and drip with balsam, and the flying, whirling seeds, escaping from the ripe cones, mottle the air like flocks of butterflies. Even in the richest part of these unrivaled forests where so many noble trees challenge admiration, we linger fondly among the colossal firs and extol their beauty again and again, as if no other tree in the world could henceforth claim our love. It is in these woods the great granite domes arise that are so striking and characteristic a feature of the Sierra. Here, too, we find the best of the garden-meadows full of lilies. A dry spot a little way back from the margin of a silver fir lily-garden makes a glorious campground, especially where the slope is toward the east with a view of the distant peaks along the summit of the range. The tall lilies are brought forward most impressively like visitors by the light of your campfire, and the nearest of the trees with their whorled branches tower above you like larger lilies, and the sky seen through the garden-opening seems one vast meadow of white lily stars.

The Two-Leaved Pine

The two-leaved pine (*Pinus contorta*, var. Murrayana) [lodgepole pine, *ed.*], above the silver fir zone, forms the bulk of the alpine forests up to a height of from eight thousand to ninety-five hundred feet above the sea, growing in beautiful order on moraines scarcely changed as yet by post-glacial weathering. Compared with the giants of the lower regions this is a small tree, seldom exceeding a height of eighty or ninety feet. The largest I ever measured was ninety feet high and a little over six feet in diameter. The average height of mature trees throughout the entire belt is probably not far from fifty or sixty feet with a diameter of two feet. It is a well-proportioned, rather handsome tree with grayish-brown bark and crooked, much-divided branches, which cover the greater part of the trunk, but not so densely as to prevent it being seen. The lower limbs, like those of most other conifers that grow in snowy regions, curve downward, gradually take a horizontal position about half-way up the trunk, then aspire more and more toward the summit. The short, rigid needles in fascicles of two are arranged in comparatively long cylindrical tassels at the ends of the tough up-curving branches. The cones are about two inches long, growing in clusters among the needles without any striking effect except while very young, when the flowers are of a vivid crimson color and the whole tree appears to be dotted with brilliant flowers. The staminate flowers are still more showy on account of their great abundance, often giving a reddish-yellow tinge to the whole mass of foliage and filling the air with pollen. No other pine in the range is so regularly planted as this one, covering moraines that extend along the sides of the high rocky valleys for miles without interruption. The thin bark is streaked and sprinkled with resin as though it had been showered upon the forest like rain.

Therefore this tree more than any other is subject to destruction by fire. During strong winds, extensive forests are destroyed, the flames leaping from tree to tree in continuous belts that go surging and racing onward above the bending wood like prairie-grass fires. During the calm season of Indian summer, the fire creeps quietly along the ground, feeding on the needles and cones. Arriving at the foot of a tree, the resiny bark is ignited and the heated air ascends in a swift current, increasing in velocity and dragging the flames upward. Then the leaves catch forming an immense column of fire, beautifully spired on the edges and tinted a rose-purple hue. It rushes aloft thirty or forty feet above the top of the tree, forming a grand spectacle, especially at night. It lasts, however, only a few seconds, vanishing with magical rapidity, to be succeeded by others along the fireline at irregular intervals, tree after tree, upflashing and darting, leaving the trunks and branches scarcely scarred. The heat, however, is sufficient to kill the tree and in a few years the bark shrivels and falls off. Forests miles in extent are thus killed and left standing, with the branches on, but peeled and rigid, appearing gray in the distance like misty clouds. Later the branches drop off, leaving a forest of bleached spars. At length the roots decay and the forlorn gray trunks are blown down during some storm and piled one upon another, encumbering the ground until, dry and seasoned, they are consumed by another fire and leave the ground ready for a fresh crop.

In sheltered lake-hollows, on beds of alluvium, this pine varies so far from the common form that frequently it could be taken for a distinct species, growing in damp sods like grasses from forty to eighty feet high, bending all together to the breeze and whirling in eddying gusts more lively than any other tree in the woods. I frequently found specimens fifty feet high less than five inches in diameter. Being so slender and at the same time clad with leafy boughs, it is often bent and weighed down to the ground when laden with soft snow, thus forming fine ornamental arches, many of them to last until the melting of the snow in the spring.

The Mountain Pine
The mountain pine (*Pinus monticola*) [western white pine, *ed.*] is the noblest tree of the alpine zone—hardy and long-lived, towering grandly above its companions and becoming stronger and more imposing just where other species begin to crouch and disappear. At its best it is usually about ninety feet high and five or six feet in diameter, though you may find specimens here and there considerably larger than this. It is as massive

and suggestive of enduring strength as an oak. About two-thirds of the trunk is commonly free of limbs, but close, fringy tufts of spray occur nearly all the way down to the ground. On trees that occupy exposed situations near its upper limit, the bark is deep reddish-brown and rather deeply furrowed, the main furrows running nearly parallel to each other and connected on the old trees by conspicuous cross-furrows. The cones are from four to eight inches long, smooth, slender, cylindrical and somewhat curved. They grow in clusters of from three to six or seven and become pendulous as they increase in weight. This species is nearly related to the sugar pine and, though not half so tall, it suggests its noble relative in the way that it extends its long branches in general habit. It is first met on the upper margin of the silver fir zone, singly, in what appears as chance situations without making much impression on the general forest. Continuing up through the forests of the two-leaved pine it begins to show its distinguishing characteristic in the most marked way at an elevation of about ten thousand feet, extending its tough, rather slender arms in the frosty air, welcoming the storms and feeding on them and reaching sometimes to the grand old age of one thousand years.

The Western Juniper
The western juniper (*Juniperus occidentalis*) is preeminently a sturdy, storm-enduring, rock tree occupying the baldest domes and pavements in the upper silver fir and alpine zones, at a height of from seven thousand to ninety-five hundred feet. It never makes anything like a forest here, but stands out separate and independent in the wind, clinging by slight joints to

the rock, with scarce a handful of soil in sight of it, seeming to depend chiefly on snow and air for nourishment, and yet it has maintained tough health on this diet for two thousand years or more. In such situations, rooted in narrow cracks or fissures, it is frequently over eight feet in diameter and not much more in height. The tops of old trees are almost always dead, and large stubborn-looking limbs push out horizontally, most of them broken and dead at the end, but densely covered, and imbedded here and there with tufts or mounds of gray-green scalelike foliage. Some trees are mere storm-beaten stumps about as broad as long, decorated with a few leafy sprays, reminding one of the crumbling towers of old castles scantily draped with ivy. Its homes on bare, barren dome and ridgetop seem to have been chosen for safety against fire, for on isolated mounds of sand and gravel free from grass and bushes on which fire could feed, it is often found growing tall and unscathed to a height of forty to sixty feet, with scarce a trace of the rocky angularity and broken limbs so characteristic a feature throughout the greater part of its range. It never makes anything like a forest; seldom even a grove. Usually it stands out separate and independent, clinging by slight joints to the rocks, living chiefly on snow and thin air and maintaining sound health on this diet for two thousand years or more. Every feature or every gesture it makes expresses steadfast, dogged endurance. The bark is of a bright cinnamon color and is handsomely braided and reticulated on thrifty trees, flaking off in thin, shining ribbons that are sometimes used by the Indians for tent matting. Its fine color and picturesqueness are appreciated by artists, but to me the juniper seems a singularly strange and taciturn tree. I have spent many a day and night in its company and always have found it silent and rigid. It seems to be a survivor of some ancient race, wholly unacquainted with its neighbors. Its broad stumpiness, of course, makes wind-waving or even shaking out of the question, but it is not this rocky rigidity that constitutes its silence. In calm, sun-days the sugar pine preaches like an enthusiastic apostle without moving a leaf. On level rocks the juniper dies standing and wastes insensibly out of existence like granite, the wind exerting about as little control over it, alive or dead, as is does over a glacier boulder.

I have spent a good deal of time trying to determine the age of these wonderful trees, but as all of the very old ones are honey-combed with dry rot I never was able to get a complete count of the largest. Some are undoubtedly more than two thousand years old, for though on deep moraine soil they grow about as fast as some of the pines; on bare pavements and smoothly glaciated, overswept ridges in the dome region they grow very slowly. One on Starr King Ridge only two feet eleven inches in diameter was one thousand one hundred and forty years old—forty years ago. Another on the same ridge, only one foot seven and a half inches in diameter, had reached the age of eight hundred and thirty-four years. The first fifteen inches from the bark of a medium-size tree six feet in diameter, on the north Tenaya pavement, had eight hundred and fifty-nine layers of wood. Beyond this the count was stopped by dry rot and scars. The largest examined was thirty-three feet in girth, or nearly ten feet in diameter and, although I have failed to get anything like a complete count, I learned enough from this and many other specimens to convince me that most of the trees eight or ten feet thick, standing on pavements, are more than twenty centuries old rather than less. Barring accidents, for all I can see they would live forever; even then overthrown by avalanches, they refuse to lie at rest, lean stubbornly on their big branches as if anxious to rise, and while a single root holds to the rock, put forth fresh leaves with a grim, never-say-die expression.

The Mountain Hemlock

As the juniper is the most stubborn and unshakeable of trees in the Yosemite region, the mountain hemlock (*Tsuga mertensiana*) is the most graceful and pliant and sensitive. Until it reaches a height of fifty or sixty feet, it is sumptuously clothed down to the ground with drooping branches, which are divided again and again into delicate waving sprays, grouped and arranged in ways that are indescribably beautiful, and profusely adorned with small brown cones. The flowers also are peculiarly beautiful and effective; the female dark rich purple, the male blue, of so fine and pure a tone. The best azure of the mountain sky seems to be condensed in them. Though apparently the most delicate and feminine of all the mountain trees, it grows best where the snow lies deepest, at a height of from nine thousand to ninety-five hundred feet, in hollows on the northern slopes of mountains and ridges. But under all circumstances, sheltered from heavy winds or in bleak exposure to them, well fed or starved, even at its highest limit, ten thousand five hundred feet above the sea, on exposed ridgetops where it has to crouch and huddle close in low thickets, it still contrives to put forth its sprays and branches in forms of invincible beauty, while on moist, well-drained moraines it displays a perfectly tropical luxuriance of foliage, flowers and fruit. The snow of the first winter storm is frequently soft, and lodges in the dense leafy branches, weighing them down against the trunk, and the slender, drooping axis, bending lower and lower as the load increases, at length reaches the ground, forming an ornamental arch. Then, as storm succeeds storm and snow is heaped on snow, the whole tree is at last buried, not again to see the light of day or move leaf or limb until set free by the spring thaws in June or July. Not only the young saplings are thus carefully covered and put to sleep in the whitest of white beds for five or six months of the year, but trees thirty feet high or more. From April to May, when the snow by repeated thawing and freezing is firmly compacted, you may ride over the prostrate groves without seeing a single branch or leaf of them. No other of our alpine conifers so finely veils its strength; poised in thin, white sunshine, clad with branches from head to foot, it towers in unassuming majesty, drooping as if unaffected with the aspiring tendencies of its race, loving the ground, conscious of heaven and joyously receptive of its blessings, reaching out its branches like sensitive tentacles, feeling the light and reveling in it. The largest specimen I ever found was nineteen feet seven inches in circumference. It was growing on the edge of Lake Hollow, north of Mount Hoffman, at an elevation of ninety-two hundred and fifty feet above the level of the sea, and was probably about a hundred feet in height. Fine groves of mature trees, ninety to a hundred feet in height, are growing near the base of Mount Conness. It is widely distributed from near the south extremity of the High Sierra northward along the Cascade Mountains of Oregon and Washington and the coast ranges of British Columbia to

Alaska, where it was first discovered in 1827. Its northernmost limit, so far as I have observed, is in the icy fiords of Prince William Sound in latitude 61°, where it forms pure forests at the level of the sea, growing tall and majestic on the banks of glaciers. There, as in the Yosemite region, it is ineffably beautiful, the very loveliest of all the American conifers.

The Whitebark Pine

The dwarf pine, or whitebark pine (*Pinus albicaulis*), forms the extreme edge of the timberline throughout nearly the whole extent of the range on both flanks. It is first met growing with the two-leaved pine on the upper margin of the alpine belt, as an erect tree from fifteen to thirty feet high and from one to two feet in diameter. Hence it goes straggling up the flanks of the summit peaks, upon moraines or crumbling ledges, wherever it can get a foothold, to an elevation of from ten thousand to twelve thousand feet, where it dwarfs to a mass of crumpled branches, covered with slender shoots, each tipped with a short, close-packed, leaf tassel. The bark is smooth and purplish, in some places almost white. The flowers are bright scarlet and rose-purple, giving a very flowery appearance little looked for in such a tree. The cones are about three inches long, an inch and a half in diameter, grow in rigid clusters, and are dark chocolate in color while young, and bear beautiful pearly-white seeds about the size of peas, most of which are eaten by chipmunks and the Clarke's crows. Pines are commonly regarded as sky-loving trees that must necessarily aspire or die. This species forms a marked exception, crouching and creeping in compliance with the most rigorous demands of climate, yet enduring bravely to a more advanced age than many of its lofty relatives in the sun-lands far below it. Seen from a distance it would never be taken for a tree of any kind. For example, on Cathedral Peak there is a scattered growth of this pine, creeping like mosses over the roof, nowhere giving hint of an ascending axis. While, approached quite near, it still appears matty and heathy, and one experiences no difficulty in walking over the top of it, it is seldom absolutely prostrate, usually attaining a height of three or four feet with a main trunk, and with branches outspread above it, as if in ascending they had been checked by a ceiling against which they had been compelled to spread horizontally. The winter snow is a sort of ceiling, lasting half the year, while the pressed surface is made yet smoother by violent winds armed with cutting sandgrains that bear down any shoot which offers to rise much above the general level, and that carve the dead trunks and branches in beautiful patterns.

During stormy nights I have often camped snugly beneath the interlacing arches of this little pine. The needles, which have accumulated for centuries, make fine beds, a fact well known to other mountaineers, such as deer and wild sheep, who paw out oval hollows and lie beneath the larger trees in safe and comfortable concealment. This lowly dwarf reaches a far greater age than would be guessed. A specimen that I examined, growing at an elevation of ten thousand seven hundred feet, yet looked as though it might be plucked up by the roots, for it was only three and a half inches in diameter and its topmost tassel reached hardly three feet above the ground. Cutting it half through and counting the annual rings with the aid of a lens, I found its age to be no less than two hundred and fifty-five years. Another specimen about the same height, with a trunk six inches in diameter, I found to be four hundred twenty-six years old, forty years ago, and one of its supple branchlets hardly an eighth of an inch in diameter inside the bark, was seventy-five years old, and so filled with oily balsam and seasoned by storms that I tied it in knots like a whipcord.

The Nut Pine

In going across the range from the Tuolumne River Soda Springs to Mono Lake, one makes the acquaintance of the curious little nut pine (*Pinus monophylla*) [singleleaf pinyon, *ed.*]. It dots the eastern flank of the Sierra to which it is mostly restricted in grayish bush-like patches, from the margin of the sage-plains to an elevation of from seven thousand to eight thousand feet. A more contented, fruitful, and unaspiring conifer could not be conceived. All the species we have been sketching make departures more or less distant from the typical spire form, but none goes so far as this. Without any apparent cause it keeps near the ground, throwing out crooked, divergent branches like an orchard appletree, and seldom pushes a single shoot higher than fifteen or twenty feet above the ground.

The average thickness of the trunk is, perhaps, about ten or twelve inches. The leaves are mostly undivided, like round awls, instead of being separated, like those of other pines, into twos and threes and fives. The cones are green while growing, and are usually found over all the tree, forming quite a marked feature as seen against the bluish-gray foliage. They are quite small, only about two inches in length, and seem to have but little space for seeds. But when we come to open them, we find that about half the entire bulk of the cone is made up of sweet, nutritious nuts, nearly as large as hazelnuts. This is undoubtedly the most important food-tree on the Sierra, and furnishes the Mona, Carson, and Walker River Indians with more and better nuts than all the other species taken together. It is the Indian's own tree, and many a white man have they killed for cutting it down. Being so low, the cones are readily beaten off with poles, and the nuts procured by roasting them until the scales open. In bountiful seasons, a single Indian may gather thirty or forty bushels.

Oaks

After the conifers, the most important of the Yosemite trees are the oaks, two species; the California live oak (*Quercus agrifolia*) [coast live oak, *ed.*], with black trunks, reaching a thickness of from four to nearly seven feet, wide spreading branches and bright deeply-scalloped leaves. It occupies the greater part of the broad sandy flats of the upper end of the valley, and is the species that yields the acorns so highly prized by the Indians and woodpeckers. The other species is the mountain live oak, or goldcup oak (*Quercus chrysolepis*) [canyon live oak, *ed.*], a sturdy mountaineer of a tree, growing mostly on the earthquake taluses and benches of the sunny north wall of the valley. In tough, unwedgeable, knotty strength, it is the oak of oaks, a magnificent tree. The largest and most picturesque specimen in the valley is near the foot of Tenaya Fall, a romantic spot seldom seen on account of the rough trouble of getting to it. It is planted on three huge boulders and yet manages to draw sufficient moisture and food from this craggy soil to maintain itself in good health. It is twenty feet in circumference, measured above a large branch between three and four feet in diameter that has been broken off. The main knotty trunk seems to be made up of craggy granite boulders like those on which it stands, being about the same color as the mossy, lichened boulders and about as rough. Two moss-lined caves near the ground open back into the trunk, one on the north side, the other on the west, forming picturesque, romantic seats. The largest of the main branches is eighteen feet and nine inches in circumference, and some of the long, pendulous branchlets droop over the stream at the foot of the fall where it is gray with spray. The leaves are glossy yellow-green, ever in motion from the wind from the fall. It is a fine place to dream in, with falls, cascades, cool rocks lined with *Hypnum* three inches thick; shaded with maple, dogwood, alder, willow; grand clumps of lady ferns where no hand may touch them; light filtering through translucent leaves; oaks fifty feet high; lilies eight feet high in a filled lake basin nearby, and the finest *Libocedrus* groves and tallest ferns and goldenrods.

Riverside Trees

The principal riverside trees are poplar, alder, willow, broad-leaved maple, and Nuttall's flowering dogwood [Pacific dogwood, *ed.*]. The broad-leaved maple and mountain maple are found mostly in the cool canyons at the head of the valley, spreading their branches in beautiful arches over the foaming streams. Some of the involucres of the flowering dogwood measure six to eight inches in diameter, and the whole tree when in flower looks as if covered with snow. In the spring when the streams are in flood it is the whitest of trees. In

Indian summer the leaves become bright crimson, making a still grander show than the flowers. The poplar (*Populus trichocarpa*), often called balm-of-Gilead from the gum on its buds, is a tall tree, towering above its companions and gracefully embowering the banks of the river. Its abundant foliage turns bright yellow in the fall, and the Indian-summer sunshine sifts through it in delightful tones over the slow-gliding waters when they are at their lowest ebb.

Theodore Roosevelt and John Muir on Glacier Point

14

In Yosemite with John Muir

Theodore Roosevelt

When I first visited California, it was my good fortune to see the "big trees," the Sequoias, and then to travel down into the Yosemite, with John Muir. . . . The first night was clear, and we lay down in the darkening aisles of the great Sequoia grove. The majestic trunks, beautiful in color and in symmetry, rose round us like the pillars of a mightier cathedral than ever was conceived even by the fervor of the Middle Ages. . . .

163

Giant Sequoia

15

The Giant Sequoia

John Muir

Between the heavy pine and silver fir zones towers the Big Tree (*Sequoiadendron gigantea*), the king of all the conifers in the world, "the noblest of the noble race."

In the northern groves, there are comparatively few young trees or saplings. But here, for every old storm-beaten giant, there are many in their prime and for each of these a crowd of hopeful young trees and saplings, growing vigorously on moraines, rocky edges, along watercourses and meadows. But though the area occupied by the big tree increases so greatly from north to south, there is no marked increase in the size of the trees. The height of two hundred and seventy-five feet or thereabouts and a diameter of about twenty feet, four feet from the ground is, perhaps, about the average size of what may be called full-grown trees, where they are favorably located. The specimens twenty-five feet in diameter are not very rare and a few are nearly three hundred feet high. In the Calaveras grove there are four trees over three hundred feet in height, the tallest of which as measured by the Geological Survey is three hundred and twenty-five feet. The very largest that I have yet met in the course of my explorations is a majestic old fire-scarred monument in the Kings River forest. It is thirty-five feet and eight inches in diameter inside the bark, four feet above the ground. It is burned half through, and I spent a day in clearing away the charred surface with a sharp ax and counting the annual wood-rings with the aid of a pocket lens. I succeeded in laying bare a section all the way from the outside to the heart and counted a little over four thousand rings, showing that this tree was in its prime about twenty-seven feet in diameter at the beginning of the Christian era. No other tree in the world, as far as I know, has looked down on so many centuries as the sequoia or opens so many impressive and suggestive views into history. Under the most favorable conditions, these giants probably live five thousand years or more though few of even the larger trees are half as old. The age of one that was felled in Calaveras grove, for the sake of having its stump for a dancing-floor, was about thirteen hundred years, and its diameter measured across the stump twenty-four feet inside the bark. Another that was felled in the Kings River forest was about the same size but nearly a thousand years older (twenty-two hundred years), though not a very old-looking tree.

So harmonious and finely balanced are even the mightiest of these monarchs in all their proportions that there is never anything overgrown or monstrous about them. Seeing them for the first time you are more impressed with their beauty than their size, their grandeur being in great part invisible, but sooner or later it becomes manifest to the loving eye, stealing slowly on the senses like the grandeur of Niagara or of the Yosemite Domes. When you approach them and walk around them you begin to wonder at their colossal size and try to measure them. They bulge considerably at the base, but not more than is required for beauty and safety and the only reason that this bulging seems in some cases excessive is that only a comparatively small section is seen in near views. No description can give anything like an adequate idea of their singular majesty, much less of their beauty. Except the sugar pine, most of their neighbors with pointed tops seem ever trying to go higher, while the big tree, soaring above them all, seems satisfied. Its grand domed head seems to be poised about as lightly as a cloud, giving no impression of seeking to rise higher. Only when it is young does it show, like other conifers, a heavenward yearning, sharply aspiring with a long quick-growing top. Indeed, the whole tree for the first century or two, or until it is a hundred or one hundred and fifty feet high, is arrowhead in form, and, compared with the solemn rigidity of age, seems as sensitive to the wind as a squirrel's tail. As it grows older, the lower branches are gradually dropped and the upper ones thinned out until comparatively few are left. These, however, are developed to a great size, divide again and again and terminate in bossy, rounded masses of leafy branchlets, while the head becomes dome-shaped, and is the first to feel the touch of the rosy beams of the morning, the last to bid the sun good-night. Perfect specimens, unhurt by running fires or lightning, are singularly regular and symmetrical in general form though not in the least conventionalized, for they show extraordinary variety in the unity and harmony of their general outline. The immensely strong, stately shafts are free of limbs for one hundred and fifty feet or so. The large limbs reach out with equal boldness in every direction, showing no weather side, and no other tree has foliage so densely massed, so finely molded in outline and so perfectly subordinate to an ideal type. A particularly knotty, angular, ungovernable-looking branch, from five to seven or eight feet in diameter and perhaps a thousand years old, may occasionally be seen pushing out from the trunk as if determined to break across the bounds of the regular curve, but like all the others, it dissolves in bosses of branchlets and sprays as soon as the general outline is approached. Except in picturesque old age, after being struck by lightning or broken by thousands of snowstorms, the regularity of forms is one of their most distinguishing characteristics. Another is the simple beauty of the trunk and its great thickness as compared with its height and the width of the branches, which makes them look more like finely modeled and sculptured architectural columns than the stems of trees, while the great limbs look like rafters, sup-

porting the magnificent dome head. But though so consum-
mately beautiful, the big tree always seems unfamiliar, with
peculiar physiognomy, awfully solemn and earnest; yet with all
its strangeness it impresses us as being more at home than any
of its neighbors, holding the best right to the ground as the
oldest, strongest inhabitant. One soon becomes acquainted
with new species of pine and fir and spruce as with friendly
people, shaking their outstretched branches like shaking
hands and fondling their little ones, while the venerable aboriginal sequoia, ancient of other days, keeps you at a distance,
looking as strange in aspect and behavior among its neighbor
trees as would the mastodon among the homely bears and
deers. Only the Sierra juniper is at all like it, standing rigid and
unconquerable on glacier pavements for thousands of years,
grim and silent, with an air of antiquity about as pronounced
as that of the sequoia.

The bark of the largest trees is from one to two feet thick,
rich cinnamon brown, purplish on young trees, forming magnificent masses of color with the underbrush. Toward the end
of winter the trees are in bloom, while the snow is still eight or
ten feet deep. The female flowers are about three-eighths of an
inch long, pale green, and grow in countless thousands on the
ends of sprays. The male are still more abundant, pale yellow,
a fourth of an inch long and when the pollen is ripe, they color
the whole tree and dust the air and the ground. The cones are
bright grass-green in color, about two and a half inches long,
one and a half wide, made up of thirty or forty strong, closely-
packed, rhomboidal scales, with four to eight seeds at the base
of each. The seeds are wonderfully small and light, being only
from an eighth to a fourth of an inch long and wide, including

a filmy surrounding wing, which causes them to glint and waver in falling and enables the wind to carry them considerable distances. Unless harvested by the squirrels, the cones discharge their seed and remain on the tree for many years. In fruitful seasons the trees are fairly laden. On two small branches one and a half and two inches in diameter, I counted four hundred and eighty cones. No other California conifer produces nearly so many seeds, except, perhaps, the other sequoia, the Redwood of the Coast Mountains. Millions are ripened annually by a single tree, and in a fruitful year the product of one of the northern groves would be enough to plant all the mountain ranges in the world.

As soon as any accident happens to the crown, such as being smashed off by lightning, the branches beneath the wound, no matter how situated, seem to be excited, like a colony of bees that have lost their queen, and become anxious to repair the damage. Limbs that have grown outward for centuries at right angles to the trunk begin to turn upward to assist in making a new crown, each speedily assuming the special form of true summits. Even in the case of mere stumps, burned half through, some mere ornamental tuft will try to go aloft and do its best as a leader in forming a new head. Groups of two or three are often found standing close together, the seeds from which they sprang having probably grown on ground cleared for their reception by the fall of a large tree of a former generation. They are called "loving couples," "three graces," etc. When these trees are young, they are seen to stand twenty or thirty feet apart; by the time they are full-grown their trunks will touch and crowd against each other and in some cases even appear as one.

No species of coniferous tree in the range keeps its members so well together as the sequoia; a mile is, perhaps, the greatest distance of any straggler from the main body, and all of those stragglers that have come under my observation are young, instead of old monumental trees, relics of a more extended growth.

Again, the great trunks of the sequoia last for centuries after they fall. I have a specimen block of sequoia wood, cut from a fallen tree, which is hardly distinguishable from a similar section cut from a living tree, although the one cut from the fallen trunk has certainly lain on the damp forest floor more than three hundred and eighty years, probably thrice as long. The time-measure in the case is simply this: When the ponderous trunk to which the old vestige belonged fell, it sunk itself into the ground, thus making a long, straight ditch, and in the middle of this ditch a silver fir four feet in diameter and three hundred and eighty years old was growing, as I determined by cutting it half through and counting the rings, thus demonstrating that the remnant of the trunk that made the ditch has lain on the ground more than three hundred and eighty years. For it is evident that, to find the whole time, we must add to the three hundred and eighty years the time that the vanished portion of the trunk lay in the ditch before being burned out of the way, plus the time that passed before the seed from which the monumental fir sprang fell into the prepared soil and took root. Now, because sequoia trunks are never wholly consumed in one forest fire, and those fires recur only at considerable intervals, and because sequoia ditches after being cleared are often left unplanted for centuries, it becomes evident that the trunk-remnant in question may probably have lain a thousand years or more. And this instance is by no means a late one.

We therefore conclude that the area covered by sequoia has not been diminished during the last eight or ten thousand years, and probably not at all in post-glacial time. Nevertheless, the questions may be asked: Is the species verging toward extinction? What are its relations to climate, soil, and associated trees?

All the phenomena bearing on these questions also throw light, as we shall endeavor to show, upon the peculiar distribution of the species, and sustain the conclusion already arrived at as to the question of former extension. In the northern groups, as we have seen, there are few young trees or saplings growing up around the old ones to perpetuate the race, and inasmuch as those aged sequoias, so nearly childless, are the only ones commonly known, the species, to most observers, seems doomed to speedy extinction, as being nothing more than an expiring remnant, vanquished in the so-called struggle for life by pines and firs that have driven it into its last strongholds in moist glens where the climate is supposed to be exceptionally favorable. But the story told by the majestic continuous forests of the south creates a very different impression. No tree in the forest is more enduringly established in concordance with both climate and soil. It grows heartily everywhere—on moraines, rocky ledges, along watercourses, and in the deep, moist alluvium of meadows with, as we have seen, a multitude of seedlings and saplings crowding up around the aged, abundantly able to maintain the forest in prime vigor. So that if all the trees of any section of the main sequoia forest were ranged together according to age, a very promising curve would be presented, all the way up from last year's seedlings to giants, and with the young and middle-aged portion of the curve many times longer than the old portion. Even as far north as the Fresno, I counted five hundred and thirty-six saplings and seedlings, growing promisingly upon a landslip not exceeding two acres in area. This soil-bed was about seven years old, and had been seeded almost simultaneously by pines, firs, *Libocedrus*, and sequoia, presenting a simple and instructive illustration of the struggle for life among the rival species. It was interesting to note that the conditions thus far affecting them have enabled the young sequoias to gain a marked advantage. Toward the south, where the sequoia becomes most exuberant and numerous, the rival trees become less so; and where they mix with sequoias, they grow up beneath them like slender grasses among stalks of Indian corn. Upon a bed of sandy floodsoil I counted ninety-four sequoias, from one to twelve feet high, on a patch of ground once occupied by four large sugar pines which lay crumbling beneath them—an instance of conditions which have enabled sequoias to crowd out the pines. I also noted eighty-six vigorous saplings upon a piece of fresh ground prepared for their reception by fire. Thus fire, the great destroyer of the sequoia, also furnishes the bare ground required for its growth from the seed. Fresh ground is, however, furnished in sufficient quantities for the renewal of the forests without the aid of fire—by the fall of old trees. The soil is thus upturned and mellowed, and many trees are planted for every one that falls.

It is constantly asserted in a vague way that the Sierra was vastly wetter than now, and that the increasing drought will, of itself, extinguish the sequoia, leaving its ground to other trees capable of flourishing in a drier climate. But that the sequoia can and does grow on as dry ground as any of its present rivals is manifest in a thousand places. "Why, then," it will be asked, "are sequoias always found only in well-watered places?" Simply because a growth of sequoias creates those streams. The thirsty mountaineer knows well that in every sequoia grove he will find running water, but it is a mistake to suppose that the water is the cause of the grove being there; on the contrary, the grove is the cause of the water being there. Drain off the water and the trees will remain, but cut off the trees, and the streams will vanish. Never was cause more completely mistaken for effect than in the case of these related phenomena of sequoia woods and perennial streams.

When attention is called to the method of sequoia stream-making, it will be apprehended at once. The roots of this immense tree fill the ground, forming a thick sponge that absorbs and holds back the rain and melting snow, only allowing it to ooze and flow gently. Indeed, every fallen leaf and rootlet, as well as long clasping root, and prostrate trunk, may be regarded as a dam hoarding the bounty of storm clouds, and dispensing it as blessings all through the summer, instead of allowing it to go headlong in short-lived floods.

Since, then, it is a fact that thousands of sequoias are growing thriftily on what is termed dry ground, and even clinging like mountain pines to rifts in granite precipices, and since it has also been shown that the extra moisture found in connection with the denser growths is an effect of their presence, instead of a cause of their presence, then the notions as to the former extension of the species and its near approach to extinction, based upon its supposed dependence on greater moisture, are seen to be erroneous.

There is no absolute limit to the existence of any tree. Death is due to accidents, not, as that of animals, to the wearing out of organs. Only the leaves die of old age. Their fall is foretold in their structure, but the leaves are renewed every year, and so also are the essential organs—wood, roots, bark, buds. Most of the Sierra trees die of disease, insects, fungi, etc., but nothing hurts the big tree. I never saw one that was sick or showed the slightest sign of decay. Barring accidents, it seems to be immortal. It is a curious fact that all the very old sequoias had lost their heads by lightning strokes. "All things come to him who waits." But of all living things, sequoia is perhaps the only one able to wait long enough to make sure of being struck by lightning.

Sequoia grove

16

In California—The Big Trees

Horace Greeley

Steamboat *Cornelia*, on the San Joaquin
August 15, 1859

We went up to the Mariposa trees early next morning. The trail crosses a meadow of most luxuriant wild grass, then strikes eastward up the hills, and rises almost steadily, but in the main not steeply, for five miles, when it enters and ends in a slight depression or valley, nearly on the top of this particular mountain, where the Big Trees have been quietly nestled for I dare not say how many thousand years. That they were of very substantial size when David danced before the ark, when Solomon laid the foundations of the Temple, when Theseus ruled in Athens, when Aeneas fled from the burning wreck of vanquished Troy, when Sesostris led his victorious Egyptians into the heart of Asia, I have no manner of doubt.

The Big Trees, of course, do not stand alone. I apprehend that they could not stand at present, in view of the very moderate depth at which they are anchored to the earth. Had they stood on an unsheltered mountain top, or even an exposed hillside, they would doubtless have been prostrated, as I presume thousands like them were prostrated, by the hurricanes of centuries before Christ's advent. But the locality of these, though probably twenty-five hundred feet above the South Merced, and some forty-five hundred above the sea, is sheltered and tranquil, though several of these trees have manifestly fallen within the present century. Unquestionably, they are past their prime, though to none more than to them is applicable the complimentary characterization of "a green old age." Let me try to give as clear an idea of these forest mastodons as I can, though I know that will be but a poor one.

In measuring trees, it is so easy to exaggerate by running your line around the roots rather than the real body, that I place little dependence on the reported and recorded measurements of parties under no obligations to preserve a judicial impartiality. But I believe a fair measurement of the largest trees standing in this grove would make them not less than ninety feet in circumference, and over thirty in diameter, at a height of six feet from their respective bases, and that several of them have an altitude of more than three hundred feet. I believe the one that was last uprooted measures a little over three hundred.

But these relics of a more bounteous and magnificent world seem destined to speedy extinction. I deem them generally enfeebled by age and the racking and wrenching of their roots by the blasts that sweep through their tops. These malign influences they might withstand for ages, however, were it not for the damage they have already sustained, and are in danger of hereafter sustaining, through the devastating agency of fire. For these glorious evergreen forests, though the ground beneath them is but thinly covered with inflammable matter, are yet subject to be overrun every second or third year by forest conflagrations. For the earth, to a depth of several feet, even, is dry as an ash heap from July to October, and the hills are so steep that fire ascends them with wonderful facility. And thus the big trees are scarred, and gouged, and hollowed out at the root and upward, as the effects of successive fires, one of which, originating far southward, ran through this locality so late as last autumn, burning one of the forest kings so that it has since fallen, half destroying another already prostrate, through the hollow of which two horsemen were accustomed to ride abreast for a distance of fully one hundred feet, and doing serious damage to very many others. If the village of Mariposa, the county, or the state of California, does not immediately provide for the safety of these trees, I shall deeply deplore the infatuation, and believe that these giants might have been more happily located.

The big trees are usually accounted redwood, but bear a strong resemblance to the cedar family, so that my intelligent guide plausibly insisted that they are identical in species with their probable contemporaries, the famous cedars of Lebanon. The larger cedars in their vicinity bear a decided resemblance to the smallest of them, and yet there are quite obvious differences between them. The cedar's limbs are by far the more numerous, and come far down the trunk; they are also relatively smaller. The cedar's bark is the more deeply creased up and down the trunk, while the foliage of the big trees is nearer allied to that of certain pines than to the cedar's. The bark of the big trees is very thick—in some instances, over two feet— and is of a dry, light quality, resembling cork: hence the fatal facility of damage by running fires. The wood of the big trees is of a light red color, seeming devoid alike of sap and resin, and to burn about as freely while the tree lives as a year or more after its death.

Unless in the cedars of Lebanon, I suspect these mammoths of the vegetable world have no counterparts out of California.

Cathedral Rocks

17

Yosemite in Winter

John Muir

Yosemite Valley
January 1st, 1872

Winter has taken Yosemite, and we are snowbound. The latest leaves are shaken from the oaks and alders; the snow-laden pines, with drooping boughs, look like barbed arrows aimed at the sky, and the fern-tangles and meadows are spread with a smooth cloth of snow.

On November 28th came one of the most picturesque snowstorms I have ever seen. It was a tranquil day in Yosemite. About midday, a close-grained cloud grew in the middle of the valley, blurring the sun, but rocks and trees continued to cast shadow. In a few hours, the cloud ceiling deepened and gave birth to a rank down-growth of silky streamers. These cloud-weeds were most luxuriant about the Cathedral Rocks, completely hiding all their summits. Then heavier masses, hairy outside with a dark nucleus, appeared, and foundered almost to the ground. Toward night, all cloud and rock distinctions were blended out, rock after rock disappeared, El Capitan, the Domes and the Sentinel, and all the brows about Yosemite Falls were wiped out, and the whole valley was filled with equal, seamless gloom. There was no wind and every rock and tree and grass blade had a hushed, expectant air. The fullness of time arrived, and down came the big flakes in tufted companies of full-grown flowers. Not jostling and rustling like autumn leaves or blossom showers of an orchard whose cast-away flakes are hushed into any hollow for a grave, but they journeyed down with gestures of confident life, alighting upon predestined places on rock and leaf, like flocks of linnets or showers of summer flies. Steady, exhaustless, innumerable. The trees, and bushes, and dead brown grass were flowered far beyond summer, bowed down in blossom and all the rocks were buried. Every peak and dome, every niche and tablet had their share of snow. And blessed are the eyes that beheld morning open the glory of that one dead storm. In vain did I search for some special separate mass of beauty on which to rest my gaze. No island appeared throughout the whole gulf of the beauty. The glorious crystal sediment was everywhere. From wall to wall of our beautiful temple, from meadow to sky was one finished unit of beauty, one star of equal ray, one glowing sun, weighed in the celestial balances and found perfect.

The Cascades

18

Riding an Avalanche

John Muir

As has been already stated, the first of the great snowstorms that replenish the Yosemite fountains seldom sets in before the end of November. Then, warned by the sky, wide-awake mountaineers, together with the deer and most of the birds, make haste to the lowlands or foothills, and burrowing

marmots, mountain beavers, wood rats, and other small mountain people, go into winter quarters, some of them not again to
see the light of day until the general awakening and resurrec-
tion of the spring in June or July. The fertile clouds, drooping
and condensing in brooding silence, seem to be thoughtfully
examining the forests and streams with reference to the work
that lies before them. At length, all their plans perfected,
tufted flakes and single starry crystals come in sight, solemnly
swirling and glinting to their blessed appointed places. And
soon the busy throng fills the sky and makes darkness like
night. The first heavy fall is usually from about two to four feet
in depth then, with intervals of days or weeks of bright weather.
Storm succeeds storm, heaping snow on snow, until thirty to
fifty feet has fallen. But on account of its settling and com-
pacting, and waste from melting and evaporation, the average
depth actually found at any time seldom exceeds ten feet in the
forest regions, or fifteen feet along the slopes of the summit
peaks. After snowstorms come avalanches, varying greatly in
form, size, behavior, and in the songs they sing. Some on the
smooth slopes of the mountains are short and broad; others
long and river-like in the side canyons of Yosemite and in the
main canyons, flowing in regular channels and booming like
waterfalls, while countless smaller ones fall everywhere from
laden trees and rocks and lofty canyon walls. Most delightful it
is to stand in the middle of Yosemite on still, clear mornings
after snowstorms and watch the throng of avalanches as they
come down, rejoicing, to their places, whispering, thrilling like
birds, or booming and roaring like thunder. The noble yellow
pines stand hushed and motionless as if under a spell until the
morning sunshine begins to sift through their laden spires.

Then the dense masses on the ends of the leafy branches begin to shift and fall, those from the upper branches striking the lower ones in succession, enveloping each tree in a hollow, conical avalanche of fairy fineness while the relieved branches spring up and wave with startling effect in the general stillness, as if each tree was moving of its own volition. Hundreds of broad cloud-shaped masses may also be seen leaping over the brows of the cliffs from great heights, descending at first with regular avalanche speed until, worn into dust by friction, they float in front of the precipices like irised clouds. Those which descend from the brow of El Capitan are particularly fine, but most of the great Yosemite avalanches flow in regular channels like cascades and waterfalls. When the snow first gives way on the upper slopes of their basins, a dull rushing, rumbling sound is heard which rapidly increases and seems to draw nearer with appalling intensity of tone. Presently the white flood comes bounding into sight over bosses and sheer places, leaping from bench to bench, spreading and narrowing and throwing off clouds of whirling dust like the spray of foaming cataracts. Compared with waterfalls and cascades, avalanches are short-lived, few of them lasting more than a minute or two, and the sharp, clashing sounds so common in falling water are mostly wanting; but in their low massy thundertones and purple-tinged whiteness, and in their dress, gait, gestures, and general behavior, they are much alike.

Avalanches

Besides these common after-storm avalanches that are to be found not only in Yosemite but in all the deep, sheer-walled canyon of the range there are two other important kinds, which may be called annual and century avalanches, which still further enrich the scenery. The only place about the valley where one may be sure to see the annual kind is on the north slope of Clouds Rest. They are composed of heavy, compacted snow, which has been subjected to frequent alternations of freezing and thawing. They are developed on canyon and mountainsides at an elevation of from nine to ten thousand feet, where the slopes are inclined at an angle too low to shed off the dry winter snow, and which accumulates until the spring thaws sap their foundations and make them slippery. Then away in grand style go the ponderous icy masses without any fine snowdust. Those of Clouds Rest descend like thunderbolts for more than a mile.

The great century avalanches and the kind that mow wide swaths through the upper forests occur on mountainsides about ten or twelve thousand feet high, where under ordinary weather conditions the snow accumulated from winter to winter lies at rest for many years, allowing trees, fifty to a hundred feet high, to grow undisturbed on the slopes beneath them. On their way down through the woods they seldom fail to make a perfectly clean sweep, stripping off the soil as well as the trees, clearing paths two or three hundred yards wide from the timberline to the glacier meadows or lakes, and piling their uprooted trees, head downward, in rows along the sides of the gaps like lateral moraines. Scars and broken branches of the trees standing on the sides of the gaps record the depth of the overwhelming flood. And when we come to count the annual woodrings on the uprooted trees we learn that some of these immense avalanches occur only once in a century, or even at still wider intervals.

A Ride on an Avalanche

Few Yosemite visitors ever see snow avalanches and fewer still know the exhilaration of riding on them. In all my mountaineering I have enjoyed only one avalanche ride, and the start was so sudden and the end came so soon I had but little time to think of the danger that attends this sort of travel, though at such times one thinks fast. One fine Yosemite morning after a heavy snowfall, being eager to see as many avalanches as possible and wide views of the forest and summit peaks in their new white robes before the sunshine had time to change them, I set out early to climb by a side canyon to the top of a commanding ridge a little over three thousand feet above the valley. On account of the looseness of the snow that blocked the canyon, I knew the climb would require a long time, some three or four hours as I estimated, but it proved far more difficult than I had anticipated. Most of the way I sank waist deep, almost out of sight in some places. After spending the whole day to within half an hour or so of sundown, I was still several hundred feet below the summit. Then my hopes were reduced to getting up in time to see the sunset. But I was not to get summit views of any sort that day, for deep trampling near the canyon head, where the snow was strained, started an avalanche, and I was swished down to the foot of the canyon as if by enchantment. The wallowing ascent had taken nearly all day, the descent only about a minute. When the avalanche started, I threw myself on my back and spread my arms to try to keep from sinking. Fortunately, though the grade of the canyon is very steep, it is not interrupted by precipices large enough to cause outbounding or free plunging. On no part of the rush was I buried. I was only moderately imbedded on the surface or at times a little below it, and covered with a veil of back-streaming dust particles, and as the whole mass beneath and about me joined in the flight, there was no friction, though I was tossed here and there and lurched from side to side. When the avalanche swedged and came to rest, I found myself on top of the crumpled pile without bruise or scar. This was a fine experience. Hawthorne says somewhere that steam has spiritualized travel, though unspiritual smells, smoke, etc., still attend steam travel. This flight, in what might be called a milky way of snow-stars, was the most spiritual and exhilarating of all the modes of motion I have ever experienced. Elijah's flight in a chariot of fire could hardly have been more gloriously exciting.

The Minarets

19

Snow Banners

John Muir

It is on the mountain tops, when they are laden with loose, dry snow and swept by a gale from the north, that the most magnificent storm scenery is displayed. The peaks along the axis of the range are then decorated with resplendent banners, some of them more than a mile long, shining, streaming, waving with solemn exuberant enthusiasm as if celebrating some surpassingly glorious event.

The snow of which these banners are made falls on the high Sierra in most extravagant abundance, sometimes to a depth of fifteen or twenty feet, coming from the fertile clouds, not in large angled flakes such as one oftentimes sees in Yosemite, seldom even in complete crystals, for many of the starry blossoms fall before they are ripe, while most of those that attain perfect development as six-petaled flowers are more or less broken by glinting and chafing against one another on the way down to their work. This dry, frosty snow is prepared for the grand banner-waving celebrations by the action of the wind. Instead of at once finding rest like that which falls into the tranquil depths of the forest, it is shoved and rolled and beaten against boulders and out-jutting rocks, swirled in pits and hollows like sand in river potholes, and ground into sparkling dust. And when storm winds find this snowdust in a loose condition on the slopes above the timberline, they toss it back into the sky and sweep it onward from peak to peak in the form of smooth regular banners, or in cloudy drifts, according to the velocity and direction of the wind, and the conformation of the slopes over which it is driven. While thus flying through the air, a small portion escapes from the mountains to the sky as vapor, but far the greater part is, at length, locked fast in bossy, overcurling cornices along the ridges or in stratified sheets in the glacier cirques, some of it to replenish the small residual glaciers and remain silent and rigid for centuries before it is finally melted and sent singing down home to the sea.

Sentinel Meadow

20

Caught in a Sierra Storm

Clarence King

From every commanding eminence around the Yosemite, no distant object rises with more inspiring greatness than the Obelisk of Mount Clark. Seen from the west it is a high, isolated peak, having a dome-like outline very much flattened upon its west side, the precipice sinking deeply down to an old glacier ravine. From the north this peak is a slender, single needle, jutting two thousand feet from a rough-hewn pedestal of rocks and snowfields. Forest-covered heights rise to its base from east and west. To the south it falls into a deep saddle, which rises again, after a level outline of a mile, sweeping up in another noble granite peak. On the north the spur drops abruptly down, overhanging an edge of the great Merced gorge, its base buried beneath an accumulation of morainal matter deposited by ancient Merced glaciers. From the region of Mount Hoffmann, looming in most impressive isolation, its slender needle-like summit had long fired us with ambition, and, having finished my agreeable climb round the Yosemite walls, I concluded to visit the mountain with Cotter, and, if the weather should permit, to attempt a climb. We packed our two mules with a week's provisions and a single blanket each, and on the tenth of November left our friends at the headquarter's camp in Yosemite Valley and rode out upon the Mariposa trail, reaching the plateau by noon. Having passed Meadow Brook, we left the path and bore off in the direction of Mount Clark, spending the afternoon in riding over granite ridges and open stretches of frozen meadow, where the ground was all hard, and the grass entirely cropped off by numerous herds of sheep that had ranged here during the summer. The whole earth was bare, and rang under our mules' hoofs almost as clearly as the granite itself.

For the first time in many months, a mild, moist wind sprang up from the south, and with it came slowly creeping over the sky a dull, leaden bank of ominous-looking cloud. Since April we had had no storm. The perpetually cloudless sky had banished all thought, almost memory, of foul weather. But winter tempests had already held off remarkably, and we knew that at any moment they might set in, and in twenty-four hours

192

render the plateaus impassable. It was with some anxiety that I closed my eyes that night, and, sleeping lightly, often awoke as a freshening wind moved the pines. At dawn we were up, and observed that a dark, heavy mass of storm cloud covered the whole sky, and had settled down over the Obelisk, wrapping even the snowfields at its base in gray folds. The entire peak was lost, except now and then, when the torn vapors parted for a few moments and disclosed its sharp summit, whitened by new-fallen snow. A strange moan filled the air. The winds howled pitilessly over the rocks, and swept in deafening blasts through the pines. It was my duty to saddle up directly and flee for Yosemite. But I am naturally an optimist, a sort of geological Micawber, so I dodged my duty, and determined to give the weather every opportunity for a clear-off. Accordingly, we remained in camp all day, studying the minerals of the granite as the thickly strewn boulders gave us material. At nightfall I climbed a little rise back of our meadow, and looked out over the basin of Illilouette and up in the direction of the Obelisk. Now and then the parting clouds opened a glimpse of the mountain, and occasionally an unusual blast of wind blew away the deeply settled vapors from the canyon to westward, but each time they closed in more threateningly, and before I descended to camp, the whole land was obscured in the cloud which settled densely down.

The mules had made themselves comfortable with a repast of rich mountain grasses, which, though slightly frosted, still retained much of their original juice and nutriment. We ourselves made a deep inroad on the supply of provisions, and, after chatting awhile by the firelight, went to bed, taking the precaution to pile our effects carefully together, covering them with an india-rubber blanket. Our bivouac was in the middle of a cluster of firs, quite well protected overhead, but open to the sudden gusts which blew roughly hither and thither. By nine o'clock the wind died away altogether, and in a few moments a thick cloud of snow was falling. We had gone to bed together, pulled the blankets as a cover over our heads, and in a few moments fell into a heavy sleep. Once or twice in the night I woke with a slight sense of suffocation, and cautiously lifted the blanket over my head, but each time found it growing heavier and heavier with a freight of snow. In the morning we awoke quite early, and, pushing back the blanket, found that we had been covered by about a foot and a half of snow. The poor mules had approached us to the limit of their rope, and stood within a few feet of our beds, anxiously waiting our first signs of life.

We hurried to breakfast, and hastily putting on the saddles and wrapping ourselves from head to foot in our blankets, mounted and started for the crest of the moraine. I had taken the precaution to make a little sketchmap in my notebook, with the compass directions of our march from Yosemite, and we had now the difficult task of retracing our steps in a storm so blinding and fierce that we could never see more than a rod in advance. But for the regular form of the moraine, with whose curve we were already familiar, I fear we must have lost our way in the real labyrinth of glaciated rocks which covered the whole Illilouette basin. Snow blew in every direction, filling our eyes and blinding the poor mules, who often turned quickly from some sudden gust, and refused to go on. It was a cruel necessity, but we spurred them inexorably forward, guiding them to the right and left to avoid rocks and trees which, in their blindness, they were constantly threatening to strike. Warmly rolled in our blankets, we suffered little from cold, but the driving sleet and hail very soon bruised our cheeks and eyelids most painfully. It required real effort of will to face the storm, and we very soon learned to take turns in breaking trail. The snow constantly balled upon our animals' feet, and they slid in every direction. Now and then, in descending a sharp slope of granite, the poor creatures would get sliding, and rush to the bottom, their legs stiffened out, and their heads thrust forward in fear. After crossing the Illilouette, which we did at our old ford, we found it very difficult to climb the long, steep hillside, for the mules were quite unable to carry us, obliging us to lead them, and to throw ourselves upon the snowdrifts to break a pathway.

This slope almost wore us out, and when at last we reached its summit, we threw ourselves upon the snow for a rest, but were in such a profuse perspiration that I deemed it unsafe to lie there for a moment, and, getting up again, we mounted the mules and rode slowly on toward open plateaus near great meadows. The snow gradually decreased in depth as we descended upon the plain directly south of Yosemite. The wind abated somewhat, and there were only occasional snow flurries, between half-hours of tolerable comfort. Constant use of the compass and reference to my little map at length brought us to the Mariposa trail, but not until after eight hours of anxious, exhaustive labor—anxious from the constant dread of losing our way in the blinding confusion of storm; exhausting, for we had more than half of the way acted as trailbreakers, dragging our frightened and tired brutes after us. The poor creatures instantly recognized the trail, and started in a brisk trot toward Inspiration Point. Suddenly an icy wind swept up the valley, carrying with it a storm of snow and hail. The wind blew with such violence that the whole freight of sleet and ice was carried horizontally with fearful swiftness, cutting the bruised faces of the mules, and giving our own eyelids exquisite torture. The brutes refused to carry us farther. We were obliged to dismount and drive them before us, beating them constantly with clubs.

Fighting our way against this bitter blast, half blinded by hard, wind-driven snow-crystals, we at last gave up and took refuge in a dense clump of firs which crown the spur by Inspiration Point. Our poor mules cowered under shelter with us, and turned tail to the storm. The fir trees were solid cones of snow, which now and then unloaded themselves when severely bent by a sudden gust, half burying us in dry, white powder. Wind roared below us in the Yosemite gorge. It blew from the west, rolling up in waves which smote the cliffs, and surged on up the valley. While we sat still, the drifts began to pile up at our backs; the mules were belly-deep, and our situation began to be serious. Looking over the cliff brink we saw but the hurrying snow, and only heard a confused tumult of wind. A steady increase in the severity of the gale made us fear that the trees might crash down over us, so we left the mules and crept cautiously over the edge of the cliff, and ensconced ourselves in a sheltered nook, protected by walls of rock which rose at our back.

We had been in this position about an hour, half frozen and soaked through, when I at length gathered conscience enough to climb back and take a look at our brutes. The forlorn pair were frosted over with a thick coating, their pitiful eyes staring eagerly at me. I had half a mind to turn them loose, but, considering that their obstinate nature might lead them back to our Obelisk camp, I patted their noses, and climbed back to the shelf by Cotter, determined to try it for a quarter of an hour more, when, if the tempest did not lull, I thought we must press on and face the snow for an hour more, while we tramped down to the valley.

Suddenly there came a lull in the storm; its blinding fury of snow and wind ceased. Overhead, still hurrying eastward, the white bank drove on, unveiling, as it fled, the Yosemite walls, plateau, and every object to the eastward as far as Mount Clark. As yet, the valley bottom was obscured by a layer of mist and cloud, which rose to the height of about a thousand feet, submerging cliff-foot and debris pile. Between these strata, the cloud above and the cloud below, every object was in clear, distinct view. The sharp, terrible fronts of precipices, capped with a fresh cover of white, plunged down into the still, gray river of cloud below, their stony surfaces clouded with purple, salmon-color, and bandings of brown, all hues unnoticeable in everyday light. Forest, and crag, and plateau, and distant mountain were snow-covered to a uniform whiteness; only the dark gorge beneath us showed the least traces of color. There all was rich, deep, gloomy. Even over the snowy surfaces above there prevailed an almost ashen gray, which reflected itself from the dull, drifting sky. A few torn locks of vapor poured over the cliff edge at intervals, and crawled down like wreaths of smoke, floating gracefully and losing themselves at last in the bank of cloud which lay upon the bottom of the valley.

All of a sudden, the whole gray roof rolled away like a scroll, leaving the heavens from west to far east one expanse of pure, warm blue. Setting sunlight smote full upon the stony walls below, and shot over the plateau country, gilding here a snowy forest group, and there a wave-crest of whitened ridge. The whole air sparkled with diamond particles. Red light streamed in through the open Yosemite gateway, brightening those vast, solemn faces of stone, and intensifying the deep neutral blue of shadowed alcoves. The luminous cloudbank in the east rolled from the last Sierra summit, leaving the whole chain of peaks in broad light, each rocky crest strongly red, the newly fallen snow marbling it over with a soft, deep rose, and wherever a canyon carved itself down the rocky fronts, its course was traceable by a shadowy band of blue. The middle distance glowed with a tint of golden yellow; the broken heights along the canyon brinks and edges of the cliff in front were of an intense, spotless white. Far below us the cloud stratum melted away, revealing the floor of the valley, whose russet and emerald and brown and red burned in the broad evening sun. It was a marvelous piece of contrasted lights—the distance so pure, so soft in its rosy warmth, so cool in the depth of its shadowy blue, the foreground strong in fiery orange, or sparkling in absolute whiteness. I enjoyed, too, looking up at the pure, unclouded sky, which now wore an aspect of intense serenity. For half an hour, Nature seemed in entire repose. Not a breath of wind stirred the white, snow-laden shafts of the trees. Not a sound of animate creature or the most distant reverberation of waterfall reached us. No film of vapor moved across the tranquil, sapphire sky. Absolute quiet reigned until a loud roar proceeding from El Capitan turned our eyes in that direction. From the round, dome-like cap of its summit there moved down an avalanche, gathering volume and swiftness as it rushed to the brink, and then, leaping out two or three hundred feet into space, fell, slowly filtering down through the lighted air, like a silver cloud, until within a thousand feet of the earth it floated into the shadow of the cliff and sank to the ground as a faint blue mist. Next the Cathedral snow poured from its lighted summit in resounding avalanches. Then the Three Brothers shot off their loads, and afar from the east a deep roar reached us as the whole snow-cover thundered down the flank of Clouds Rest. The light, already pale, left the distant heights in still more glorious contrast. A zone of amber sky rose behind the glowing peaks, and a cold steel-blue plain of snow skirted their bases. Mist slowly gathered again in the gorge below us and overspread the valley floor, shutting it out from our view.

We ran down the zigzag trail until we came to that shelf of bare granite immediately below the final descent into the valley. Here we paused just above the surface of the clouds, which, swept by fitful breezes, rose in swells, floating up and sinking again like waves of the sea. Intense light, more glowing than ever, streamed in upon the upper half of the cliffs, their bases sunken in the purple mist. As the cloud-waves crawled upward in the breeze they here and there touched a red-purple light and fell back again into the shadow. We watched these effects with greatest interest, and, just as we were about moving on again, a loud burst as of heavy thunder arrested us, sounding as if the very walls were crashing in. We looked, and from the whole brow of El Capitan rushed over one huge avalanche, breaking into the finest powder and floating down through orange light, disappearing in the sea of purple cloud beneath us. Clouds which had enfolded the heavens rolled off to the east in torn fillets of gold. The stars came out full and flashing in the darkling sky of evening.

The vast valley walls, light in contrast with the deep nocturnal violet heavens, rose far into the night, apparently holding up a roof of stars whose brilliancy faded quite rapidly, until finally the last blinking points of light died out, and cold, hard gray stretched from cliff to cliff. Far up canyons and in the heart of the mountains, we could hear terrible tempest gusts crashing among the trees, and breaking in deep, long surges against faces of granite. Coming nearer and nearer, they swept down the gorges, with volume increasing every moment, until they poured into the upper end of the valley and fell upon its groves with terrible fury. The wind shrieked wild and high among the summit crags, it tore through the pine belts, and now and then a sudden, sharp crash resounded through the valley as, one after another, old, infirm pines were hurled down before its blast. The very walls seemed to tremble; the air was thick with flying leaves and dead branches. The snow of the summits, hard frozen by a sudden chill, was blown from the walls, and filled the air with its keen, cutting crystals. At last, the very clouds, torn into wild flocks, were swept down into the valley, filling it with opaque, hurrying vapors. Rocks, loosening themselves from the plateau, came thundering down precipice faces, crashing upon debris piles and forest groups below. Sleet and snow and rain fell fast, and the boom of falling trees and crashing avalanches followed one another in an almost uninterrupted roar. In the Sentinel gorge, back of our camp, an avalanche of rock was suddenly let loose, and came down with a harsh rattle, the boulders bounding over debris piles and tearing through the trees by our camp. A vivid belt of blue lightning flashed down through the blackness, and for a moment, every outline of cliff and forest forms, and the rushing clouds of snow and sleet, were lighted up with a cold, pallid gleam. The burst of thunder which followed rolled but for a moment, and was silenced by the furious storm. In the moment of lightning, I saw that the Yosemite Fall, which had been dry for a month, had suddenly sprung into life again. Vast volumes of water and ice were pouring over and beating like sea waves upon the granite below. Our mules came up to the cabin, and stood on its lee side trembling, and uttering suppressed moans.

After hours, the fitfulness of the tempest passed away, leaving a grand, monotonous roar. It had torn off all the rotten branches of the year, and prostrated every decrepit tree, and at last settled down to a continuous gale, laden with torrents of rain. We lay down upon our bunks in our clothes, watching and listening through all the first hours of the night. Sleep was impossible; angry winds and the fury of drifting rain shook our little shelters, and kept us wide awake. Toward morning a second thunderstorm burst, and by the light of its flashes I saw that the river had risen nearly to our cabin door, covering the broad valley in front of us with a sheet of flood. Gradually the sound of Yosemite Fall grew louder and stronger, the throbs, as it beat upon the rocks, rising higher and higher till the whole valley rung with its pulsations. By dawn the storm had spent its fury, rain ceased, and around us the air was perfectly still. But aloft, among cliffs and walls, the gale might still be heard sweeping across the forest and tearing itself among granite needles. Fearing that so continuous a storm might block up our mountain trails, Hyde and Cotter and Wilmer, with instruments and pack-animals, started early and went out to Clark's Ranch.

So dense and impenetrable a fog overhung us that daylight came with extreme slowness, and it was nine o'clock before we rose for breakfast, and at ten a gloomy sea of mist still hung over the valley. The Merced had overflowed its banks, and ran wild. Toward noon the mist began to draw down the valley, and finally all drifted away, leaving us shut in by a gray canopy of cloud which stretched from wall to wall, hanging down here and there in deep blue sags. In this stratum of gray were lost many higher summits, but the whole form of valley and cliff could be seen with terrible distinctness, the walls apparently drawn together, their bases at one or two points pushed into yellow floods of water which lay like lakes upon the level expanse. The whole lip of Yosemite was filled to the brim, and through it there poured a broad, full torrent of white. Shortly after noon, a few rifts opened overhead, showing a fair sky, from which poured gushes of strong, yellow sunlight, touching here and there upon somber faces of cliff, and occasionally gilding the falling torrent. A wind still blew, smiting the Yosemite precipice, and playing strangest games with the fall itself. At one time a gust rushed upon the lip of the fall with such violence as to dam back all its waters. We could see its white pile in the lip mounting higher and higher, still held back by the wind, until there must have been a front of from a hundred and fifty to two hundred feet of boiling white water. For a whole minute not a drop poured down the wall. But, gathering strength, the torrent overcame the wind, rushed out with tremendous violence, leaped one hundred and fifty feet straight out into air, and fell clear to the rocks below, dashing high and white again, and breaking into a cloud of spray that filled the lower air of the valley for a mile.

While the water was held back in the gorge, there was a moment of complete silence, but when it finally burst out again, a crash as of sudden thunder shook the air. At times gusts of wind would drive upon the Three Brothers cliff, and be deflected toward Yosemite, swinging the whole mighty cataract like a pendulum. And again, pouring upon the rocks at the bottom of the valley, it would gather up the whole fall in midair, whirl it in a festoon, and carry it back over the very summit of the walls. I got out the theodolite to measure the angle of its deflection, and, while watching, it swung over an entire semicircle, now carried from the cliffs to the right, and then whirled back in a cloud of foam over the head of the Three Brothers. A very frequent prank was to loop the whole twenty-six hundred feet of cataract into a single, semicircular festoon, which fell in the form of fine fringe.

Throughout the afternoon, we did little else than watch these ever-changing forms of falling water, until toward evening, when we walked up to see the Merced. I never beheld such a rapid rise in any river; from a mere brook, hiding itself away under overhanging banks and among shrubby islands, it sprang in one night to the size of a full, large river, flowing with the rapidity of a torrent and whirling in its eddies huge trunks of stormblown pines. As twilight gathered, the scene deepened into a most indescribable gloom. Dark blue shadows covered half the precipices, and sullen, unvaried sky stretched over us its implacable gray. There was something positively fearful in this color; such an impenetrable sky might overarch the

Inferno. As we looked, it slowly sank, creeping down precipices, filling the whole gorge, coming down, down, and fitting the cliffs like the piston of an air-pump, till within a thousand feet of us it became stationary, and then slowly lifted again, clearing the summit and rising to an almost infinite remoteness. Slowly, a few hard, sharp crystals of snow floated down. Later, the air became intensely chilly, and by dark was full of slowly falling snow, giving prospect of a great mountain storm which might close the Sierras.

On the following morning, we determined at all costs to pack our remaining instruments and escape. The ground was covered with snow to the depth of seven or eight inches, and through drifting fogbanks we could occasionally get glimpses and see that every cliff was deeply buried in snow. We had still a few barometrical observations along the Mariposa trail which were necessary to complete our series of altitudes. I started in advance of Gardiner and Clark to break the trail, expecting that when I stopped to make readings they would easily overtake me. Two hours' hard work was needed to reach the ascent. It was not until noon that I made Inspiration Point, snow having deepened to eighteen inches, entirely obliterating the trail, and had it not been for the extreme frequency of our journeys I should never have been able to follow it. As it was, with occasional mistakes which were soon remedied, I kept the way very well, and my tracks made it easy for the party behind. Having reached the plateau, I made my two barometrical stations, and then started alone through forests for Westfall's cabin. Every fir tree was a solid cone of white, and often clusters of five or six were buried together in one common pile. Now and then a little sunlight broke through

the clouds, and in these intervals the scene was one of wonderful beauty. Tall shafts of fir, often one hundred and eighty
feet high, trimmed with white branches, cast their blue
shadows upon snowy ground.

At about four o'clock, after nine hours of hard tramping, I
reached Westfall's cabin, built a fire, and sat down to warm
myself and wait for my friends. In half an hour they made their
appearance, looking haggard and weary, declaring they would
go no farther that night. They led their mule into the cabin,
and unpacked, and began to make themselves comfortably at
home. At about five, the darkness of night had fairly settled
down, and with it came a gentle but dense snowstorm. It
seemed to me a terrible risk for us to remain in the mountains,
and I felt it to be absolutely necessary that one, at least, should
press on to Clark's, so that, if a really great storm should come,
he could bring up aid. Accordingly, I volunteered to go on
myself, Clark and Gardiner expressing their determination to
remain where they were at all costs.

At this juncture, Cotter's well-known voice sounded through
the woods as he approached the cabin. He had been all day
climbing from Clark's, and had come to lend a hand in getting
the things down. He was of my opinion, that it was absolutely
necessary for one of us, at least, to go back to Clark's, and
offered, if I thought best, to try to accompany me. I had come
from Yosemite and he from Clark's, having traveled all day, and
it was no slight task for us to face storm and darkness in the
forest, and among complicated spurs of the Sierra.

We ate our lunch by the cabin fire, bade our friends good-
night, and walked out together into the darkness. For the first
mile there was no danger of missing our way. Even in the

darkness of night, Cotter's tracks could be seen, but after about half an hour it began to be very difficult to keep the trail. The storm increased to a tempest, and exhaustion compelled us to travel slower and slower. It was with intense anxiety that we searched for well-known blazed trees along the trail, often thrusting our arms down in the snow to feel for a blaze that we knew of. If it was not there, we had for a moment an overpowering sense of being lost, but we were ordinarily rewarded after searching upon a few trees, and the blaze once found animated us with new courage. Hour after hour we traveled down the mountain, falling off high banks now and then, for in the dark all ideas of slope were lost. It must have been about midnight when we reached what seemed to be the verge of a precipice. If our calculations were right, we must have come to the edge of the South Fork Canyon. Here Cotter sank with exhaustion and declared that he must sleep. I rolled him over and implored him to get up and struggle on for a little while longer, when I felt sure that we must get down to the South Fork Canyon. He utterly refused, and lay there in a drowsy condition, fast giving up to the effects of fatigue and cold. I unbound a long scarf, which was tied round his neck, put it under his arms like a harness, and, tying it round my body, started on, dragging him through the snow, to see if by that means I might not exasperate him to rise and labor on. In a few minutes it had its effect, and he sprang to his feet and fell upon me in a burst of indignation. A few words were enough to bring him to himself, when the old, calm courage was reasserted, and we started together to make our way down the cliff. Happily, we at length found the right ridge, and rapidly descended through forest to the river side.

Believing that we must still be below the bridge, we walked rapidly up the bank until at last we found it, and came quickly to Clark's. We pounded upon the cabin door, and waked up our friends, who received us with joy, and set about cooking us a supper. It was two o'clock when we arrived, and by three we all went off again to our bunks. My anxiety about Gardiner and Clark prevented my sleeping. Every few minutes I went to the door.

Before dawn it had cleared again, and remained fair till the next noon, when the two made their appearance. No sooner were they quietly housed than the storm burst again with renewed strength, howling among the forest trees grandly. Snow drifted heavily all the afternoon, and through the night it still fell, reaching an average depth of about two feet by the following morning.

We were up early, and packed upon the animals our instruments, notebooks, and personal effects, leaving all the blankets and heavy luggage to be gotten out in the following spring. We toiled slowly and heavily up Chowchilla trail. The branches of the great pines and firs were overloaded with snow, which now and then fell in small avalanches upon our heads. Here and there an old bough gave way under its weight, and fell with a soft thud into the snow. We took turns breaking trail, Napoleon, the one-eyed mule, distinguishing himself greatly by following its intricate crooks, while the bravest of us, by turns, held to his tail. There is something deeply humiliating in this process. All the domineering qualities of mankind vanished before the quick, subtle instinct of that noble animal, the mule, and his superior strength came out in magnificent style. With a sublime scorn of his former master, he started ahead, dragging me proudly after him. I had sometimes thrashed that mule with unsympathetic violence, and I fancied it was something very like poetic justice thus submissively to follow in his wake.

Midday found us upon the Chowchilla summit, following a trail deeply buried and often obliterated, and undiscoverable but for our long-eared leader. As we descended the west slope, the snow grew more and more moist, less deep, and gradually turned into rain. An hour's tramp found us upon bare ground, under the fiercely driving rain, which quickly soaked us to the bone. The streams, as we descended, were found to be more and more swollen, until at last it required some nerve to ford the little brooklets, which the mule had drunk dry on our upward journey. The earth was thoroughly softened, and here and there the trail was filled with brimming brooks, which rapidly gullied it out.

A more drowned and bedraggled set of fellows never walked out upon the wagon road and turned toward Mariposa. Streams of water flowed from every fold of our garments, our soaked hats clung to our cheeks, the baggage was a mass of pulp, and the mules smelled violently of wet hide. Fortunately, our notebooks, carefully strapped in oilcloth, so far resisted wetting. It was three o'clock in the afternoon when we reached Dulong's house, and were surprised to see the water flowing over the top of the bridge. In ordinary times, a dry arroyo traverses this farm, and runs under a bridge in front of the house. Clark, our only mounted man, rode out, as he supposed, upon the bridge, but unfortunately it was gone, and he and his horse plunged splendidly into the stream. They came to the surface, Clark with a look of intense astonishment on his face, and the mare sputtering and striking out wildly for the other side.

Being a strong swimmer, she reached the bank, climbed out, and Clark politely invited us to follow. The one-eyed Napoleon was brought to the brink and induced to plunge in by an application of fence-rails *a tergo*, his cyclopean organ piloting him safely across, when he was quickly followed by the other mules. We watched the load of instruments with some anxiety, and were not reassured when their heavy weight bore the mule quite under. But she climbed successfully out, and we ourselves, half swimming, half floundering, managed to cross.

A little way farther we came upon another stream rushing violently across the road, sweeping down logs and sections of fence. Here Clark dismounted, and we drove the whole train in. Three animals got safely over, but the instrument mule was swept down stream and badly snagged, lying upon one side with his head under water. Cotter and Gardiner and Clark ran up stream and got across upon a log. I made a dash for the snagged mule, and by strong swimming managed to catch one of his feet, and then his tail, and worked myself toward the shore. It was something of a task to hold his head out of the water, but I was quickly joined by the others, and we managed to drag him out by the head and tail. There he lay upon the bank on his side, tired of life, utterly refusing to get upon his feet, the most abominable specimen of inertia and indifference. While I was pricking him vigorously with a tripod, the ground caved under my feet and I quickly sank. Cotter, who was standing close by, seized me by the cape of my soldier's overcoat, and landed me as carefully as he would a fish. As we marched down the road, unconsciously keeping step, the sound of our boots had quite a symphonic effect; they were full of water, and with soft, melodious slushing acted as a calmer upon our spirits.

The road in some places was cut out many feet deep, and we were obliged to climb upon the wooded banks, and make laborious detours. At last we reached a branch of the Chowchilla, which was pouring in a flood between a man's house and his barn. Here we formed a line, a mule between each two men. Our line was swept frightfully down stream, but the leader gained his feet, and we came out safe and dripping upon terra firma on the other side. A mile farther we came upon the main Chowchilla, which was running a perfect flood. From being a mere brooklet, it had swollen to a considerable river, with waves five and six feet high sweeping down its center. We formed our line and attempted the passage, but were thrown back. It would have been madness to try it again, and we turned sorrowfully back to the last ranch. Cotter and I piloted the animals over to the barn, and, upon returning, threw a rope to our friends upon the other side, and were drawn through the swift water.

In the ranch house we found two bachelors, typical California partners, who were quietly partaking of their supper of bacon, fried onions, Japanese tea, and biscuits, which, like "Harry York's," had too much saleratus [sodium bicarbonate, *ed.*]. We stood upon their threshold awhile and dripped, quite a rill descending over the two steps, trickling down the dooryard as a new fork of the Chowchilla.

We asked for supper and shelter, but were met with such a gruff, inhospitable reply that we lost all sense of modesty, and walked in with all our moisture. We stretched a rope across the middle of the sitting room before a huge fire in an open chimney, then, stripping ourselves to the buff, we hung up our steaming clothes upon the line, and turned solemnly round and round before the fire, drying our persons.

In the meanwhile, our inhospitable landlords made the best of the situation, and proceeded to achieve more onions and more saleratus biscuit for our entertainment. Upon our departure in the morning, the generous rancher charged us first-class hotel prices.

The flood had utterly disappeared, and we passed over the Chowchilla with surprise and dry shoes.

At Mariposa we parted from Clark, and devoted two whole days to struggling through the mud of San Joaquin Valley to San Francisco, where we arrived, wet and exhausted, just in time to get on board the New York steamer.

On the morning of the twelfth day out, Gardiner and I seated ourselves under the grateful shadow of palm trees, a bewitching black-and-tan sister thrumming her guitar while the chocolate for our breakfast boiled. The slumberous haze of the tropics hung over Lake Nicaragua; but high above its indistinct, pearly vale rose the smooth cone of the volcano of Omatepec, robed in a cover of pale emerald green. Warmth, repose, the verdure of eternal spring, the poetical whisper of palms, the heavy odor of the tropical blooms, banished the grand, cold fury of the Sierra, which had left a permanent chill in our bones.

Tunnel View in December

21

A Winter Earthquake

John Muir

Earthquake Storms

The avalanche taluses, leaning against the walls at intervals of a mile or two, are among the most striking and interesting of the secondary features of the valley. They are from about three to five hundred feet high, made up of huge, angular, well-pre-

213

served, unshifting boulders, and instead of being slowly weathered from the cliffs like ordinary taluses, they were all formed suddenly and simultaneously by a great earthquake that occurred at least three centuries ago. And though thus hurled into existence in a few seconds or minutes, they are the least changeable of all the Sierra soil-beds. Excepting those which were launched directly into the channels of swift rivers, scarcely one of their wedged and interlacing boulders has moved since the day of their creation. And though mostly made up of huge blocks of granite, many of them from ten to fifty feet cube weighing thousands of tons with only a few small chips, trees and shrubs make out to live and thrive on them and even delicate herbaceous plants—*Draperia, Collomia, Zauschneria* [fuchsia or hummingbird trumpet, *ed.*]—soothing and coloring their wild rugged slopes with gardens and groves.

I was long in doubt on some points concerning the origin of those taluses. Plainly enough they were derived from the cliffs above them, because they are of the size of scars on the wall, the rough angular surface of which contrasts with the rounded, glaciated, unfractured parts. It was plain, too, that instead of being made up of material slowly and gradually weathered from the cliffs like ordinary taluses, almost every one of them had been formed suddenly in a single avalanche, and had not been increased in size during the last three or four centuries, for trees three or four hundred years old are growing on them, some standing at the top close to the wall without a bruise or broken branch. Furthermore, all these taluses throughout the range seemed by the trees and lichens growing on them to be of the same age. All the phenomena thus pointed straight to a grand ancient earthquake. But for years I left the question open, and went on from canyon to canyon, observing again and again, measuring the heights of taluses throughout the range on both flanks, and the variations in the angles of their surface slopes, studying the way their boulders had been assorted and related and brought to rest, and their correspondence in size with the cleavage joints of the cliffs from whence they were derived, cautious about making up my mind. But at last, all doubt as to their formation vanished.

At half-past two o'clock of a moonlit morning in March, I was awakened by a tremendous earthquake, and though I had never before enjoyed a storm of this sort, the strange thrilling motion could not be mistaken, and I ran out of my cabin, both glad and frightened, shouting, "A noble earthquake! A noble earthquake!" feeling sure I was going to learn something. The shocks were so violent and varied, and succeeded one another so closely, that I had to balance myself carefully in walking as if on the deck of a ship among waves, and it seemed impossible that the high cliffs of the valley could escape being shattered. In particular, I feared that the sheer-fronted Sentinel Rock, towering above my cabin, would be shaken down, and I took shelter back of a large yellow pine, hoping that it might protect me from at least the smaller outbounding boulders. For a minute or two the shocks became more and more violent—flashing horizontal thrusts mixed with a few twists and battering, explosive, upheaving jolts—as if Nature were wrecking her Yosemite temple, and getting ready to build a still better one.

I was now convinced before a single boulder had fallen that earthquakes were the talus-makers and positive proof soon came. It was a calm moonlight night, and no sound was heard for the first minute or so, save low, muffled, underground, bubbling rumblings, and the whispering and rustling of the agitated trees, as if Nature were holding her breath. Then, suddenly, out of the strange silence and strange motion there came a tremendous roar. The Eagle Rock on the south wall, about a half a mile up the valley, gave way and I saw it falling in thousands of the great boulders I had so long been studying, pouring to the valley floor in a free curve luminous from friction, making a terribly sublime spectacle—an arc of glowing, passionate fire, fifteen hundred feet span, as true in form and as serene in beauty as a rainbow in the midst of the stupendous, roaring rock-storm. The sound was so tremendously deep and broad and earnest, the whole earth like a living creature seemed to have at last found a voice and to be calling to her sister planets. In trying to tell something of the size of this awful sound it seems to me that if all the thunder of all the storms had ever heard were condensed into one roar it would not equal this rock-roar at the birth of a mountain talus. Think, then, of the roar that arose to heaven at the simultaneous birth of all the thousands of ancient canyon-taluses throughout the length and breadth of the range!

The first severe shocks were soon over, and eager to examine the new-born talus I ran up the valley in the moonlight and climbed upon it before the huge blocks, after their fiery flight, had come to complete rest. They were slowly settling into their places, chafing, grating against one another, groaning, and whispering; but no motion was visible except in a stream of small fragments pattering down the face of the cliff. A cloud of dust particles, lighted by the moon, floated out across the whole breadth of the valley, forming a ceiling that lasted until after sunrise, and the air was filled with the odor of crushed Douglas spruces [Douglas fir, *ed.*] from a grove that had been mowed down and mashed like weeds.

After the ground began to calm I ran across the meadow to the river to see in what direction it was flowing and was glad to find that down the valley was still down. Its waters were muddy from portions of its banks having given way, but it was flowing around its curves and over its ripples and shallows with ordinary tones and gestures. The mud would soon be cleared away and the raw slips on the banks would be the only visible record of the shaking it suffered.

The Upper Yosemite Fall, glowing white in the moonlight, seemed to know nothing of the earthquake, manifesting no change in form or voice, as far as I could see or hear.

After a second startling shock, about half-past three o'clock, the ground continued to tremble gently, and smooth, hollow rumbling sounds, not always distinguishable from the rounded, bumping, explosive tones of the falls, came from deep in the mountains in a northern direction.

The few Indians fled from their huts to the middle of the valley, fearing that angry spirits were trying to kill them. And, as I afterward learned, most of the Yosemite tribe, who were spending the winter at their village on Bull Creek forty miles away, were so terrified that they ran into the river and washed themselves, getting themselves clean enough to say their prayers, I suppose, or to die. I asked Dick, one of the Indians with whom I was acquainted, "What made the ground shake and jump so much?" He only shook his head and said, "No good. No good," and looked appealingly to me to give him hope that his life was to be spared.

In the morning I found the few white settlers assembled in front of the old Hutchings Hotel comparing notes and meditating flight to the lowlands, seemingly as sorely frightened as the Indians. Shortly after sunrise, a low, blunt, muffled rumbling, like distant thunder, was followed by another series of shocks, which, though not nearly so severe as the first, made the cliffs and domes tremble like jelly, and the big pines and oaks thrill and swish and wave their branches with startling effect. Then the talkers were suddenly hushed, and the solemnity on their faces was sublime. One in particular of these winter neighbors, a somewhat speculative thinker with whom I had openly conversed, was a firm believer in the cataclysmic origin of the valley, and I now jokingly remarked that his wild tumble-down-and-engulfment hypothesis might soon be proved, since these underground rumblings and shakings might be the forerunners of another Yosemite-making cataclysm, which would perhaps double the depth of the valley by swallowing the floor, leaving the ends of the roads and trails dangling three or four thousand feet in the air. Just then came the third series of shocks, and it was fine to see how awfully silent and solemn he became. His belief in the existence of a mysterious abyss, into which the suspended floor of the valley and all the domes and battlements of the walls might at any moment go roaring down, mightily troubled him. To diminish his fears and laugh him into something like reasonable faith, I said, "Come, cheer up. Smile a little and clap your hands, now that kind Mother Earth is trotting us on her knee to amuse us and make us good." But the well-meant joke seemed irreverent and utterly failed, as if only prayerful terror could rightly belong to the wild beauty-making business. Even after all the heavier shocks were over, I could do nothing to reassure him. On the contrary, he handed me the keys of his little store to keep, saying that with a companion of like mind he was going to the lowlands to stay until the fate of poor, trembling Yosemite was settled. In vain I rallied them on their fears, calling attention to the strength of the granite walls of our valley home, the very best and solidest masonry in the world, and less likely to collapse and sink than the sedimentary lowlands to which they were looking for safety, and saying that in any case they sometime would have to die, and so grand a burial was not to be slighted. But they were too seriously panic-stricken to get comfort from anything I could say.

During the third severe shock, the trees were so violently shaken that the birds flew out with frightened cries. In particular, I noticed two robins flying in terror from a leafless oak, the branches of which swished and quivered as if struck by a heavy battering ram. Exceedingly interesting were the flashing and quivering of the elastic needles of the pines in the sunlight and the waving up and down of the branches while the trunks stood rigid. There was no swaying, waving or swirling as in windstorms, but quick, quivering jerks, and at times the heavy tasseled branches moved as if they had all been pressed down against the trunk and suddenly let go, to spring up and vibrate until they came to rest again. Only the owls seemed to be undisturbed. Before the rumbling echoes had died away, a hollow-voiced owl began to hoot in philosophical tranquility from near the edge of the new talus as if nothing extraordinary had occurred, although, perhaps, he was curious to know what all the noise was about. His "hoot-too-hoot-too-whoo" might have meant, "what's a' the steer, kimmer?"

It was long before the valley found perfect rest. The rocks trembled more or less every day for over two months, and I kept a bucket of water on my table to learn what I could of the movements. The blunt thunder in the depths of the mountains was usually followed by sudden jarring, horizontal thrusts from the northward, often succeeded by twisting, upjolting movements. More than a month after the first great shock, when I was standing on a fallen tree up the valley near Lamon's winter cabin, I heard a distinct bubbling thunder from the direction of Tenaya Canyon. Carlo, a large intelligent Saint Bernard dog standing beside me seemed greatly astonished, and looked intently in that direction with mouth open and uttered a low *Wouf!* as if saying, "What's that?" He must have known that it was not thunder, though like it. The air was perfectly still, not the faintest breath of wind perceptible, and a fine, mellow, sunny hush pervaded everything, in the midst of which came that subterranean thunder. Then, while we gazed and listened, came the corresponding shocks, distinct as if some mighty hand had shaken the ground. After the sharp horizontal jars died away, they were followed by a gentle rocking and undulating of the ground so distinct that Carlo looked at the log on which he was standing to see who was shaking it. It was the season of flooded meadows and the pools about me, calm as sheets of glass, were suddenly thrown into low ruffling waves.

Judging by its effects, this Yosemite, or Inyo earthquake, as it is sometimes called, was gentle as compared with the one that gave rise to the grand talus system of the range and did so much for the canyon scenery. Nature, usually so deliberate in her operations, then created, as we have seen, a new set of features, simply by giving the mountains a shake, changing not only the high peaks and cliffs, but the streams. As soon as these rock avalanches fell, the streams began to sing new songs, for in many places, thousands of boulders were hurled into their channels, roughening and half damming them, compelling the waters to surge and roar in rapids where before they glided smoothly. Some of the streams were completely dammed; driftwood, leaves, etc., gradually filling the interstices between the boulders, thus giving rise to lakes and level reaches. These again, after being gradually filled in, were changed to meadows, through which the streams are now silently meandering, while at the same time some of the taluses took the places of old meadows and groves. Thus rough places were made smooth, and smooth places rough. But, on the whole, by what at first sight seemed pure confounded confusion and ruin, the landscapes were enriched, for gradually every talus was covered with groves and gardens, and made a finely proportioned and ornamental base for the cliffs. In this work of beauty, every boulder is prepared and measured and put in its place more thoughtfully than are the stones of temples. If for a moment you are inclined to regard these taluses as mere draggled, chaotic dumps, climb to the top of one of them, and run down without any haggling, puttering hesitation, boldly jumping from boulder to boulder with even speed. You will then find your feet playing a tune, and quickly discover the music and poetry of these magnificent rock piles—a fine lesson. All Nature's wildness tells the same story—the shocks and outbursts of earthquakes, volcanoes, geysers, roaring, thundering waves and floods, the silent uprush of sap in plants, storms of every sort—each and all are the orderly beauty-making love-beats of Nature's heart.

Blue Lupine

22

The Flowers

John Muir

Yosemite was all one glorious flower garden before plows and scythes and trampling, biting horses came to make its wide open spaces look like farmers' pasture fields. Nevertheless, countless flowers still bloom every year in glorious profusion on the grand talus slopes, wall benches and tablets, and in all the fine, cool side-canyons up to the rim of the valley, and beyond, higher and higher, to the summits of the peaks. Even on the open floor and in easily-reached side-nooks, many common flowering plants have survived and still make a brave show in the spring and early summer. Among these we may mention tall *Oenotheras* [evening-primrose, *ed.*], *Pentstemon lutea* [beardtongue, *ed*], and *P. douglasii* (*sic*) with fine blue and red flowers; *Spraguea* [purslane, *ed*], scarlet *Zauschneria* [fuchsia, *ed*], with its curious radiant rosettes characteristic of the sandy flats; *Mimulus* [monkeyflower, *ed.*], blue and white violets, geranium, columbine, *erythraea* [centaury, *ed.*], larkspur, collomia, *Draperia*, gilias, *Heleniums* [sneezeweed, *ed.*], bahia, goldenrods, daisies, honeysuckle; *Heuchera* [alumroot, *ed.*], bolandra, saxifrages, gentians. In cool canyon nooks and on Clouds Rest and the base of Starr King Dome you may find *Primula suffrutescens*, the only wild primrose discovered in California, and the only known shrubby species in the genus. And there are several fine orchids, *Habenaria* and *Cypripedium*, the latter very rare, once common in the valley near the foot of Glacier Point, and in a bog on the rim of the valley near a place called Gentry's Station, now abandoned. It is a very beautiful species, the large oval lip white, delicately veined with purple; the other petals and the sepals purple, strap-shaped, and elegantly curled and twisted.

Of the lily family, *Fritillaria*, *Smilacina*, *Chlorogalum*, and several fine species of *Brodaea*, Ithuriel's spear, and others less prized are common, and the favorite *Calochortus*, or Mariposa lily, a unique genus of many species, something like the tulips of Europe but far finer. Most of them grow on the warm foothills below the valley, but two charming species, *C. oeruleus* and *C. nudus,* dwell in springy places on Wawona Road a few miles beyond the brink of the walls.

The snow plant (*Sarcodes sanguinea*) is more admired by tourists than any other in California. It is red, fleshy and watery, and looks like a gigantic asparagus shoot. Soon after the snow is off the ground, it rises through the dead needles and humus in the pine and fir woods like a bright glowing pillar of fire. In a week or so, it grows to a height of eight or twelve inches with a diameter of an inch and a half or two inches. Then its long fringed bracts curl aside, allowing the twenty- or thirty-five-lobed, bell-shaped flowers to open and look straight out from the axis. It is said to grow up through the snow; on the contrary, it always waits until the ground is warm, though with other early flowers it is occasionally buried or half-buried for a day or two by spring storms. The entire plant—flowers, bracts, stem, scales, and roots—is fiery red. Its color could appeal to one's blood. Nevertheless, it is a singularly cold and unsympathetic plant. Everybody admires it as a wonderful curiosity, but nobody loves it as lilies, violets, roses, daisies are loved. Without fragrance, it stands beneath the pines and firs, lonely and silent, as if unacquainted with any other plant in the world, never moving in the wildest storms, rigid as if lifeless, though covered with beautiful rosy flowers.

Far the most delightful and fragrant of the valley flowers is the Washington lily, white, moderate in size, with from three- to ten-flowered racemes. I found one specimen in the lower end of the valley at the foot of the Wawona grade that was eight feet high, the raceme two feet long, with fifty-two flowers, fifteen of them open. The others had faded or were still in the bud. This famous lily is distributed over the sunny portions of the sugar pine woods, never in large meadow-garden companies like the large and the small tiger lilies (*pardalinum* and *parvum*), but widely scattered, standing up to the waist in dense *Ceanothus* and manzanita chaparral, waving its lovely flowers above the blooming wilderness of brush, and giving their fragrance to the breeze. It is now becoming scarce in the most accessible parts of its range on account of the high price paid for its bulbs by gardeners through whom it has been distributed far and wide over the flower-loving world. For, on account of its pure color and delicate, delightful fragrance, all lily-lovers at once adopted it as a favorite.

The principal shrubs are manzanita and *Ceanothus*, several species of each, azalea, *Rubus nutkanus* [brambles, *ed.*], brier rose, choke-cherry, *Philadelphus* [mock orange, *ed.*], *Calycanthus* [spicebush, *ed.*], *Garrya* [silk tassle bush, *ed.*], *Rhamnus* [coffeeberry, *ed.*], etc.

The manzanita never fails to attract particular attention. The species common in the valley is usually about six or seven feet high, round-headed with innumerable branches, red or chocolate-color bark, pale green leaves set on edge, and a rich profusion of small, pink, narrow-throated, urn-shaped flowers, like those of *Arbutus* [madrone, *ed.*]. The knotty, crooked, angular branches are about as rigid as bones, and the red bark is so thin and smooth on both trunk and branches, they look as if they had been peeled and polished and painted. In the spring, large areas on the mountain up to a height of eight or nine thousand feet are brightened with the rosy flowers, and in autumn with their red fruit. The pleasantly acid berries, about the size of peas, look like little apples, and a hungry mountaineer is glad to eat them, though half their bulk is made up of hard seeds. Indians, bears, coyotes, foxes, birds, and other mountain people live on them for weeks and months. The different species of *Ceanothus* usually associated with manzanita are flowery fragrant and altogether delightful shrubs, growing in glorious abundance, not only in the valley, but high up in the forest on sunny or half-shaded ground. In the sugar pine woods, the most beautiful species is *C. integerrimus,* often called Californian lilac, or deer brush. It is five or six feet high with slender branches, glossy foliage, and abundance of blue flowers in close, showy panicles. Two species, *C. prostrates* and *C. procumbens,* spread smooth, blue-flowered mats and rugs beneath the pines, and offer fine beds to tired mountaineers. The commonest species, *C. cordulatus* [whitethorn, *ed.*], is most common in the silver fir woods. It is white-flowered and thorny, and makes dense thickets of tangled chaparral, difficult to wade through or to walk over. But it is pressed flat every winter by ten or fifteen feet of snow. The western azalea makes glorious beds of bloom along the riverbank and meadows. In the valley, it is from two to five feet high, has fine green leaves, mostly hidden beneath its rich profusion of large, fragrant white and yellow flowers, which are in their prime in June, July, and August, according to the elevation, ranging from three thousand to six thousand feet. Near the azalea-bordered streams, the small wild rose, resembling *R. blanda,* makes large thickets, deliciously fragrant, especially on a dewy morning and after showers. Not far from these azalea and rose gardens, *Rubus nutkanus* covers the ground with broad, soft, velvety leaves, and pure white flowers as large as those of its neighbor and relative, the rose, and much finer in texture, followed at the end of summer by soft red berries good for everybody. This is the commonest and the most beautiful of the whole blessed, flowery, fruity *Rubus* genus.

There are a great many interesting ferns in the valley and about it. Naturally enough, the greater number are rock ferns—*Pelaea* [cliffbrake, *ed.*], *Cheilanthes* [lip fern, *ed.*], *Polypodium, Adiantum* [maidenhair fern, *ed.*], *Woodsia* [cliff fern, *ed.*], *Cryptogramma* [parsley fern, *ed.*], etc.—with small tufted fronds, lining cool glens and fringing the seams of the cliffs. The most important of the larger species are *Woodwardia* [chain fern, *ed.*], *Aspidium* [sword fern, *ed.*], *Asplenium* [spleenwort, *ed.*], and, above all, the common *Pteris* [bracken, *ed.*]. *Woodwardia radicans* is a superb, broad-shouldered fern five to eight feet high, growing in vase-shaped clumps where the ground is nearly level and on some of the benches of the north wall of the valley where it is watered by a broad, trickling stream. It thatches the sloping rocks, frond overlapping frond, like roof shingles. The broad-fronded, hardy *Pteris aquilina*, the commonest of ferns, covers large areas on the floor of the valley. No other fern does so much for the color glory of autumn, with its browns and reds and yellows, even after lying dead beneath the snow all winter. It spreads a rich brown mantle over the desolate ground in the spring before the grass has sprouted, and at the first touch of sun heat, its young fronds come rearing up full of faith and hope through the midst of the last year's ruins.

Of the five species of *Pelaea, P. breweri* [Brewer's cliffbrake, *ed.*] is the hardiest as to enduring high altitudes and stormy weather, and at the same time it is the most fragile of the genus. It grows in dense tufts in the clefts of storm-beaten rocks, high up on the mountainside on the very edge of the fern line. It is a handsome little fern about four or five inches high, has pale green pinnate fronds, and shining bronze-colored stalks about as brittle as glass. Its companions on the lower part of its range are *Cryptogramma acrostichoides* and *Phegopteris alpestris*, the latter with soft, delicate fronds, not in the least like those of rock fern, though it grows on the rocks where the snow lies longest. *Pellaea bridgesii*, with blue-green, narrow, simple pinnate fronds, is about the same size as *breweri* and ranks next to it as a mountaineer, growing in fissures, wet or dry, and around the edges of boulders that are resting on glacier pavements with no fissures whatever. About a thousand feet lower we find the smaller, more abundant *P. densa* on ledges and boulder-strewn, fissured pavements, watered until late in summer from oozing currents derived from lingering snowbanks. It is, or rather was, extremely abundant between the foot of Nevada and the head of Vernal Fall, but visitors with great industry have dug out almost every root, so that now one has to scramble in out-of-the-way places to find it. The three species of *Cheilanthes* in the valley, *C. californica*, *C. gracillima*, and *myriophylla*, with beautiful two-to-four-pinnate fronds, an inch to five inches long, adorn the stupendous walls however dry and sheer. The exceedingly delicate *californica* is so rare that I have found it only once. The others are abundant and are sometimes accompanied by the little gold fern, *Gymnogramme triangularis*, and rarely by the curious little *Botrychium simplex* [Yosemite moonwort, *ed.*], some of them less than an inch high. The finest of all the rock ferns is *Adiantum pedatum*, lover of waterfalls and the finest spray-dust. The homes it loves best are over-leaning, cave-like hollows, beside the larger falls, where it can wet its fingers with their dewy spray. Many of these moss-lined chambers contain thousands of these delightful ferns, clinging to mossy walls by the slightest hold, reaching out their delicate finger-fronds on dark, shining stalks, sensitive and tremulous, throbbing in unison with every movement and tone of the falling water, moving each division of the frond separately at times, as if fingering the music.

Toward the end of March, *Carex* [sedge, *ed.*] sprouts on the warmer portions of the meadows are about an inch high, the aments of the alders along the banks of the river are nearly ripe, the *Libocedrus* [incense-cedar, *ed.*] is sowing its pollen, willows put forth their silky catkins, and a multitude of happy insects and swelling buds proclaim the promise of spring. May and June are the main bloom-months of the year. Both the flowers and falls are then at their best. Wild strawberries are ripe in May. The early flowers are in bloom, the birds are busy in the groves, and frogs in the shallow meadow pools. In June and July, the Yosemite summer is in all its glory. It is the prime time of plant-bloom and water-bloom, and the lofty domes and battlements are then bathed in divine purple light. By the first of August, the midsummer glories of the valley are past their prime. The young birds are then out of their nests and most of the plants have gone to seed. August is the season of ripe nuts and berries—raspberries, blackberries, thimbleberries, gooseberries, shadberries, blackcurrants, puckery chokecherries, pinenuts, etc., offering a royal feast to squirrels, bears, Indians, and birds of every feather. Autumn tints begin to kindle and burn over meadow and grove, and a soft mellow haze in the morning sunbeams heralds the approach of Indian summer. The shallow river is now at rest, its floodwork done. It is now but little more than a series of pools united by trickling, whispering currents that steal softly over brown pebbles and sand with scarcely an audible murmur. Each pool has a character of its own and, though they are nearly currentless, the night air and tree shadows keep them cool. Their shores curve in and out in bay and promontory, giving the appearance of miniature lakes, their banks in most places embossed with brier and azalea, sedge and grass and fern. Above these, in their glory of autumn colors, a mingled growth of alder, willow, dogwood and balm-of-Gilead, mellow sunshine overhead, cool shadows beneath, light filtered and strained in passing through the ripe leaves like that which passes through colored windows. The surface of the water is stirred, perhaps, by whirling water beetles, or some startled trout, seeking shelter beneath fallen logs or roots. The falls, too, are quiet; no wind stirs, and the whole valley floor is a mosaic of greens and purples, yellows and reds. Even the rocks seem strangely soft and mellow, as if they, too, had ripened.

Eastern Sierras

23

The Birds

John Muir

The songs of the Yosemite winds and waterfalls are delight-fully enriched with bird song, especially in the nesting time of spring and early summer. The most familiar and best known of all is the common robin, who may be seen every day, hopping about briskly on the meadows and uttering his cheery, enlivening call. The black-headed grosbeak, too, is here, with the Bullock oriole, and western tanager, brown song-sparrow, hermit thrush, the purple finch—a fine singer, with head and throat of a rosy-red hue—several species of warblers and vireos, kinglets, flycatchers, etc. But the most wonderful singer of all the birds is the water ouzel that dives into foaming rapids and feeds at the bottom, holding on in a wonderful way, living a charmed life.

Several species of hummingbirds are always to be seen, darting and buzzing among the showy flowers. The little red-bellied nuthatches, the chickadees, and little brown creepers, threading the furrows of the bark of the pines, searching for food in the crevices. The large Steller's jay makes merry in the pinetops. Flocks of beautiful green swallows skim over the streams, and the noisy Clarke's crow [Clark's nutcracker, *ed.*] may oftentimes be seen on the highest points around the valley. In the deep woods beyond the walls you may frequently hear and see the dusky grouse and the pileated woodpecker, or woodcock almost as large as a pigeon. The junco or snowbird builds its nest on the floor of the valley among the ferns; several species of sparrow are common and the beautiful lazuli bunting, a common bird in the underbrush, flitting about among the azalea and *Ceanothus* bushes and enlivening the groves with his brilliant color; and on gravelly bars, the spotted sandpiper is sometimes seen. Many woodpeckers dwell in the valley; the familiar flicker, the Harris woodpecker, and the species which so busily stores up acorns in the thick bark of the yellow pines.

The short, cold days of winter are also sweetened with the music and hopeful chatter of a considerable number of birds.

No cheerier choir ever sang in snow. First and best of all is the water ouzel, a dainty, dusky little bird about the size of a robin, that sings in sweet fluty song all winter and all summer, in storms and calms, sunshine and shadow, haunting the rapids and waterfalls with marvelous constancy, building his nest in the cleft of a rock bathed in spray. He is not web-footed, yet he dives fearlessly into foaming rapids, seeming to take the greater delight the more boisterous the stream, always as cheerful and calm as any linnet in a grove. All his gestures as he flits about amid the loud uproar of the falls bespeak the utmost simplicity and confidence—bird and stream one and inseparable. What a pair, yet well related. A yet finer bloom than the foambell in an eddying pool is this little bird. Like some delicate flower growing on a tree of rugged strength, the little ouzel grows on the booming stream, showing savage power changed to terms of sweetest love, plain and easily understood to human hearts. We may miss the meaning of the loud, resounding torrent, but the flute-like voice of the bird—only love is in it.

A few robins, belated on their way down from the upper meadows, linger in the valley and make out to spend the winter in comparative comfort, feeding on the mistletoe berries that grow on the oaks. In the depths of the great forests, on the high meadows, in the severest solitudes, they seem as much at home as in the old apple orchards about the busy habitations of man. They ascend the Sierra as the snow melts, following the green footsteps of spring, until in July or August the highest glacier meadows are reached on the summit of the range. Then, after the short summer is over, and their work in cheering and sweetening these lofty wilds is done, they gradually make their way down again in accord with the weather, keeping below the snowstorms, lingering here and there to feed on huckleberries and frost-nipped wild cherries growing on the upper slopes. Thence, down to the vineyards and orchards of the lowlands to spend the winter.

The kingfisher winters in the valley, and the flicker and, of course, the carpenter woodpecker [acorn woodpecker, *ed.*], that lays up large stores of acorns in the bark of trees; wrens also, with a few brown and gray linnets, and flocks of the arctic bluebird, making lively pictures among the snow-laden mistletoe. Flocks of pigeons are often seen, and about six species of ducks, as the river is never wholly frozen over. Among these are the mallard and the beautiful wood duck, now less abundant than formerly on account of being so often shot at. Flocks of wandering geese usually visit the valley in March and April, driven down by hunger, or weariness, or stress of weather while on their way across the range. They come in by the river canyon, but oftentimes are sorely bewildered in trying to get out again. I have frequently seen them try to fly over the walls of the valley until tired out and compelled to re-alight. Yosemite magnitudes seem to be as deceptive to geese as to men, for after circling to a considerable height and forming regular arrow-shaped ranks they would suddenly find themselves in danger of being dashed against the face of the cliff, much nearer the bottom than the top. Then turning in confusion with loud screams they would try again and again until exhausted and compelled to descend. I have occasionally observed large flocks on their travels crossing the summits of the range at a height of twelve thousand to thirteen thousand feet above the level of the sea, and even in so rare an atmosphere as this they seemed to be sustaining themselves without extra effort. Strong, however, as they are of wind and wing, they cannot fly over Yosemite walls, starting from the bottom.

A pair of golden eagles have lived in the valley ever since I first visited it, hunting all winter along the northern cliffs and down the river canyon. Their nest is on a ledge of the cliff over which pours Nevada Fall.

One wild, stormy winter morning after five feet of snow had fallen on the floor of the valley and the flying flakes driven by a strong wind still thickened the air, making darkness like the approach of night, I sallied forth to see what I might learn and enjoy. It was impossible to go very far without the aid of snow-shoes, but I found no great difficulty in making my way to a part of the river where one of my ouzels lived. I found him at home busy about his breakfast, apparently unaware of anything uncomfortable in the weather. Presently he flew out to a stone against which the icy current was beating, and turning his back to the wind, sang as delightfully as a lark in springtime.

After spending an hour or two with my favorite, I made my way across the valley, boring and wallowing through the loose snow, to learn as much as possible about the way the other birds were spending their time. In winter one can always find them because they are then restricted to the north side of the valley, especially the Indian Canyon groves, which from their peculiar exposure are the warmest.

I found most of the robins cowering on the lee side of the larger branches of the trees, where the snow could not fall on them, while two or three of the more venturesome were making desperate efforts to get at the mistletoe berries by clinging to the underside of the snow-crowned masses, back downward, something like woodpeckers. Every now and then some of the loose snow was dislodged and sifted down on the hungry birds, sending them screaming back to their companions in the grove, shivering and muttering like cold, hungry children.

Some of the sparrows were busy scratching and pecking at the feet of the larger trees where the snow had been shed off, gleaning seeds and benumbed insects, joined now and then by a robin weary of his unsuccessful efforts to get at the snow-covered mistletoe berries. The brave woodpeckers were clinging to the snowless sides of the larger boles and overarching branches of the camp trees, making short flights from side to side of the grove, pecking now and then at the acorns they had stored in the bark, and chattering aimlessly as if unable to keep still, evidently putting in the time in a very dull way. The hardy nuthatches were threading the open furrows of the barks in their usual industrious manner and uttering their quaint notes, giving no evidence of distress. The Steller's jays were, of course, making more noise and stir than all the other birds combined, ever coming and going with loud bluster, screaming as if each had a lump of melting sludge in his throat, and taking good care to improve every opportunity afforded by the darkness and confusion of the storm to steal from the acorn stores of the woodpeckers. One of the golden eagles made an impressive picture as he stood bolt upright on the top of a tall pine stump, braving the storm, with his back to the wind and a tuft of snow piled on his broad shoulders, a monument of passive endurance. Thus every storm-bound bird seemed more or less uncomfortable, if not in distress. The storm was reflected in every gesture, and not one cheerful note, not to say song, came from a single bill. Their cowering, joyless endurance offered striking contrasts to the spontaneous, irrepressible gladness of the ouzel, who could no more help giving out sweet song than a rose sweet fragrance. He must sing, though the heavens fall.

Yosemite Falls

24

A Close Call on the Obelisk

Clarence King

Delightful oaks cast protecting shadows over our camp on the 1st of June, 1866. Just beyond a little cook-fire where Hoover was preparing his mind and pan for an omelet stood Mrs. Fremont's Mariposa cottage, with doors and windows wide open, still keeping up its air of hospitable invitation, though now deserted and fallen into decay. A little farther on, through an opening, a few clustered roofs and chimneys of the Bear Valley village showed their distant red-brown tint among heavy masses of green. Eastward swelled up a great ridge, upon whose grassy slopes were rough, serpentine outcrops—groups of pines, and oak groves with pale green foliage and clean white bark. Under the roots of this famous Mount Bullion have been mined those gold veins whose treasure enriched so few, whose promise allured so many.

So now in June, I climbed on a Sunday morning to my old retreat, found the same stone seat, with leaning oak-tree back, and wide, low canopy of boughs. A little down to the left, welling among tufts of grass and waving tulips, is the spring which Mrs. Fremont found for her campground. North and south for miles extends our ridge in gently rising or falling outline, its top broadly round, and for the most part an open oak grove with grass carpet and mountain flowers in wayward loveliness of growth. West, you overlook a wide panorama. Oak and pine-mottled foothills, with rusty groundwork and cloudings of green, wander down in rolling lines to the ripe plain; beyond are plains, then Coast Ranges, rising in peaks, or curved down in passes, through which gray banks of fog drift in and vanish before the hot air of the plains. East, the Sierra slope is rent and gashed in a wilderness of canyons, yawning deep and savage. Miles of chaparral tangle in dense growth over walls and spurs, covering with kindly olive-green the staring red of riven mountainside and gashed earth. Beyond this swells up the more refined plateau and hill country made of granite and trimmed with pine, bold domes rising above the green cover; and there the sharp, terrible front of El Capitan, guarding

Yosemite and looking down into its purple gulf. Beyond, again, are the peaks, and among them one looms sharpest. It is that Obelisk from which the great storm drove Cotter and me in 1864. We were now bound to push there as soon as grass should grow among the upper canyons.

Mountain oaks, less wonderful than great, straight pines, but altogether domestic in their generous way of reaching out low, long boughs, roofing in spots of shade, are the only trees on the Pacific slope which seem to me at all allied to men. And these quiet foothill summits, these islands of modest, lovely verdure floating in an ocean of sunlight, lifted enough above San Joaquin plains to reach pure, high air and thrill your blood and brain with mountain oxygen, are yet far enough below the rugged wildness of pine and ice and rock to leave you in peace, and not forever challenge you to combat. They are almost the only places in the Sierras impressing me as rightly fitted for human company. I cannot find in wholesale vineyards and ranches dotted along the Sierra foot anything which savors of the eternal indigenous perfume of home. They are scenes of speculation and thrift, of immense enterprise and comfort, with no end of fences and square miles of grain, with here and there astounding specimens of modern upholstery, to say nothing of pianos with elaborate legs and always discordant keys; but they never comfort the soul with that air of sacred household reserve, of simple human poetry, which elsewhere greets you under plainer roofs, and broods over your days and nights familiarly.

Here on these still summits the oaks lock their arms and gather in groves around open slopes of natural park, and you are at home. A cottage or a castle would seem in keeping, nor would the savage gorges and snowcapped Sierras overcome the sober kindliness of these affectionate trees. It is almost as hard now, as I write, to turn my back on Mount Bullion and descend to camp again, as it was that afternoon in 1866.

From some upsurging crag upon its brink you look out over wide expanse of granite swells, upon whose solid surface the firs climb and cluster, and afar on the skyline only darken together in one deep green cover. Upward heave the eastern ridges; above them looms a white rank of peaks. Into this plateau is rent a chasm; the fresh-splintered granite falls down, down, thousands of feet in sheer, blank faces or giant crags broken in cleft and stair, gorge and bluff, down till they sink under that winding ribbon of park with its flash of river among sunlit grass, its darkness, where, within shadows of jutting wall, cloud-like gather the pine companies, or, in summer opening, stand oak and cottonwood, casting together their lengthening shadow over meadow and pool. The falls, like torrents of snow, pour in white lines over purple precipice, or, as the wind wills, float and drift in vanishing film of airy lacework.

Two leading ideas are wrought here with a force hardly to be seen elsewhere. First, the titanic power, the awful stress, which has rent this solid table-land of granite in twain; secondly, the magical faculty displayed by vegetation in redeeming the aspect of wreck and masking a vast geological tragedy behind draperies of fresh and living green. I can never cease marveling how all this terrible crush and sundering is made fair, even lovely, by meadow, by wandering groves, and by those climbing files of pine which thread every gorge and camp in armies over every brink.

The three great falls of America—Niagara, Shoshone, and Yosemite—all, happily, bearing Indian names, are as characteristically different as possible. There seems little left for a cataract to express.

Niagara rolls forward with something like the inexorable sway of a natural law. It is force, power; forever banishing before its irresistible rush all ideas of restraint.

No sheltering pine or mountain distance of up-piled Sierras guards the approach to the Shoshone. You ride upon a waste—the pale earth stretched in desolation. Suddenly you stand upon a brink, as if the earth had yawned. Black walls flank the abyss. Deep in the bed, a great river fights its way through labyrinths of blackened ruins, and plunges in foaming whiteness over a cliff of lava. You turn from the brink as from a frightful glimpse of the Inferno, and when you have gone a mile, the earth seems to have closed again. Every trace of canyon has vanished, and the stillness of the desert reigns.

As you stand at the base of those cool walls of granite that rise to the clouds from the green floor of Yosemite, a beautiful park, carpeted with verdure, expands from your feet. Vast and stately pines band with their shadows the sunny reaches of the pure Merced. An arch of blue bridges over from cliff to cliff. From the far summit of a wall of pearly granite, over stains of purple and yellow—leaping, as it were, from the very cloud— falls a silver scarf, light, lace-like, graceful, luminous, swayed by the wind. The cliffs' repose is undisturbed by the silvery fall, whose endlessly varying forms of wind-tossed spray lend an element of life to what would otherwise be masses of inanimate stone. The Yosemite is a grace. It is an adornment. It is a ray of light on the solid front of the precipice.

From Yosemite our course was bent toward the Merced Obelisk. An afternoon in early July brought us to camp in the self-same spot where Cotter and I had bivouacked in the storm more than two years before. I remembered the crash and wail of those two dreary nights, the thunderous fullness of tempest beating upon cliffs, and the stealthy, silent snow-burial, and perhaps to the memory of that bitter experience was added the contrasting force of today's beauty.

A warm afternoon sun poured through cloudless skies into one rocky amphitheater. The little alpine meadow and full, arrowy brook were flanked upon either side by broad, rounded masses of granite, and margined by groups of vigorous upland trees: firs for the most part, but watched over here and there by towering pines and great, aged junipers whose massive red trunks seemed welded to the very stone.

For the first time that year we found ourselves slowly zigzagging to and fro, following a grade with that peculiarly deliberate gait to which mountaineering experience very soon confines one. Black firs and thick-clustered pines covered in clumps all the lower slope, but, ascending, we came more and more into open ground, walking on glacial debris among trains of huge boulders and occasional thickets of slender, delicate young trees. Emerging finally into open granite country, we came full in sight of our goal, whose great western precipice rose sheer and solid above us.

From the south base of the Obelisk a sharp mural ridge curves east, surrounding an amphitheater whose sloping, rugged sides were picturesquely mottled in snow and stone. From the summit of this ridge we knew we should look over into the upper Merced basin, a great, billowy, granite depression lying between the Merced group and Mount Lyell, the birthplace of all those ice rivers and deep-canyoned torrents which join in the Little Yosemite and form the river Merced. Toward this we pressed, hurrying rapidly, as the sun declined, in hopes of making our point before darkness should obscure the terra incognita beyond.

It put us at our best to hasten over the rough, rudely piled blocks and up cracks among solid bluffs of granite, but with the sun fully half an hour high we reached the Obelisk foot and looked from our ridgetop eastward into the new land.

From our feet, granite and ice in steep, roof-like curves fell abruptly down to the Merced Canyon brink, and beyond, over the great gulf, rose terraces and ridges of sculptured stone, dressed with snowfield, one above another, up to the eastern rank of peaks whose sharp, solid forms were still in full light.

From below, it is always a most interesting feature of the mountaineer's daily life to watch fading sunlight upon the summit rocks and snow. There is something peculiarly charming in the deep carmine flush and in the pale gradations of violet and cool blue-purple into which it successively fades. We were now in the very midst of this alpine glow. Our rocky amphitheater, opening directly to the sun, was crowded full of this pure, red light. Snowfields warmed to deepest rose, gnarled stems of dead pines were dark vermilion, the rocks yellow, and the vast body of the Obelisk at our left one spire of gold piercing the sapphire zenith. Eastward, far below us, the Illilouette basin lay in a peculiarly mild haze, its deep carpet of forest warmed into faint bronze, and the bare domes and rounded, granite ridges which everywhere rise above the trees were yellow, of a soft, creamy tint. Farther down, every foothill was perceptibly reddened under the level beams. Sunlight reflecting from every object shot up to us, enriching the brightness of our amphitheater.

We drank and breathed the light, its mellow warmth permeating every fiber. We spread our blankets under the lee of an overhanging rock, sheltered from the keen east wind, and in full view of the broad western horizon.

After a short half-hour of this wonderful light the sun rested for an instant upon the Coast Ranges, and sank, leaving our mountains suddenly dead, as if the very breath of life had ebbed away, cold, gray shadows covering their rigid bodies, and pale sheets of snow half shrouding their forms.

For a full hour after the sun went down we did little else than study the western sky, watching with greatest interest a wonderful permanence and singular gradation of lingering light. Over two hundred miles of horizon, a low stratum of pure orange covered the sky for seven or eight degrees; above that another narrow band of beryl-green, and then the cool, dark evening blue.

I always notice, whenever one gets a very wide view of remote horizon from some lofty mountaintop, the sky loses its high domed appearance, the gradations reaching but a few degrees upward from the earth, creating the general form of an inverted saucer. The orange and beryl bands occupied only about fifteen degrees in altitude, but swept around nearly from north to south. It was as if a wonderfully transparent and brilliant rainbow had been stretched along the skyline. At eleven, the colors were still perceptible, and at midnight, when I rose to observe the thermometer, they were gone, but a low faint zone of light still lingered.

At gray dawn we were up and cooking our rasher of bacon, and soon had shouldered our instruments and started for the top.

The Obelisk is flattened, and expands its base into two sharp, serrated ridges, which form its north and south edges. The broad faces turned to the east and west are solid and utterly inaccessible, the latter being almost vertical, the former quite too steep to climb. We started, therefore, to work our way up the south edge, and, having crossed a little ravine from whose head we could look down eastward upon steep thousand-foot névé, and westward along the forest-covered ridge up which we had clambered, began in good earnest to mount rough blocks of granite.

The edge here is made of immense, broken rocks poised on each other in delicate balance, vast masses threatening to topple over at a touch. This blade has from a distance a considerably smooth and even appearance, but we found it composed of pinnacles often a hundred feet high, separated from the main top by a deep, vertical cleft. More than once, after struggling to the top of one of these pinnacles, we were obliged to climb down the same way in order to avoid the notches. Finally, when we had reached the brink of a vertical cul-de-sac, the edge no longer afforded us even a foothold. There were left but the smooth, impossible western face and the treacherous, cracked front of the eastern precipice. We were driven out upon the latter, and here forced to climb with the very greatest care, one of us always in advance making sure of his foothold, the other passing up instruments by hand, and then cautiously following.

In this way we spent nearly a full hour going from crack to crack, clinging by the least protruding masses of stone, now and then looking over our shoulders at the wreck of granite, the slopes of ice, and frozen lake thousands of feet below, and then upward to gather courage from the bold, red spike which still rose grandly above us.

At last we struggled up to what we had all along believed the summit, and found ourselves only on a minor turret, the great needle still a hundred feet above. From rock to rock and crevice to crevice we made our way up a fractured edge until within fifty feet of the top, and here its sharp angle rose smooth and vertical, the eastern precipice carved in a flat face upon the one side, the western broken by a smoothly curved recess like the corner of a room. No human being could scale the edge. An arctic bluebird fluttered along the eastern slope in vain quest of a foothold, and alighted, panting, at our feet. One step more and we stood together on a little, detached pinnacle, where, by steadying ourselves against the sharp, vertical Obelisk edge, we could rest, although the keen sense of steepness below was not altogether pleasing.

About seven feet across the open head of a cul-de-sac (a mere recess in the west face) was a vertical crack riven into the granite not more than three feet wide, but as much as eight feet deep; in it were wedged a few loose boulders; below, it opened out into space. At the head of this crack a rough crevice led up to the summit.

Summoning nerve, I knew I could make the leap, but the life and death question was whether the debris would give way under my weight, and leave me struggling in the smooth recess, sure to fall and be dashed to atoms.

Two years we had longed to climb that peak, and now, within a few yards of the summit, no weak-heartedness could stop us. I thought, should the debris give way, by a very quick turn and powerful spring I could regain our rock in safety.

There was no discussion, but, planting my foot on the brink, I sprang, my side brushing the rough, projecting crag. While in the air I looked down, and a picture stamped itself on my brain never to be forgotten. The debris crumbled and moved. I clutched both sides of the cleft, relieving all possible weight from my feet. The rocks wedged themselves again, and I was safe.

It was a delicate feat of balancing for us to bridge that chasm with a transit and pass it across. The view it afforded down the abyss was calculated to make a man cool and steady.

Barometer and knapsack were next passed over. I placed them all at the crevice head, and flattened myself against the rock to make room for Gardiner. I shall never forget the look in his eye as he caught a glimpse of the abyss in his leap. It gave me such a chill as no amount of danger, or even death, coming to myself could ever give. The debris grated under his weight an instant and wedged itself again.

We sprang up on the rocks like chamois, and stood on the top shouting for joy.

Our summit was four feet across, not large enough for the transit instrument and both of us, so I, whose duties were geological, descended to a niche a few feet lower and sat down to my writing.

The sense of aerial isolation was thrilling. Away below, rocks, ridges, crags, and fields of ice swell up in jostling confusion to make a base from which springs the spire of stone eleven thousand six hundred feet high. On all sides I could look right down at the narrow pedestal. Eastward, great ranks of peaks, culminating in Mount Lyell, were in full, clear view. All streams and canyons tributary to the Merced were beneath us in map-like distinctness. Afar to the west lay the rolling plateau gashed with canyons; there the white line of Yosemite Fall; and beyond, half submerged in warm haze, my Sunday mountain.

The same little arctic bluebird came again and perched close by me, pouring out his sweet, simple song with a gayety and freedom which wholly charmed me.

During our four hours' stay, the thought that we must make that leap again gradually intruded itself, and whether writing or studying the country I could not altogether free myself from its pressure.

It was a relief when we packed up and descended to the horrible cleft to actually meet our danger. We had now an unreliable footing to spring from, and a mere block of rock to balance us after the jump.

We sprang strongly, struck firmly, and were safe. We worked patiently down the east face, wound among blocks and pinnacles of the lower descent, and hurried through moraines to camp, well pleased that the Obelisk had not vanquished us.

Half Dome from Glacier Point

25

How Best To Spend One's Yosemite Time

John Muir

One-Day Excursions—No. 1

If I were so time-poor as to have only one day to spend in
Yosemite, I should start at daybreak, say at three o'clock in mid-
summer, with a pocketful of any sort of dry breakfast stuff, for
Glacier Point, Sentinel Dome, the head of Illilouette Fall,

Nevada Fall, the top of Liberty Cap, Vernal Fall and the wild boulder-choked river canyon. The trail leaves the valley at the base of Sentinel Rock, and as you slowly saunter from point to point along its many accommodating zigzags, nearly all the valley rocks and falls are seen in striking, ever-changing combinations. At an elevation of about five hundred feet, a particularly fine, wide-sweeping view down the valley is obtained, past the sheer face of the Sentinel and between the Cathedral Rocks and El Capitan. At a height of about fifteen hundred feet, the great Half Dome comes full in sight, overshadowing every other feature of the valley to the eastward. From Glacier Point you look down three thousand feet over the edge of its sheer face to the meadows and groves and innumerable yellow pine spires, with the meandering river sparkling and spangling through the midst of them. Across the valley, a great telling view is presented of the Royal Arches, North Dome, Indian Canyon, Three Brothers and El Capitan, with the dome-paved basin of Yosemite Creek and Mount Hoffman in the background. To the eastward, Half Dome close beside you looking higher and more wonderful than ever; southeastward the Starr King, girdled with silver firs, and the spacious garden-like basin of the Illilouette and its deeply sculptured fountain-peaks, called "The Merced Group"; and beyond all, marshaled along the eastern horizon, the icy summits on the axis of the range and broad swaths of forests growing on ancient moraines, while the Nevada, Vernal, and Yosemite Falls are not only full in sight but are distinctly heard as if one were standing beside them in their spray.

The views from the summit of Sentinel Dome are still more extensive and telling. Eastward, the crowds of peaks at the head of the Merced, Tuolumne and San Joaquin Rivers are presented in bewildering array; westward, the vast forests, yellow foothills and the broad San Joaquin plains and the Coast Ranges, hazy and dim in the distance.

From Glacier Point, go down the trail into the lower end of the Illilouette basin, cross Illilouette Creek and follow it to the Fall where from an outjutting rock at its head you will get a fine view of its rejoicing waters and wild canyon and Half Dome. Thence returning to the trail, follow it to the head of Nevada Fall. Linger here an hour or two, for not only have you glorious views of the wonderful fall, but of its wild, leaping, exulting rapids and, greater than all, the stupendous scenery into the heart of which the white passionate river goes wildly thundering, surpassing everything of its kind in the world. After an unmeasured hour or so of this glory, all your body aglow, nerve currents flashing through you never before felt, go to the top of Liberty Cap, only a glad saunter now that your legs as well as head and heart are awake and rejoicing with everything. Liberty Cap, a companion of Half Dome, is sheer and inaccessible on three of its sides, but on the east, a gentle, ice-burnished, juniper-dotted slope extends to the summit where other wonderful views are displayed: the south side and shoulders of Half Dome and Clouds Rest, the beautiful Little Yosemite Valley and its many domes, the Starr King cluster of domes, Sentinel Dome, Glacier Point, and, perhaps the most tremendously impressive of all, the views of the hopper-shaped canyon of the river from the head of Nevada Fall to the head of the valley.

Returning to the trail, you descend between Nevada Fall and Liberty Cap with fine side views of both the fall and the rock, pass on through clouds of spray and along the rapids to the lead of Vernal Fall, about a mile below Nevada. Linger here if night is still distant, for views of this favorite fall and the stupendous rock scenery about it. Then descend a stairway by its side, follow a dim trail through its spray, and a plain one along the border of the boulder-dashed rapids and so back to the wide, tranquil valley.

One-Day Excursions—No. 2

Another grand one-day excursion is to Upper Yosemite Fall, the top of the highest of the Three Brothers, called Eagle Peak on the Geological Survey maps; the brow of El Capitan; the head of Ribbon Fall; across the beautiful Ribbon Creek Basin; and back to the valley by the Big Oak Flat wagon-road.

The trail leaves the valley on the east side of the largest of the earthquake taluses immediately opposite Sentinel Rock, and as it passes within a few rods of the foot of the great fall, magnificent views are obtained as you approach it and pass through its spray. When the snow is melting fast you will be well drenched. From the foot of the fall, the trail zigzags up a narrow canyon between the fall and a plain mural cliff that is burnished here and there by glacial action.

You should stop a while on a flat iron-fenced rock a little below the head of the fall beside the enthusiastic throng of starry comet-like waters to learn something of their strength, their marvelous variety of forms, and above all, their glorious music, gathered and composed from the snow-, hail-, rain-, and wind-storms that have fallen on their glacier-sculptured, domey, ridgy basin. Refreshed and exhilarated, you follow your trailway through silver fir and pine woods to Eagle Peak, where the most comprehensive of all the views to be had on the north-wall heights are displayed. After an hour or two of gazing, dreaming, studying the tremendous topography, trace the rim of the valley to the grand El Capitan ridge and go down to its brow, where you will gain everlasting impressions of Nature's steadfastness and power combined with ineffable fineness of beauty.

Dragging yourself away, go to the head of Ribbon Fall, thence across the beautiful Ribbon Creek Basin to the Big Oak Flat stage-road, and down its fine grades to the valley, enjoying glorious Yosemite scenery all the way to the foot of El Capitan and your camp.

Two-Day Excursions—No. 1

For a two-day trip, I would go straight to Mount Hoffman, spend the night on the summit, next morning go down by May Lake to Tenaya Lake and return to the valley by Clouds Rest and Nevada and Vernal Falls. As on the foregoing excursion, you leave the valley by the Yosemite Falls trail and follow it to the Tioga wagon-road, a short distance east of Porcupine Flat. From that point, push straight up to the summit. Mount Hoffman is a mass of gray granite that rises almost in the center of Yosemite Park, about eight or ten miles in a straight line from the valley. Its southern slopes are low and easily climbed, and adorned here and there with castle-like crumbling piles and long jagged crests that look like artificial masonry. On the north side, it is abruptly precipitous and banked with lasting snow. Most of the broad summit is comparatively level and thick sown with crystals, quartz, mica, hornblende, feldspar, granite, zircon, tourmaline, etc., weathered out and strewn closely and loosely as if they had been sown broadcast. Their radiance is fairly dazzling in sunlight, almost hiding the multitude of small flowers that grow among them. At first sight, only these radiant crystals are likely to be noticed, but looking closely you discover a multitude of very small gilias, phloxes, *Mimulus*, etc., many of them with more petals than leaves. On the borders of little streams larger plants flourish—lupines, daisies, asters, goldenrods, harebell, mountain columbine, *Potentilla*, *Astragalus*, and a few gentians; with charming heathwort—*Bryanthus*, *Cassiope*, *Kalmia*, *Vaccinium* in boulder-fringing rings or bank covers. You saunter among the crystals and flowers as if you were walking among stars. From the summit, nearly all Yosemite Park is displayed like a map: forests, lakes, meadows, and snowy peaks. Northward lies Yosemite's wide basin with its domes and small lakes, shining like larger crystals; eastward the rocky, meadowy Tuolumne region, bounded by its snowy peaks in glorious array; southward Yosemite and westward the vast forest. On no other Yosemite Park mountain are you more likely to linger. You will find it a magnificent sky camp. Clumps of dwarf pine and mountain hemlock will furnish resin roots and branches for fuel and light, and the rills, sparkling water. Thousands of the little plant people will gaze at your campfire with the crystals and stars, companions and guardians as you lie at rest in the heart of the vast serene night.

The most telling of all the wide Hoffman views is the basin of the Tuolumne with its meadows, forests, and hundreds of smooth rock-waves that appear to be coming rolling on towards you like high heaving waves ready to break, and beyond these, the great mountains. But best of all are the dawn and the sunrise. No mountain top could be better placed for this most glorious of mountain view—to watch and see the deepening colors of the dawn and the sunbeams streaming through the snowy High Sierra passes, awakening the lakes and crystals, the chilled plant people and winged people, and making everything shine and sing in pure glory.

With your heart aglow, spangling Lake Tenaya and Lake May will beckon you away for walks on their ice-burnished shores. Leave Tenaya at the west end, cross to the south side of the outlet, and gradually work your way up in an almost straight south direction to the summit of the divide between Tenaya Creek and the main upper Merced River or Nevada Creek and follow the divide to Clouds Rest. After a glorious view from the crest of this lofty granite wave, you will find a trail on its western end that will lead you down past Nevada and Vernal Falls to the valley in good time, provided you left your Hoffman sky camp early.

Two-Day Excursions—No. 2

Another grand two-day excursion is the same as the first of the one-day trips, as far as the head of Illilouette Fall. From there, trace the beautiful stream up through the heart of its magnificent forests and gardens to the canyons between the Red and Merced Peaks, and pass the night where I camped forty-one years ago. Early next morning, visit the small glacier on the north side of Merced Peak, the first of the sixty-five that I discovered in the Sierra.

Glacial phenomena in the Illilouette Basin are on the grandest scale, and in the course of my explorations I found that the canyon and moraines between the Merced and Red

Mountains were the most interesting of them all. The path of the vanished glacier shone in many places as if washed with silver, and pushing up the canyon on this bright road I passed lake after lake in solid basins of granite and many a meadow along the canyon stream that links them together. The main lateral moraines that bound the view below the canyon are from a hundred to nearly two hundred feet high and wonderfully regular, like artificial embankments covered with a magnificent growth of silver fir and pine. But this garden and forest luxuriance is speedily left behind, and patches of *Bryanthus*, *Cassiope*, and arctic willows begin to appear. The small lakes, which a few miles down the valley are so richly bordered with flowery meadows, have at an elevation of ten thousand feet only small brown mats of *Carex*, leaving bare rocks around more than half their shores. Yet, strange to say, amid all this arctic repression, the mountain pine on ledges and buttresses of Red Mountain seems to find the climate best suited to it. Some specimens that I measured were over a hundred feet high and twenty-four feet in circumference, showing hardly a trace of severe storms, looking as fresh and vigorous as the giants of the lower zones. Evening came on just as I got fairly into the main canyon. It is about a mile wide and a little less than two miles long. The crumbling spurs of Red Mountain bound it on the north, the somber cliffs of Merced Mountain on the south and a deeply-serrated, splintered ridge curving around from mountain to mountain shuts it in on the east. My camp was on the brink of one of the lakes in a thicket of mountain hemlock, partly sheltered from the wind. Early next morning, I set out to trace the ancient glacier to its head. Passing around the north shore of my camp lake I followed the main stream from one lakelet to another. The dwarf pines and hemlocks disappeared and the stream was bordered with icicles. The main lateral moraines that extend from the mouth of the canyon are continued in straggling masses along the walls. Tracing the streams back to the highest of its little lakes, I noticed a deposit of fine gray mud, something like the mud corn from a grindstone. This suggested its glacial origin, for the stream that was carrying it issued from a raw-looking moraine that seemed to be in process of formation. It is from sixty to over a hundred feet high in front, with a slope of about thirty-eight degrees. Climbing to the top of it, I discovered a very small but well-characterized glacier swooping down from the shadowy cliffs of the mountain to its terminal moraine. The ice appeared on all the lower portion of the glacier; farther up it was covered with snow. The uppermost crevasse was from twelve to fourteen feet wide. The melting snow and ice formed a network of rills that ran gracefully down the surface of the glacier, merrily singing in their shining channels. After this discovery, I made excursions over all the High Sierra and discovered that what at first sight looked like snowfields were in great part glaciers which were completing the sculpture of the summit peaks.

Rising early—which will be easy, as your bed will be rather cold and you will not be able to sleep much anyhow—after visiting the glacier, climb Red Mountain and enjoy the magnificent views from the summit. I counted forty lakes from one standpoint on this mountain, and the views to the westward over the Illilouette Basin, the most superbly forested of all the basins whose waters rain into Yosemite, and those of the Yosemite rocks, especially Half Dome and the upper part of the north wall, are very fine. But, of course, far the most imposing view is the vast array of snowy peaks along the axis of the range. Then from the top of this peak, light and free and exhilarated with mountain air and mountain beauty, you should run lightly down the northern slope of the mountain, descend the canyon between Red and Gray Mountains, thence northward along the bases of Gray Mountain and Mount Clark, and go down into the head of Little Yosemite, and thence down past Nevada and Vernal Falls to the valley, a truly glorious two-day trip!

A Three-Day Excursion

The best three-day excursion, as far as I can see, is the same as the first of the two-day trips until you reach Lake Tenaya. There instead of returning to the valley, follow Tioga Road around the northwest side of the lake, over to Tuolumne Meadows and up to the west base of Mount Dana. Leave the road there and make straight for the highest point on the timberline between Mounts Dana and Gibbs and camp there.

On the morning of the third day, go to the top of Mount Dana in time for the glory of the dawn and the sunrise over the gray Mono Desert and the sublime forest of High Sierra peaks. When you leave the mountain, go far enough down the north side for a view of the Dana Glacier, then make your way back to Tioga Road, follow it along Tuolumne Meadows to the crossing of Budd Creek where you will find the Sunrise trail branching off up the mountainside through the forest in a southwesterly direction past the west side of Cathedral Peak, which will lead you down to the valley by Vernal and Nevada Falls. If you are a good walker, you can leave the trail where it begins to descend a steep slope in the silver fir woods and bear off to the right and make straight for the top of Clouds Rest. The walking is good and almost level, and from the west end of Clouds Rest take the Clouds Rest Trail, which will lead direct to the valley by Nevada and Vernal Falls. To any one not desperately time-poor this trip should have four days instead of three; camping the second night at Soda Springs; thence to Mount Dana and return to Soda Springs, camping the third night there; thence by the Sunrise trail to Cathedral Peak, visiting the beautiful Cathedral Lake which lies about a mile to the west of Cathedral Peak, eating your luncheon, and thence to Clouds Rest and the valley as above. This is one of the most interesting of all the comparatively short trips that can be made in the whole Yosemite region. Not only do you see all the grandest of the Yosemite rocks and waterfalls and the High Sierra with their glaciers, glacier lakes, and glacier meadows, etc., but sections of the magnificent silver fir, two-leaved pine, and dwarf pine zones; with the principal alpine flowers and shrubs, especially sods of dwarf *Vaccinium* covered with flowers and fruit though less than an inch high, broad mats of dwarf willow scarce an inch high with catkins that rise straight from the ground, and glorious beds of blue gentians—grandeur enough and beauty enough for a lifetime.

The Upper Tuolumne Excursion

We come now to the grandest of all the Yosemite excursions, one that requires at least two or three weeks. The best time to make it is from about the middle of July. The visitor entering Yosemite in July has the advantage of seeing the falls not perhaps in their very flood prime, but next thing to it, while the glacier meadows will be in their glory and the snow on the mountains will be firm enough to make climbing safe. Long ago I made these Sierra trips, carrying only a sackful of bread with a little tea and sugar and was thus independent and free, but now that trails or carriage roads lead out of the valley in almost every direction, it is easy to take a pack animal, so that the luxury of a blanket and a supply of food can easily be had.

The best way to leave the valley will be by the Yosemite Fall trail, camping the first night on Tioga Road opposite the east end of the Hoffman Range. Next morning climb Mount Hoffman. Thence push on past Tenaya Lake into Tuolumne Meadows and establish a central camp near Soda Springs, from which glorious excursions can be made at your leisure. For here, in this upper Tuolumne Valley, is the widest, smoothest, most serenely spacious and in every way the most delightful summer pleasure-park in all the High Sierra. And since it is connected with Yosemite by two good trails, and a fairly good carriage road that passes between Yosemite and Mount Hoffman, it is also the most accessible. It is in the heart of the High Sierra east of Yosemite, eighty-five hundred to nine thousand feet above the level of the sea. The gray, picturesque Cathedral Range bounds it on the south; a similar range or spur, the highest peak of which is Mount Conness, on the north; the noble Mounts Dana, Gibbs, Mammoth, Lyell, McClure and others on the axis of the range on the east; a heaving, billowing crowd of glacier-polished rocks and Mount Hoffman on the west. Down through the open sunny meadow-levels of the valley flows the Tuolumne River, fresh and cool from its many glacial fountains, the highest of which are the glaciers that lie on the north sides of Mount Lyell and Mount McClure.

Along the river a series of beautiful glacier-meadows extend with but little interruption, from the lower end of the valley to its head, a distance of about twelve miles, forming charming sauntering-grounds from which the glorious mountains may be enjoyed as they look down in divine serenity over the dark forests that clothe their bases. Narrow strips of pine woods cross the meadow carpet from side to side, and it is somewhat roughened here and there by moraine boulders and dead trees brought down from the heights by snow avalanches. But for miles and miles it is so smooth and level that a hundred horsemen may ride abreast over it.

The main lower portion of the meadows is about four miles long and from a quarter to half a mile wide, but the width of the valley is, on an average, about eight miles. Tracing the river, we find that it forks a mile above Soda Springs, the main fork turning southward to Mount Lyell, the other eastward to Mount Dana and Mount Gibbs. Along both forks, strips of meadow extend almost to their heads. The most beautiful portions of the meadows are spread over lake basins, which have been filled up by deposits from the river. A few of these river-lakes still exist, but they are now shallow and are rapidly approaching extinction. The sod in most places is exceedingly fine and silky and free from weeds and bushes, while charming flowers abound, especially gentians, dwarf daisies, *Potentillas*, and the pink bells of dwarf *Vaccinium*. On the banks of the river and its tributaries, *Cassiope* and *Bryanthus* may be found where the sod curls over stream banks and around boulders. The principal grass of these meadows is a delicate *Calamagrostis* with very slender filiform leaves, and when it is in flower, the ground seems to be covered with a faint purple mist, the stems of the panicles being so fine that they are almost invisible, and offer no appreciable resistance in walking through them. Along the edges of the meadows beneath the pines and throughout the greater part of the valley, tall ribbon-leaved grasses grow in abundance, chiefly *Bromus*, *Triticum*, and *Agrostis*.

In October, the nights are frosty, and then the meadows at sunrise, when every leaf is laden with crystals, are a fine sight. The days are still warm and calm, and bees and butterflies continue to waver and hum about the late-blooming flowers until the coming of the snow, usually in November. Storm then follows storm in quick succession, burying the meadows to a depth of from ten to twenty feet, while magnificent avalanches descend through the forests from the laden heights, depositing huge piles of snow mixed with uprooted trees and boulders. In the open sunshine the snow usually lasts until the end of June, but the new season's vegetation is not generally in bloom until late in July. Perhaps the best all-round excursion-time after winters of average snowfall is from the middle of July to the middle or end of August. The snow is then melted from the woods and southern slopes of the mountains, and the meadows and gardens are in their glory, while the weather is mostly all-reviving, exhilarating sunshine. The few clouds that rise now and then and the showers they yield are only enough to keep everything fresh and fragrant.

The groves about Soda Springs are favorite camping grounds on account of the cold, pleasant-tasting water charged with carbonic acid, and because of the views of the mountains across the meadow—Glacier Monument, Cathedral Peak, Cathedral Spires, Unicorn Peak, and a series of ornamental nameless companions, rising in striking forms and nearness above a dense forest growing on the left lateral moraine of the ancient Tuolumne glacier, which, broad, deep, and far-reaching, exerted vast influence on the scenery of this portion of the Sierra. But there are fine camping grounds all along the meadows, and one may move from grove to grove every day all summer, enjoying new homes and new beauty to satisfy every roving desire for change.

There are five main capital excursions to be made from here—to the summits of Mounts Dana, Lyell and Conness, and through the Bloody Canyon Pass to Mono Lake and the volcanoes, and down Tuolumne Canyon, at least as far as the foot of the wonderful series of river cataracts. All of these excursions are sure to be made memorable with joyful health-giving experiences, but perhaps none of them will be remembered with keener delight than the days spent sauntering on the broad velvet lawns by the river, sharing the sky with the mountains and trees, gaining something of their strength and peace.

The excursion to the top of Mount Dana is a very easy one, for though the mountain is thirteen thousand feet high, the ascent from the west side is so gentle and smooth that one may ride a mule to the very summit. Across many a busy stream, from meadow to meadow, lies your flowery way, mountains all about you, few of them hidden by irregular foregrounds. Gradually ascending, other mountains come in sight, peak rising above peak with their snow and ice in endless variety of grouping and sculpture. Now your attention is turned to the moraines, sweeping in beautiful curves from the hollows and canyons, now to the granite waves and pavements rising here and there above the heathy sod, polished a thousand years ago and still shining. Towards the base of the mountain you note the dwarfing of the trees, until at a height of about eleven thousand feet you find patches of the tough, whitebark pine, pressed so flat by the ten or twenty feet of snow piled upon them every winter for centuries that you may walk over them as if walking on a shaggy rug. And, if curious about such things, you may discover specimens of this hardy tree-mountaineer not more than four feet high and about as many inches in diameter at the ground, that are from two hundred to four hundred years old, still holding bravely to life, making the most of their slender summers, shaking their tasseled needles in the breeze right cheerily, drinking the thin sunshine and maturing their fine purple cones as if they meant to live forever. The general view from the summit is one of the most extensive and sublime to be found in all the range. To the eastward, you gaze far out over the desert plains and mountains of the Great Basin, range beyond range extending with soft outlines, blue and purple in the distance. More than six thousand feet below you lies Lake Mono, ten miles in diameter from north to south, and fourteen from west to east, lying bare in the treeless desert like a disk of burnished metal, though at times it is swept by mountain storm winds and streaked with foam. To the southward, there is a well-defined range of pale-gray extinct volcanoes, and though the highest of them rises nearly two thousand feet above the lake, you can look down from here into their circular, cup-like craters, from which a comparatively short time ago ashes and cinders were showered over the surrounding sage plains and glacier-laden mountains.

To the westward, the landscape is made up of exceedingly strong, gray, glaciated domes and ridge waves, most of them comparatively low, but the largest high enough to be called mountains; separated by canyons and darkened with lines and fields of forest, Cathedral Peak, and Mount Hoffman in the distance; small lakes and innumerable meadows in the foreground. Northward and southward, the great snowy mountains, marshaled along the axis of the range, are seen in all their glory, crowded together in some places like trees in groves, making landscapes of wild, extravagant, bewildering magnificence, yet calm and silent as the sky.

Some eight glaciers are in sight. One of these is the Dana Glacier on the north side of the mountain, lying at the foot of a precipice about a thousand feet high, with a lovely pale-green lake a little below it. This is one of the many, small, shrunken remnants of the vast glacial system of the Sierra that once filled the hollows and valleys of the mountains and covered all the lower ridges below the immediate summit fountains, flowing to right and left away from the axis of the range, lavishly fed by the snows of the glacial period.

In the excursion to Mount Lyell, the immediate base of the mountain is easily reached on meadow walks along the river. Turning to the southward above the forks of the river, you enter the narrow Lyell branch of the valley, narrow enough and deep enough to be called a canyon. It is about eight miles long and from two thousand to three thousand feet deep. The flat meadow bottom is from about three hundred to two hundred yards wide, with gently curved margins about fifty yards wide from which rise the simple massive walls of gray granite at an angle of about thirty-three degrees, mostly timbered with a light growth of pine and streaked in many places with avalanche channels. Towards the upper end of the canyon, the Sierra crown comes in sight, forming a finely-balanced picture framed by the massive canyon walls. In the foreground, when the grass is in flower, you have the purple meadow willow-thickets on the river banks; in the middle distance huge swelling bosses of granite that form the base of the general mass of the mountain, with fringing lines of dark woods marking the lower curves, smoothly snow-clad except in the autumn.

If you wish to spend two days on the Lyell trip, you will find a good campground on the east side of the river, about a mile above a fine cascade that comes down over the canyon wall in telling style and makes good camp music. From here to the top of the mountains is usually an easy day's work. At one place near the summit, careful climbing is necessary, but it is not so dangerous or difficult as to deter any one of ordinary skill, while the views are glorious. To the northward are Mammoth Mountain, Mounts Gibbs, Dana, Warren, Conness, and others, unnumbered and unnamed; to the southeast the indescribably wild and jagged range of Mount Ritter and the Minarets; south-westward stretches the dividing ridge between the north fork of the San Joaquin and the Merced, uniting with the Obelisk or Merced group of peaks that form the main fountains of the Illilouette branch of the Merced; and to the northwestward extends the Cathedral spur. These spurs like distinct ranges meet at your feet. Therefore, you look at them mostly in the direction of their extension, and their peaks seem to be massed and crowded against one another, while immense amphitheaters, canyons, and subordinate ridges with their wealth of lakes, glaciers, and snowfields, maze and cluster between them. In making the ascent in June or October, the glacier is easily crossed, for then its snow mantle is smooth or mostly melted off. But in midsummer, the climbing is exceedingly tedious because the snow is then weathered into curious and beautiful blades, sharp and slender, and set on edge in a leaning position. They lean towards the head of the glacier and extend across from side to side in regular order in a direction at right angles to the direction of greatest declivity, the distance between the crests being about two or three feet, and the depth of the troughs between them about three feet. A more interesting problem than a walk over a glacier thus sculptured and adorned is seldom presented to the mountaineer.

The Lyell Glacier is about a mile wide and less than a mile long, but presents, nevertheless, all the essential characters of large, river-like glacier—moraines, earth-bands, blue veins, crevasses, etc., while the streams that issue from it are, of course, turbid with rock-mud, showing its grinding action on its bed. And it is all the more interesting since it is the highest and most enduring remnant of the great Tuolumne Glacier, whose traces are still distinct fifty miles away, and whose influence on the landscape was so profound. The McClure Glacier, once a tributary of the Lyell, is smaller. Thirty-eight years ago I set a series of stakes in it to determine its rate of motion. Towards the end of summer, in the middle of the glacier, it was only a little over an inch in twenty-four hours.

The trip to Mono from Soda Springs can be made in a day, but many days may profitably be spent near the shores of the lake, out on its islands and about the volcanoes.

In making the trip down the Big Tuolumne Canyon [Grand Canyon of the Tuolumne, *ed.*], animals may be led as far as a small, grassy, forested lake-basin that lies below the crossing of the Virginia Creek trail. And from this point, any one accustomed to walking on earthquake boulders, carpeted with canyon chaparral, can easily go down as far as the big cascades and return to camp in one day. Many, however, are not able to do this, and it is better to go leisurely, prepared to camp anywhere, and enjoy the marvelous grandeur of the place.

The canyon begins near the lower end of the meadows and extends to Hetch Hetchy Valley, a distance of about eighteen miles, though it will seem much longer to any one who scrambles through it. It is from twelve hundred to about five thousand feet deep, and is comparatively narrow, but there are several roomy, park-like openings in it, and throughout its whole extent, Yosemite natures are displayed on a grand scale—domes, El Capitan rocks, gables, Sentinels, Royal Arches, Glacier Points, Cathedral Spires, etc. There is even a Half Dome among its wealth of rock forms, though far less sublime than Yosemite Half Dome. Its falls and cascades are innumerable. The sheer falls, except when the snow is melting in early spring, are quite small in volume as compared with those of Yosemite and Hetch Hetchy, though in any other country many of them would be regarded as wonders. But it is the cascades or sloping falls on the main river that are the crowning glory of the canyon, and these in volume, extent, and variety surpass those of any other canyon in the Sierra. The most showy and interesting of them are mostly in the upper part of the canyon, above the point of entrance of Cathedral Creek and Hoffman Creek. For miles, the river is one wild, exulting, on-rushing mass of snowy purple bloom, spreading over glacial waves of granite without any definite channel, gliding in magnificent silver plumes, dashing and foaming through huge boulder-dams, leaping high into the air in wheel-like whirls, displaying glorious enthusiasm, tossing from side to side, doubling, glinting, singing in exuberance of mountain energy.

Everyone who is anything of a mountaineer should go on through the entire length of the canyon, coming out by Hetch Hetchy. There is not a dull step all the way. With wide variations, it is a Yosemite Valley from end to end.

Besides these main, far-reaching, much-seeing excursions from the main central camp, there are numberless, lovely little saunters and scrambles and a dozen or so not so very little. Among the best of these are to Lambert [Lembert Dome, *ed.*] and Fair View Domes; to the topmost spires of Cathedral Peak, and to those of the North Church, around the base of which you pass on your way to Mount Conness; to one of the very loveliest of the glacier-meadows imbedded in the pine woods about three miles north of the Soda Springs, where forty-two years ago I spent six weeks. It trends east and west, and you can find it easily by going past the base of Lambert's Dome to Dog Lake and thence up northward through the woods about a mile or so; to the shining rock-waves full of ice-burnished feldspar crystals at the foot of the meadows; to Lake Tenaya; and, last but not least, a rather long and very hearty scramble down by the end of the meadow along Tioga Road toward Lake Tenaya to the crossing of Cathedral Creek, where you turn off and trace the creek down to its confluence with the Tuolumne. This is a genuine scramble much of the way but one of the most wonderfully telling in its glacial rockforms and inscriptions.

If you stop and fish at every tempting lake and stream you come to, a whole month, or even two months, will not be too long for this grand High Sierra excursion.

My own Sierra trip was ten years long.

Biographical Sketches

Ralph Waldo Emerson

Ralph Waldo Emerson (1803–1882) is considered America's preeminent essayist, orator, poet, and philosopher. He was a founding member of the Transcendental Club, center of the Transcendentalist movement, a philosophy that he first expressed in his 1840 essay *Nature*. Emerson attempted, with some difficulty, to retain a strict social and political independence that reflected his individualism. His doctrine of "the infinitude of the private man" remained central to his thinking. He wanted no followers, but rather, sought to give man back to himself, as a self-reliant individual. Much of Emerson's writing shows the strong influence of nondualism, best exemplified in his 1841 essay, *The Over-Soul*:

We live in succession, in division, in parts, in particles. Meantime within man is the soul of the whole; the wise silence; the universal beauty, to which every part and particle is equally related, the eternal

ONE. And this deep power in which we exist and whose beatitude is all accessible to us, is not only self-sufficing and perfect in every hour, but the act of seeing and the thing seen, the seer and the spectacle, the subject and the object, are one. We see the world piece by piece, as the sun, the moon, the animal, the tree; but the whole, of which these are shining parts, is the soul.

Horace Greeley

Horace Greeley (1811–1872), editor of the *New York Tribune,* a founder of the Republican Party, and presidential nominee, is one of the most interesting and unusual figures in American history. His life-long concern for the working man touched nearly all political and social reform movements of his era. As editor, he used the highly respected *Tribune* to voice his opposition to slavery and his support of temperance and women's rights, and to crusade against the corruption of the Ulysses S. Grant Republican administration. Wherever he went, even on the hottest days, Horace Greeley wore a long, dark coat and carried a brightly colored umbrella.

James Mason Hutchings

James Mason Hutchings (1820–1902), gold miner and publisher, led the second tourist party into Yosemite on July 5, 1855. It was said, ". . . upon the return of Hutchings party, the descriptions staggered the skeptics and silenced the croakers. From this time forward can be considered the commencement of the visits of tourists." Hutchings settled in the valley and published the illustrated *Hutchings' California Magazine,* promoting Yosemite and the High Sierra. His many articles and illustrations were collected in his major comprehensive work, *In the Heart of the Sierras,* which includes natural and human history, personal accounts of adventure and discovery, mining stories, travel tips, and descriptions of various routes to Yosemite.

Clarence King

Clarence King (1842–1901), American geologist and mountaineer, founded the United States Geological Survey, and from 1879–1881 was its first director. King's particular interest was the exploration of the Sierra Nevada. In 1864, he and Richard Cotter reported the first ascent of Mount Tyndall, mistakenly believing it to be the highest peak in the range. As a member of the California Geological Society in 1866, King, with geologist James T. Gardiner, conceived of the idea for The 40th Parallel Survey at Yosemite, which was approved by Congress in 1867. In this government-sponsored project, King and his team explored the 40th parallel from the 120th meridian to the 105th, a swath one hundred miles wide, along the route of the transcontinental railroad.

Joaquin Miller

Joaquin Miller (1837–1913), known as "The Poet of The Sierras," was born Cincinnatus Hiner Miller, but soon took the name of the legendary California bandit, Joaquin Murietta. He was a colorful figure, well known in California literary and social circles. A terrific fabricator of his own adventures, he had a life-long fascination with the lure of the gold fields, moving around frequently in Oregon, Idaho, and California. Miller's first book, *Song of The Sierras,* was published in London in 1871. Later titles include *Life Among The Modocs* and *Selected Writings of Joaquin Miller.* Six volumes of his collected poems and other writing were published in 1909. Eventually, Joaquin Miller settled in Oakland Hills, California, in full view of the Golden Gate Bridge. He named his seventy-five acre estate "The Hermitage, Oakland Heights," but later renamed it "The Hights." The odd spelling was, of course, intentional.

John Muir

John Muir (1838–1914), conservationist, naturalist, philosopher, and author, spent a lifetime of study in what he termed "the University of the Wilderness." Muir examined assumptions about man's relationship to nature, concluding that all forms of life have inherent significance, with humans no more or less significant than others. Muir urged, "Let us do something to make the mountains glad," and so in 1892, he founded the Sierra Club, one of the first major organizations in history dedicated to the preservation of wild nature. No one has written so widely and so well about a national park as John Muir wrote about Yosemite.

Frederick Law Olmsted

Frederick Law Olmsted (1822–1903) is widely recognized as the founder of American landscape architecture and the nation's foremost urban parkmaker. Olmsted's design ideals, philosophy, and influence are realized throughout the nation:

Central Park, New York City; Prospect Park, New York City; Niagara Reservation, Niagara Falls, New York; Emerald Necklace, Boston; Jackson Park, Chicago; Washington Park, Chicago; Midway Plaisance, Chicago; landscape design for the United States Capitol building and the Biltmore Estate in North Carolina.

Theodore Roosevelt

Theodore Roosevelt (1858–1919), 26th President of the United States (1901–1909) and in 1906, the first American winner of the Nobel Peace Prize, is considered by historians to be one of this country's greatest leaders. His legacy of wide-ranging accomplishments is far too extensive to review in detail here: historian, naturalist, ornithologist, explorer, soldier, and writer of thirty-five books. With the possible exception of Thomas Jefferson, he is considered the most well-read of any American politician.

As President, Roosevelt emerged as a "trust buster," and as "steward of the people," he promised the average citizen a "Square Deal". Aware of America's strategic need for a shortcut between the Atlantic and Pacific, Roosevelt secured U.S. control of the construction of the Panama Canal, which he considered his most important and historically-significant international achievement.

Roosevelt was the first President to consider the long-term, negative effects of human activity on the planet, and put his concern high on the national agenda. He worked with all major figures of the conservationist movement to determine the most efficient use of natural resources. In 1903, Roosevelt toured the Yosemite Valley with John Muir, founder of the Sierra Club. Roosevelt urged Congress to establish the United States Forest Service, thereby protecting more land for national forests, national parks, and nature preserves than all of his predecessors combined—194 million acres. The Theodore Roosevelt National Park in North Dakota commemorates his numerous achievements as conservationist; his image stands with George Washington, Thomas Jefferson and Abraham Lincoln at the Mount Rushmore Memorial.

Mark Twain

Mark Twain (1835–1910), born Samuel Langhorne Clemens, is one America's best-loved writers. His early life was filled with adventure; he was successively a journeyman printer, a steamboat pilot, and a prospector, miner, and newspaper reporter in the western territories of the United States. With the 1865 publication of *The Celebrated Jumping Frog of Calaveras County*, set in the gold country of the Sierra foothills, Twain captured national attention as a brilliant humorist. His memoir *Life on the Mississippi* (1883), *The Adventures of Huckleberry Finn* (1885), and the many other classic works that followed secured his stature in the literary world as one of America's greatest writers.

Sources

Chapter 1: *The Great Chasm of Yosemite* from the introduction to *Yosemite and the Mariposa Grove: A Preliminary Report*, Frederick Law Olmsted, 1865

Chapter 2: *The Sierra Nevada Range* from *Mountaineering in the Sierra Nevada*, "The Range," Clarence King, 1872

Chapter 3: *John Muir: An Appreciation* from "John Muir: An Appreciation," Theodore Roosevelt, *Outlook*, January 16, 1915

Chapter 4: *Yosemite Glaciers* from "Yosemite Glaciers," *New York Tribune*, December 5, 1871. This was John Muir's first published work, pieced together from letters sent to his friends, for which he was paid $200.

Chapter 5: *How the Valley Was Formed*, from *The Yosemite*, "The Ancient Yosemite Glaciers: How the Valley Was Formed," John Muir, 1912

Chapter 6: *The Incomparable Valley*, from *Picturesque California*, "The Yosemite Valley," 1888–1890; *The Century Magazine*, August, 1890; "The Treasures of the Yosemite"; and *The Yosemite*, "The Approach to the Valley," 1912, John Muir

Chapter 7: *Climbing Half Dome*, from *The Yosemite*, "The South Dome," John Muir, 1912

Chapter 8: In the Heart of the Sierras, from *In the Heart of the Sierras*, James Mason Hutchings, 1888

Chapter 9: *In California—The Yosemite*, from *An Overland Journey from New York to San Francisco in the Summer of 1859*, "California—The Yosemite," Horace Greeley, 1860

Chapter 10: *Waterfalls and Rainbows*, from *Picturesque California*, "The Yosemite Valley," 1888–1890; "The Treasures of the Yosemite," *The Century Magazine*, August, 1890; and *The Yosemite*, "The Approach to the Valley," 1912, John Muir

Chapter 11: *Around Yosemite Walls*, from *Mountaineering in the Sierra Nevada*, "Around Yosemite Walls," Clarence King, 1864

Chapter 12: *The Domes of the Yosemite*, a letter published in the San Francisco newspaper *Alta California*, Mark Twain, August 4, 1867

Chapter 13: *The Trees of the Valley*, from *The Yosemite*, "The Trees of the Valley" and "The Forest Trees in General," John Muir, 1912

Chapter 14: *In Yosemite with John Muir* from *Theodore Roosevelt, An Autobiography*, "Outdoors and Indoors," Theodore Roosevelt, 1913

Chapter 15: *The Giant Sequoia* from *Picturesque California*, "The Yosemite Valley," John Muir, 1888–1890; "The Treasures of the Yosemite," *The Century Magazine*, August, 1890; and *The Yosemite*, "The Big Trees," 1912, John Muir

Chapter 16: *In California—The Big Trees* from *An Overland Journey from New York to San Francisco in the Summer of 1859,* "California—The Big Trees," Horace Greeley, 1860

Chapter 17: *Yosemite in Winter* from "Yosemite in Winter," originally published as "In the Yosemite: Holidays among the Rocks," *New York Tribune,* John Muir, January 1, 1872

Chapter 18: *Riding an Avalanche* from *The Yosemite,* "Snow Storms," John Muir, 1912

Chapter 19: *Snow Banners* from *The Yosemite,* "Snow Banners," John Muir, 1912

Chapter 20: *Caught in a Sierra Storm* from *Mountaineering in the Sierra Nevada,* "A Sierra Storm," Clarence King, 1864

Chapter 21: *A Winter Earthquake* from *The Yosemite,* "Snow Banners," John Muir, 1912

Chapter 22: *The Flowers* from *Picturesque California,* "The Yosemite Valley," 1888–1890, and *The Yosemite,* "The Flowers," John Muir, 1912

Chapter 23*: The Birds* from *Picturesque California,* "The Yosemite Valley," (1888-1890), and *The Yosemite,* "The Birds," 1912, John Muir

Chapter 24: *A Close Call on the Obelisk* from *Mountaineering in the Sierra Nevada,* "Merced Ramblings," Clarence King, 1866

Chapter 25: *How Best to Spend One's Yosemite Time* from *The Yosemite,* "How Best to Spend One's Yosemite Time," John Muir, 1912